Published by
Resistance Books
PO Box 62732
London SW2 9GQ

Design: Ed Fredenburgh
Cover design: Hannah Ley
Set in 11/14pt Monotype Joanna
Printed by Lightning Source UK
Published November 2014 by Socialist Resistance

ISBN   978-0-902869-38-7
EAN   9780902869387

THE DYNAMIC OF REVOLUTION
IN SOUTH AFRICA

SPEECHES AND WRITINGS OF
I.B. TABATA

BY DORA TAYLOR

This book is dedicated to the men and women throughout the world who have lived and died in the cause of liberation.

Dora Taylor, 1969

I B Tabata: speeches and writings

THE DYNAMIC OF REVOLUTION IN SOUTH AFRICA

Contents

I.B.Tabata and Dora Taylor: biographical notes   viii

Foreword: *Norman Traub*   xiii

Introduction: *Dora Taylor*   xvii

Chapter One:
The revolutionary road for South Africa   1

Chapter Two:
The policy of apartheid

     I.   The problem of slave mentality   21
     II.   Teachers join the struggle   29
     III. Bantu education in South Africa   35
     IV. Christian-National education: origins   46
     V.   Bantu education must fail   50
     VI. Let us rally   57

Chapter Three:
The political situation and perspectives

     I.   Political programme of unity   64
     II.   The boycott as weapon of struggle   75
     III. Letter to Nelson Mandela: problem of
         organisational unity (16 June 1948)   91
     IV. Address to the first national conference of the
         African People's Democratic Union of Southern Africa
         (APDUSA): 1962, Cape Town   98
     V.   Verwoerd's assassination   115

Chapter Four:
The political forces and their orientation

I.   New methods of struggle   121

II. The role of the Communist Party
     of South Africa   134

III. The Pan-Africanist Congress adventure
     in perspective   141

IV. Thoughts on workers' democracy   156

V.   Conspiracy against Southern Africa's
     liberation   162

Bibliography   174

Appendix I   176

Appendix II   178

I.B.Tabata and Dora Taylor: biographical notes

I.B.Tabata 1909–1990   Dora Taylor 1899–1976

Tabata's early years were spent in the village of Bailey in the Eastern Cape, where he attended the local school. Not wishing to be a farmer he shrugged off rural life and entered Fort Hare University, where he caught the attention of Bishop Smythe, the College Warden, who gave him free access to his library, thus helping him to widen his knowledge and develop an intellectual approach to life. He later said: If the Bishop taught me one thing it was that in life it was most important to live according to ones' own ideals. You live to make a contribution to the development of mankind, and for the good of mankind; that no other things matter provided you make a contribution to mankind.

These words were given on the occasion of Tabata's funeral address in 1976 for Dora Taylor, in which he honours the part she played in his life. When Tabata's father died he moved to Cape Town in search of work. Here he met Clare Goodlatte, a former nun who had just retired as Principal of Grahamstown Training College. 'And she too showed us how to live. She had one thing in common with Dora: she was one who was always pushing others forward and not herself. She was the first person to encourage Dora to go out and fulfil herself, in that she had to do what she was qualified for,' namely writing.

In Cape Town Tabata joined the Truck Drivers' Union, soon becoming a member of the executive. In 1933 he attended the newly formed Lenin Club (of which Clare Goodlatte was the Secretary). Here, in 1935, he met Dora and Jim Taylor, Jane Gool, her brother Goolam Gool, and many other progressive thinkers who discussed political matters from a Marxist-Leninist viewpoint. It was here he developed his knowledge of Marxism and dialectical analysis which enabled him to become such a powerful political figure.

Tabata was also greatly influenced by Dora Taylor and her family, from whom he learned about science, philosophy, the arts and intellectual rigour. JG Taylor, Senior Lecturer in Psychology at UCT, had drawn attention to himself for denying that black people were less intelligent than whites (a widely held view at the time), while Dora published literary criticism in Trek, an intellectual magazine, and through which she became well known.

Tabata was accustomed to visit the Transkei annually and in 1940 he was asked by the All African Convention, of which he was a member, to make contact with people in the Transkei. By this time, however, restrictions had tightened so that he was not allowed to travel on his own account. As a solution Goolam offered to lend Tabata his new car, with Dora posing as a tourist, and Tabata being her smartly dressed chauffeur. It was their association on this trip which brought them together in a way which profoundly changed their lives. Later he travelled on his own, continuing to visit the Eastern Cape until 1956 when he was banned. On these trips he would speak to large gatherings on a mountainside where he was always watched by the police, whom he took delight in mocking.

His banning forbade him attending any gathering, political or social, and confined him to Cape Town. He was the first person in South Africa to receive a 5-year ban, which prevented him from playing any public political role for the duration of the banning order.

These were hard and difficult years for him but, observation being lax, he was able to able to visit the Taylors' home, where he was welcomed. He could not only discuss political matters with other visitors but he was also exposed to the cultural life of the family and friends, both young and old.

Dora and Tabata each took cultural food from the other, Tabata speaking of the national and international situations, while Dora contributed literature and music, together with her own plays and stories. They soon came to share the creation of Tabata's writings, with Dora using her writing skills (she had taken her English Literature degree at Aberdeen University) to shape the discourse. Through this close symbiotic relationship Tabata came to write with greater ease, while in due course Dora became a politician in her own right, as Tabata freely acknowledged. A milestone in Dora's contribution was reached when, at Tabata's suggestion, she wrote *The Role of the Missionaries in Conquest*. Research for this book alerted Dora to the lies about the supposed benign nature of imperial conquest, increasing her resolve to help change an oppressive system.

Much of their time together was spent in creating Tabata's many letters, books and other documents, and in these Tabata's political acumen stands out, while their shared affection for Shakespeare is clearly evident.

In later years she wrote "I held the pen", but this remark reflects her typical modesty. In fact she did far more than hold the pen, for the editing involved close discussion, which in turn led to greater refinement of ideas and their expression.

Doreen Muskett (née Taylor), Michael Muskett   2013

I.B. TABATA, 1909–1990

DORA TAYLOR, 1899–1976

Foreword

This book of selected writings and speeches of I.B.Tabata, edited by Dora Taylor, covers a turbulent period in the history of South Africa. It traces the development of the Unity Movement of South Africa (UMSA) and its role in the political struggle from its formation in 1943 (at the height of the Second World War) up to 1969, the year the book was completed. Both Tabata and Taylor were founder members of UMSA. Their collaboration in the production and editing of Tabata's writings was unique, spanning a period of over thirty years which ended with Taylor's death in 1976. In the early 60's, when the racist regime was carrying out a systematic policy of repression of the organisations of the national liberation movement, Taylor was driven into exile in England and Tabata, together with Jane Gool, his partner, and Nathaniel Honono, escaped to Tanzania to pursue UMSA's case for recognition by the newly formed Organisation of African Unity (OAU).

Taylor's introduction and editorial notes are an integral part of the book. In her introduction to this work she stated that she had chosen extracts from Tabata's writings and speeches 'because they are typical of a leadership which acted in the traditions of scientific socialism.' The founders of UMSA laid the basis for a national movement, which united all sections of the oppressed blacks, African, Coloured and Indian, together with all whites who accepted equality between black and white. The federal structure of UMSA was designed to bring together all the organisations of the blacks under one roof. The Ten Point programme, a minimum programme for action, was drawn up to mobilise the population in the struggle for full democratic rights. It was understood that without the support of the landless peasantry, who were the chief sources of labour for the gold mines, the white farms and heavy industry, there could be no successful struggle against national oppression. The agitational slogan, "Land and Liberty" brought home to the peasants that they could not solve the problem of their land hunger without the fight for democratic rights. A policy of non-collaboration with the oppressor, free from the control of the ruling class was applied. Unlike the South African Communist Party (SACP), which had formed an alliance with the ANC and believed in a two stage theory of revolution (first the democratic stage and in some distant future the socialist stage), the founders of UMSA believed in the theory of uninterrupted revolution.

According to this theory, the leadership of the proletariat, assisted by the peasantry, is necessary in the democratic revolution in a backward country. There is then the possibility of the growing over of the democratic into the socialist revolution. The founders of UMSA were imbued with the spirit of internationalism. They linked the struggle of the oppressed blacks in South Africa to the struggle of the oppressed all over the world trying to free themselves from the shackles of colonialism, imperialism and capitalism.

There were numerous obstacles to the editing of this book, not least of which was the onerous responsibility of Tabata as president of UMSA with a punishing schedule of work and travel. There was also the great distance separating him from Taylor, he being based in Zambia and she in England. When the manuscript was finally completed, repeated attempts to have it published failed. It may seem surprising that this work did not find a publisher, considering Tabata's stature as a political figure and writer and at a time when the world's attention was focused on the struggle being conducted by the blacks in South Africa against the apartheid regime.

Pertinent to this is that Tabata and Taylor were championing political ideas which were opposed to the ANC, which was being fêted both by the Stalinists, led by the former Soviet Union in the East, and bourgeois circles in the West. In correspondence with Taylor in December 1968 and in reference to the present work, Tabata wrote 'I feel we have, or you have, done something great. I am not sanguine about immediate results. I think of the future. Our contribution to future generations.'

Within a few years of Tabata's death in October 1990, the racist South African regime was compelled to grant democratic rights to the blacks. A 'government of national unity' was formed in 1994, which consummated the marriage between the representatives of the bourgeoisie, the National Party and the petty bourgeois leadership of the ANC. While the bourgeoisie were prepared to accept deep-going political change in South Africa, they ruled out any measures which posed a threat to their control of the economy.

A specific clause in the new constitution guaranteed their property rights. They maintained their ownership of most of the mines, factories and land in South Africa and the accumulated wealth that went with it. In the years that followed the first democratic elections, the ANC leadership in government promoted the interests of its class through the policy of black empowerment, whereby a small number of blacks was able to acquire ownership or part ownership of big companies in industry and mining, and so became incorporated into the bourgeoisie. They, together with a much bigger black middle class, constitute a base of support for the ANC. It is the interests of the workers and landless peasantry that go unattended.

South Africa remains one of the most unequal societies in the world. The vast majority of blacks are poverty stricken. Millions live in squatter camps and unemployment is soaring. While there have been some small reforms which have improved the lives of the people, the great expectations of the 'rainbow nation' following the first democratic elections have long since disappeared. However, the neoliberal policies of the ANC government are being resisted by the population. The people are looking for a way out of a system that blights their lives. New generations are growing up who have not experienced the evils of the white supremacist regimes.

The class struggles are intensifying. In the townships and squatter camps, the protests and demonstrations over the lack of proper housing and services, are becoming more widespread and bitter. The heroic strike of 28,000 African mineworkers at the Lonmin Platinum mine captured the attention of the world. In spite of arrests, dismissals and the police massacre at Marikana of 34 of their fellow workers and wounding of a further 78, the strikers held on until their bosses agreed to a substantial increase in wages, ending the 5-week strike. This strike precipitated a number of strikes in other platinum, gold, coal and chrome mines, involving 100,000 workers.

Strikes also broke out in the transport industry and among farm workers in the Western Cape. The strikes represent the greatest challenge to the ANC and the bosses since the ANC-led government came to power in 1994.

What the situation demands is a broad based socialist party, that can give a political direction to the unfolding struggles.

In South Africa there is a great history of resistance to oppression and exploitation. If the youth examine their past, they will find rich pickings to inspire them in the battles that lie ahead. We believe that the writings and speeches of Tabata will be a lasting contribution to the understanding of the forces shaping present day South Africa, and the necessity of propelling the struggle forward to socialism.

Norman Traub
2013

Introduction

A new period is opening up in the African continent. Under the present fascist regime in South Africa it might seem that the oppressed Blacks, who comprise four fifths of the population of that country, would be the last to achieve liberation. Yet historically South Africa is destined to play a significant role in the liberation of the African continent south of the Sahara. Here we speak not of self-government or neo-colonialist regimes but of real and total independence, economic and political, that is, freedom from the dominance of capitalism-imperialism.

In the last decade the African stage has been dominated by leaders of nationalist movements whose only aim was the replacement of the foreign white invaders by indigenous rulers. They have taken over the machinery of state created by the imperialist powers which in the 19th century had carved up Africa. This meant that the petit-bourgeois section, lacking a clear conception of the liberatory struggle and the nature of the forces at work in society, were tricked into maintaining neo-colonialist regimes. The new rulers found themselves prisoners within an economic structure geared to continued exploitation by the very powers from whose domination they thought to free themselves.

But the very nature of neo-colonialist states – the contradictions, the unsolved problems of the masses, their unrelieved poverty and discontent – creates instability. New forces are set in motion in an attempt to solve problems which cannot be solved within the existing framework. These states are faced with almost insuperable tasks. Centuries of imperialist exploitation have resulted in a systematic denudation of the continent in every sphere both human and material. It is well nigh impossible for any one of these states to break out of the noose of capitalism-imperialism and forge a path to socialism. And yet it is only under socialism that Africa can begin to solve its problems. It is in these circumstances that South Africa is destined to play a vital role in the liberation of the continent of Africa, for it holds the key to the next stage of development that is opening up.

South Africa is of great strategic importance as an armed bastion of imperialism in the whole complex of Africa south of the Sahara. But at the same time what happens in South Africa is of crucial significance for the unfolding of the revolutionary process throughout Africa, that is, the overthrowing of imperialist domination. The nature of the South African economy contains all the elements leading to the development of a revolutionary situation. It is an industrialised economy with all the contradictions of capitalism. It is the most highly industrialised country in Africa. A revolutionary overthrow of the system must come from the workers and peasants of South Africa.

And if they should succeed in their historical task of liberating South Africa, then it is inevitable that the tide of revolution would not stop at the boundaries of South Africa but would sweep northwards. Moreover, a liberated South Africa, where real democracy for the masses prevailed, that is, socialist democracy, would be in a position with its highly developed industrial potential to enable the countries to the north of it to advance with an unprecedented rapidity. Such a perspective underlines the prime importance of a South African revolution for the development of the continent as a whole.

Now there has been a surfeit of books about South Africa describing the crimes of apartheid or presenting interesting personalities. But in all but this one is left with only a vague idea of the nature of South African society. There is all too little examination of the basic economic structure of the system that gives rise to all those social iniquities and within which the political organisations function.

Yet it is essential to understand the development of the productive forces in South Africa, the clash of class and sectional interests and therefore the nature of the developing struggles which foreshadow the shape of things to come. After the Second World War there was a rapid economic expansion in South Africa. Today the process of industrialisation has reached such a stage that South African financiers are exporting capital for investment in foreign countries jointly with international financiers. Even agriculture is being commercialised to such an extent that a new phenomenon is emerging. Large industrial concerns are buying up the land and controlling all produce, with the result that independent white farmers are either being ousted or becoming virtual tenants.

At the same time a vast army of African landless peasantry is being turned into an agricultural proletariat. With this economic expansion there is an ever-increasing demand for cheap Black labour. All the inhuman laws passed against the Black man by whatever government is in power are designed for the regimentation of labour, drawing them into the vortex of the industrial, mining and agricultural complex of the capitalist system, rendering them rightless helots who must be channelled into the various branches of the industrial machine in the required quotas.

The mining industry, the chief earner of foreign exchange, is based almost entirely on African migrant labour, that is, on the mass of landless peasantry. A great part of the labour in commerce and manufacturing industry, including heavy industry, is drawn from the Black population. In the engineering industry 75 per cent of the workers are Africans who, by definition, are excluded from the category of workers and therefore are excluded from all the protection and privileges to which workers are entitled. There is a very large wage gap between white and all non-white workers, and a still greater wage-gap between the Whites and the mass of the Africans. For example, in industry the ratio of white to non-white wages is about 5 to 1; in 1966 the ratio of white to African cash earnings on the gold mines was 17 to 1.

All these factors contain the elements of an explosive situation. This, however, must not be allowed to obscure the basic conflict in South Africa. The basic conflict is a class conflict and the fundamental struggle is a class struggle. Yet it is the failure to understand this fundamental fact that has been responsible for the conflicting policies amongst the organisations of the oppressed and caused them to follow different paths in their attempt to solve their problem.

It is true that at present the white working class in South Africa looks on the black worker as the Roman proletarian regarded the slave. He is unaware of the identity of his interests with those of the Blacks and in the main supports the ruling-class in their oppressive policies. Thus the working class is split asunder. The policy of 'divide and rule' has in the past worked well also in keeping separate the different sections of the Non-whites – Africans, Coloured and Indian. As successive white governments steadily eroded the minimal rights of the oppressed, they attacked first those of the Africans, while the Coloureds and Indians looked on passively in the false hope of retaining their few remaining privileges. They used to send separate deputations to the government appealing for redress of their grievances; that is, they appealed for justice to their common oppressor.

In the complex situation in South Africa it is necessary to look into the objective political role of various movements. Chief amongst these is one of the oldest organisations, the African National Congress (ANC), with the youngest, the Pan African Congress (PAC), a splinter of the ANC. There is also the All-African Convention federating African organisations, which at one time included the ANC. It was the All-African Convention, together with the National Anti-CAD, a federal organisation of Coloured people, which laid the foundations of the Unity Movement of South Africa. It will be necessary also to consider the role of the Communist Party of South Africa. (CPSA).

THE AFRICAN NATIONAL CONGRESS

If we consider the policy of the African National Congress since its birth in 1912 we find first of all that its leaders are by tradition strongly attached to the white liberals and this from the outset deprived them of an independent course of action. As the agents of the liberal bourgeoisie representing the interests of British finance capital, the liberals in effect have tied them to the ruling-class. The logic of their position and outlook has led the ANC leaders into opportunism; they represent the interests of a frustrated petit-bourgeoisie. Their activities therefore stem from a reformist position. This has dictated their attitude to the masses, whom they organise into demonstrations or days of mourning in order to bring pressure on the Government for reform. They have not thought in terms of building up an organisation into a fighting instrument.

In their passive resistance campaigns they continued to protest against separate aspects of oppression without attempting to co-ordinate the struggle. Such tactics are bound up with the lack of a clear concept of the forces at work in society and of the unity of oppression affecting all sections of the Blacks, in other words, of the sum total of national oppression. Still less were they aware that racial oppression is itself an instrument of class exploitation. That is why the summit of their protest is anti-apartheid. They have never thought in terms of the overthrow of the whole exploitive (capitalist) system in South Africa.

Even now when the leaders of the African National Congress outside South Africa are talking about the armed struggle, for them it is a means of mobilising international public opinion to bring pressure to bear upon the fascistic wing of the herrenvolk in South Africa, the present Nationalist

Government. It is their understanding of this fact that prompts the imperialist powers to place their propaganda machine so readily at the disposal of the African National Congress leadership. Pressure politics also dictate their repeated appeals to the United Nations to apply sanctions on the Nationalist Government. This is not only to ignore the function of the United Nations as an instrument of United States imperialism; it is apparently to be unaware that this is to ask the imperialists of Britain and America, who have large investments in South Africa, to apply sanctions against themselves. Such pressure politics are totally inconsistent with undertaking a serious armed struggle for the liberation of all the oppressed of South Africa. All the signs are that the real political content of the African National Congress struggle is to ensure the sectional interests of an African petit-bourgeoisie under capitalism.

The anti-apartheid campaign pursued by the ANC leaders outside South Africa follows logically from their position at home. The anti-apartheid struggle, if successful, would lead to a neo-colonialist regime, and this means simply the entrenchment of imperialism in South Africa. It does not mean the liberation of the oppressed workers and peasants.

Now it is not generally understood what this anti-apartheid struggle is. This is one of the points that the Unity Movement Statement, The Revolutionary Road For South Africa, considers important to clarify. It marks in fact a conflict between two sections of the white ruling-class in South Africa, between the Afrikaner Nationalists (the descendants of the Dutch Boers), who have been in power since 1948, and the representatives of international finance capital.

The tragic misdirection of a section of the Blacks is that they have been drawn into this conflict that has nothing to do with their liberation. In terms of the South African political situation, the anti-apartheid struggle means ousting the Afrikaner Nationalists and replacing them with the real spokesman of imperialism, namely the English-speaking liberal bourgeoisie. It is of course understood that in the present world climate it would be necessary to incorporate in such a neo-colonialist government a few Black faces. Thus it becomes clear why British and United States imperialism supports the anti-apartheid campaign with its high-powered press propaganda.

THE COMMUNIST PARTY OF SOUTH AFRICA

Nowhere in the world did a Communist Party so completely embrace the Stalinist theory of "socialism in one country", with all that it involves in class collaboration and counter-revolution, as the Communist Party of South Africa.

This was not accidental. For the abandonment of the class struggle implied in this theory accurately expresses the political and social position of the leadership of the Communist Party in South Africa. Little wonder that this party followed most slavishly over the years all the shifts of the Stalinist bureaucracy from the period of Popular Frontism, the Hitler Pact, the ardent nationalism and chauvinism of the period of World War II to the role of counter-revolution in the aftermath of that war.

The white petit-bourgeois elite which dominated the Communist Party in South Africa reflected the most conservative, reactionary elements inherent in Stalinism. In a system where racialism was generated by the white ruling minority as a means of preserving its dominant position, the class origins and connections of this leadership reinforced its reactionary tendencies. It could not withstand the social weight of white herrenvolkism.

The world today knows how costly to mankind, how heavy is the price paid by humanity as a result of the policies pursued by the Stalinist bureaucracy: the defeat of the German revolution which led to the triumph of Hitlerite fascism; the betrayal of the Spanish revolution; the treachery of counterposing to fascism bourgeois democracy instead of the dictatorship of the proletariat immediately after the second World War, thus bringing about the crushing of the revolution in Greece, in France, in Indo-China, in short the betrayal of the workers in Europe and the Far East.

Even where there was a successful socialist revolution, in China, the abandonment by the Stalinist bureaucracy of the concept of internationalism of the struggle had serious consequences on the relationship between the two socialist countries.

These events are today well known because they happened on the world arena. What is not known is the consistent reactionary role of the Communist Party of South Africa. Its relationship with the African National Congress and the merchant-dominated South African Indian Congress (SAIC), and on the other hand its hostility to the All-African Convention and its still more virulent obstruction of the federal organisation embracing all sections of the oppressed, the Unity Movement of South Africa; its relationship also to the ruling class and its readiness to support segregatory institutions by putting up white candidates as "Native representatives" − all these reveal the political physiognomy of the CP At every critical turn when the militancy of the Blacks threatened a unified resistance to oppression and when they gathered themselves with an unprecedented unanimity for an onslaught on white herrenvolkism, the CP stepped in on the side of the ruling-class, creating political confusion in the ranks of the oppressed. Examples of this are cited in the book itself as it unfolds the dynamic of a struggle on two fronts, against the ruling-class and against the petit-bourgeois opportunist elements within their own ranks, who were tied to the agents of the ruling-class.

It is in the sum total of its activities that the reactionary and ultimately counter-revolutionary role of the CP manifests itself. As the Statement, The Revolutionary Road For South Africa (referred to above) indicates, the Communist Party paid lip-service to the class-struggle but in actual practice carried out a policy of reformism. In the conditions of South Africa, where racial oppression reinforces class exploitation, this involved a tacit acceptance of the inferiority of the Black man.

One of its first acts was to support a strike of white miners in the early twenties, a strike that degenerated into racialism against the Africans employed on the mines. The CP ignored the agrarian problem, the question of how to solve the land hunger of the mass of the African peasantry who comprise the largest and most oppressed labour force in South Africa's industrial complex. Like the African National Congress, it was urban-oriented. It concentrated much of its energy on trade union work amongst the Blacks, yet in this field it did not go beyond economism. Its policy of "no politics in the trade unions" found the already weakened – because largely segregated – trade union movement completely exposed when the fascist Nationalist Government imposed on the unions complete racial segregation by law.

But more than this, the treachery of this policy of "no politics in the trade unions" becomes apparent when it is known that the great majority of the working-class, the Africans, are forbidden by law to form trade unions. The Unity Movement of South Africa strongly urged the necessity for the trade union movement to become an integral part of the political struggle against national oppression and for full equality in every sphere. The CP however, instructed the trade unions and other organisations under its control to stay outside the Unity Movement.

The political content of CP activity for twenty years thereafter can be assessed in the light of its opposition to the Unity Movement of South Africa and the powerful effect of the new ideas of a unified struggle for liberation, a struggle that is completely independent of any ruling class party. For the CP to run against the stream of such a movement and espouse the interests of the black petit-bourgeois reformist elements was necessarily to fall into a counter-revolutionary role. Its tactics in carrying out this role and its attempt to conceal it produced confusion in the African National Congress, including the breaking off of the Africanist youth from that body to form the Pan Africanist Congress.

But it did not divert the main stream of the struggle supported by the peasantry. It can be said that the Communist Party's reformist policy of gradualness was overtaken by events and the militancy of the awakened masses. In effect, the CP played into the hands of imperialism. Its machinations received a setback in the early sixties when it was outmanoeuvred by the die-hard Verwoerd as head of the Boer nationalist wing of the ruling-class.

Today, however, it is pursuing the same counter-revolutionary role outside South Africa and in a wider arena. Individual CP members were dedicated people, but one must view a party by its objective effect on the liberatory struggle. It is unavoidable to view the role of the CP of South Africa in the light of its relation to the overall policy of the present ruling bureaucracy in the Soviet Union towards revolutionary movements throughout the world, a policy dictated by the illusion – the revisionist tactic – of maintaining peaceful co-existence with Imperialism.

It is an instructive fact that the CP of South Africa supported two such organisations as the African National Congress, whose leaders were rooted in the practices of reformism, and the South African Indian Congress, whose merchant-class leadership was unabashed in its declaration of a policy of compromise with the Smuts (pro-British) Government.

At a preliminary meeting called by the representatives of the All-African Convention and the National Anti-CAD to discuss the principled basis which they insisted was necessary for the establishment of the Unity Movement of South Africa, an old Indian Congress leader had said: "Our only hope is in compromise. The present power in the land would take away our present rights if we started shouting 'unity' all over the country. General Smuts is a great man, but he will not tolerate your challenging of the state power."

The younger Indian Congress leaders who supplanted their elders were no less dedicated to opportunism and pressure politics. The CP supported a joint passive resistance campaign of both Congresses. Misled into thinking that this campaign was a path to freedom, many African and Indian workers found themselves jail-victims. The campaign petered out, leaving the people with a sense of deep distrust.

THE CONGRESS ALLIANCE – A LIBERAL FRONT

The Congress Alliance epitomises the CP line of action. Having through its leaders obtained control of the African National Congress, it set up a "multi-racial democratic front against apartheid", that is, against the Nationalist wing of the ruling-class which was now in power. The Indian Congress, the CP-controlled Coloured People's Congress and the Congress of Democrats, made up of white G.P. and left liberal elements, were adjuncts to this bogus unity. We say 'bogus' advisedly. The African National Congress and the Indian Congress were both racialist in outlook; in their respective constitutions they excluded from membership anyone who did not belong to their racial group. Moreover, the CP, at one of the meetings of the Central Executive, went out of its way to emphasise the undesirability of the African National Congress opening its doors to members of other Non-White groups. "This," states the report, "would undermine the specific national character of the ANC ... It would never enjoy the whole-hearted support of the Indian and Coloured people." Such a statement is blatantly reactionary and totally at variance with the historical demands of the time for unity of the oppressed peoples."

In its sum total the political meaning of making the African National Congress the centre of a bogus unity is clear. The activities of the CP in seeking to control the Congress and organise a counter-activity to the Unity Movement of South Africa ran parallel to those of the liberals and to the same end. The white leadership of the Communist Party was, politically speaking, indistinguishable from the liberals, the spokesman of international finance capital, and thus it lent itself to counter-revolution.

The Congress Alliance is correctly described as a liberal front in which the agents of imperialism, utilising chiefly the African National Congress, made a show of force because they feared the real revolutionary force of the oppressed workers and peasants. This was the political content of the anti-apartheid struggle. The opportunist leaders amongst the Blacks, by tying themselves to the liberals and the CP were relinquishing the struggle of the oppressed workers and peasants. Everywhere the Blacks were demanding equality, not only in South Africa and not only in the African continent but throughout the colonial world. To stem the revolutionary tide the imperialists were wooing the petit-bourgeois sections amongst the Blacks.

We must add that the die-hard Afrikaner Nationalists for their part were bribing the African chiefs to become the local Tshombes in the oppression of their people.

It may seem a remarkable fact that, in their attempts to unseat the Nationalist Government, the liberals and the CP both resorted to individual acts of sabotage. But it was on a carefully controlled scale and calculated to frighten the white electorate into withdrawing its support from the Nationalist wing. The Black population as a whole was neither consulted nor involved in the venture and the mass of the African peasantry completely dissociated themselves from it.

Verwoerd out-manoeuvred the liberals, the Communist Party and the African National Congress leaders, most of whom left the country. But at the same time, under the guise of being the defender of the Whites against Red Communism, he had been able to rush a blitzkrieg of fascist laws through Parliament to arm the herrenvolk against the liberatory struggle of the workers and peasants. We must add, however, that the days of the die-hard Nationalists are numbered. The productive forces themselves are hastening the class divisions and the dissensions in the Afrikaner camp; the industrialists and financiers are identifying their interests with those of imperialism. From this point of view, the CP-liberal-ANC venture might be said to have been ill-timed.

Nevertheless it underscores the true purpose of the anti-apartheid conflict in seeking to divert the oppressed from the revolutionary road. Now when we consider the role of the African National Congress leaders in all these events – we do not speak of the rank and file – it may seem surprising that, while the conservative wing under chief Luthuli remained under the influence of the liberals, its other wing should fall under the control of the Communist Party. Yet it is not so paradoxical as it seems. As we have noted, the political climate of white herrenvolkism reinforced the reactionary tendencies of the CP leadership. The significant thing is that the Communist Party and the liberals are both pursuing abroad the same tactic as they did in South Africa. They both continue to control the African National Congress. They have tied its one wing to Moscow and the other to London, which is in effect to Washington.

It might seem a grotesque piece of surgery to split the umbilical cord of the same body so that one part is attached to one system, capitalism-imperialism, and the other to its dire antithesis, a socialist system. But again this is not so incongruous as it appears. What is paradoxical is that the relationship between Moscow and London-Washington should be expressed through a nationalist organisation, the African National Congress of South Africa. Even this seeming paradox falls away when we consider the relationship of forces in the world at the present time. The Stalinist theory of "socialism in one country" has meant in effect the relinquishment of international socialism and dictated the Bureaucracy's foreign policy of "peaceful co-existence" with imperialism. But today the heirs of Stalin are confronted by the inexorable laws of social development no less than is capitalism. In increasing areas of the world, both in the metropolitan countries and in the colonial and semi-colonial countries, the peoples are demanding real democracy, socialist democracy.

THE PAN AFRICANIST CONGRESS

Before dealing with the political role of the Unity Movement of South Africa it is necessary to say a word about the emergence of the Pan Africanist Congress (PAC) which was formed in 1959 when a section of the youth broke away from the parent body, the African National Congress.

There is so much mythology bound up with the PAC story that it is difficult for those outside South Africa to separate the false from the true. When Robert Sobukwe walked into jail, and was incarcerated on Robben Island, subsequent events were to expose the disparate nature of his immediate followers. The PAC had had no time to strike roots amongst the people when it was banned and most of Sobukwe's followers left the country. While the PAC was accepted by the Organisation of African Unity as a nationalist organisation, it speaks with as many different voices as there are individuals, who have adapted themselves in their various ways to the political climate they found in Europe and Asia. The chronic dissensions that reign in the group are an embarrassment to their patrons.

It is unprofitable to cavil at the PAC for their myth-making. It is more important to understand the circumstances under which the PAC emerged and how it passed like a meteor across the political scene. It marked the profound social tensions that had been building up over a decade from below and overflowed into the urban areas, the segregated city locations. The population as a whole was no longer docile; there was a sharp conflict amongst the oppressed between the opportunist elements and those who rejected white domination. The youth of the African National Congress, responsive to the militancy of the masses, revolted against the prevarications of their elders who were losing face with the people. But, having broken away from the parent body, they displayed all the uncertainties of a rudderless ship. They were the sons of the ANC, if rebel sons; they had no ideological differences with it.

They expressed the extremes of African nationalism, with its marked undertones of racialism. Unfortunately they had been encouraged by their shrewd elders to have a supreme contempt for political theory and principle and fell into political adventurism. They accused the African National Congress of being "too much under the influence of the whites"; they denounced the "multi-racial charterism" of the Congress Alliance and the Communist Party in particular as the carrier of "a dangerous foreign ideology". They had no concept of the complex issues involved in the South African situation.

In action the PAC floundered. It thought to rival the parent body with another passive resistance campaign, with unexpected results. There was a tepid response from the people to the campaign itself, partly because the PAC was little known but also because the ANC/SAIC campaign had left a bitter memory.

On the other hand, the savage reaction of the police in the Sharpeville massacre of African men, women and children acted as fire to a powder keg. Angry outbursts throughout the country were answered by the Verwoerd Government with the declaration of a State of Emergency (1960) during which many thousands of Blacks belonging to all movements were thrown into jail.

And then a strange thing happened. The young PAC leaders found themselves being acclaimed by the liberals in their press and receiving financial assistance. Outside South Africa substantial funds have been at their disposal.

Lacking a clear policy and programme, the PAC could not answer the needs of the people; it could not be the master of events but their victim. Young PAC men outside speak today about armed struggle. But where is the organisation? Africans who in all good faith entered camps for training after the PAC was granted recognition by the Organisation of African Unity, are bitter and disillusioned exiles until such time as they shall be able to join the main stream of the workers' and peasants' struggle in South Africa.

It is pertinent to understand how this splinter group from the ANC, in expressing the extreme of African Nationalism, was looking backwards, not forwards. The historical process in South Africa points to a new development, which places its struggle in the stream of the struggle towards socialism. In other words, it is part of a global conflict with imperialism. And the battle on two fronts, which this book in part records, marks the first phase of that struggle in South Africa.

THE UNITY MOVEMENT OF SOUTH AFRICA

We must now retrace our steps and find out the nature of the Unity Movement of South Africa and its political role in the liberatory struggle. As it has been said, a political struggle is in its essence a struggle of interests and forces, not arguments. The militant leadership which entered the national movement and helped to lay the foundations of the Non-European Unity Movement (now known as the Unity Movement of South Africa) did so in a period of social ferment resulting from the second imperialist World War. The accumulated disillusionment of the Non-White people as the Government proceeded to tighten the screw of oppression on all sections made them ripe for a new development. This leadership considered it essential to base all their agitational and organisational work first of all on a clear understanding of the social and economic forces at work in South African society, the economic roots of oppression and the nature of the state power. For, they argued, a misjudgment of the objective situation leads to a false policy and programme, in other words, a new betrayal of the people.

The leadership of the Unity Movement recognised the basic divisions in South African society as class divisions and the basic struggle as a class struggle. South Africa is a capitalist economy that is linked with world capitalism-imperialism and the struggle therefore is an integral part not only of the colonial struggle but of the struggle against the world system of capitalism. It stressed at all times the internationalism of the struggle. It understood the relationship between national racial oppression and class exploitation. The colour divisions in society are an instrument for reinforcing class exploitation. This is the key to the whole approach to the liberatory struggle, their understanding of the dynamic of the revolutionary process, their recognition that it is in the main the historical task of the oppressed workers and peasants to liberate South Africa.

With this as their starting point, the leadership took into account the particular stage of development of the oppressed people and set out to mobilise the population on the basis of a ten-point programme for full democratic rights, taking care to call it a minimum programme. They understood also the paramount importance of drawing the peasantry into the national movement.

The great mass of landless African peasantry, who are the chief source of labour for the gold mines, the white farms and heavy industry, constitute the greatest revolutionary potential. With the agitational slogan, Land and Liberty they brought home to the peasants that they would have to fight to achieve national liberation before they could solve their land hunger. It expressed the dynamic inter-connection between the two struggles. To the Coloured and Indian workers they said, "The problems of the worker in town cannot be solved independently of the peasants. His own national political struggles can never progress as long as the peasant has not begun to see his struggle as a national struggle". (From a speech on "Landlessness Is A Means Of Exploitation".)

With the slogan: We Build A Nation, they expressed the interdependence of the struggles of all sections and crystallised the necessity for the involvement of the whole population in a liberatory war. This slogan has nothing in common with the anti-White, anti-Coloured African nationalism of certain intellectuals. Such slogans were dictated by the fact that in the conditions of South Africa, equality for all and land to the peasantry were revolutionary demands and would have to be fought for. This from the outset dictated also the policy of non-collaboration with the oppressors and the building of a nation-wide organisation under a unified leadership entirely free from the control of any ruling-class party.

The full implications of the revolutionary perspectives of the Unity Movement and the socialist goal as the only means of solving the agrarian and the national problems are summarised and clarified in The Revolutionary Road For South Africa. Here we see on the ideological plane the logic of the conflict of forces and interests in the different classes and sections of South African society.

The leadership's first task was to find channels for bringing the new ideas down to the grassroots, penetrating every layer of the population and at the same time welding them into a unit that would prepare them for the battles to come. "It is only in the actual struggle on the basis of the demand for full equality," they argued, "that the people will learn the meaning of unity in the fight against a whole exploitive system". This involved first strengthening the existing federal bodies, such as the All-African Convention and the national Coloured organisation, the Anti-Coloured Affairs Department (Anti-CAD), so that they should take root amongst the people. This explains the constant emphasis on building the organisation on a national scale and the formation of local co-ordinating unity committees which would take joint action when any one section was under attack. This joint action was an effective means of breaking down racial barriers. One of the first successful campaigns of the

Unity Movement was in the urban areas in the Cape Peninsula where they exposed an attempt to whip up a pogrom spirit between Africans and Coloureds with the bogey of an "influx of Natives" taking the bread out of the mouths of the Coloured people. The counter-slogan of the Unity Movement campaign was: "An attack on one of us is an attack on all of us. The battle of the African is the battle of all of us". In the same way they organised against the extension of the Pass Laws to the Africans in the Cape Province. The joint campaign of the African and Coloureds together took the opportunity to explain how the regimentation of African labour was a threat to all workers, White as well as Non-White. These were small beginnings, but within a few years the effect of the new ideas on the people was such that, amongst the enemies of the movement, none dared stand up and expect a hearing unless he used the language of unity and the demand for equality.

By implementing the policy of non-collaboration the leadership of the All-African Convention and the Unity Movement assisted in setting in motion among the different strata of the oppressed, the peasantry, the workers, the intellectuals, the dynamic of resistance inherent in the objective situation. Its function was to deepen political consciousness through action. It is this policy which clearly identified the historical trend of the movement towards the socialist goal. It signified the refusal of the Blacks to operate the machinery of segregation for their own oppression; it involved turning their backs on the establishment and building their own independent organisations for the struggle. It is this policy which demarcated the Unity Movement from the opportunists and collaborators, exposing both them and the agents of oppression in the eyes of the people. The political content of the resulting clash with the Government on the one hand and the opportunists on the other was at all times the defence of the workers and peasants. These are some of the facts which emerge from the writings and speeches forged in the heat of the struggle itself.

Now among the many misrepresentations of the Unity Movement by its opponents, it was commonly slandered as anti-white. This was a deliberate distortion of its policy of noncollaboration with the Government in its segregatory institutions. When one bears in mind Marx's observation that ideas themselves become a revolutionary force as soon as they have gripped the masses, it was not only the collaborators who had cause to be alarmed — and hence their ceaseless efforts to keep especially the Congress youth from contamination with its dangerous ideas. The boycott struggle, which was a practical application of the policy of non-collaboration in conditions of colonial oppression, served to bring home to the peasants and workers the total irreconcilability of their interests with those of the oppressors and exploiters. In other words, inherent in this policy was the recognition of the state as an instrument of class domination. The ensuing battle on two fronts has been well documented by several hands in the literature of the All-African Convention and the Unity Movement, in a considerable body of speeches, pamphlets, polemics and books, in the struggling independent press of the movement, in conference discussions and reports. The record speaks for itself precisely because one hears the voice of the leadership addressing peasants, workers, intellectuals at every stage in its involvement with the issues which agitated them. It constitutes an arsenal of ideas hammered out on the anvil of the day-to-day struggles for over quarter of a century. It is a criminal offence in South Africa to reproduce any of this literature. Its significance for today lies in the fact that it clearly marks the historical trend of the liberatory struggle, serves as a key to understanding the present and provides directives for the future. It deals with the first phase of an unfinished struggle, the outcome of which must profoundly affect the future of South Africa and with it the future of the African continent. That is why the Unity Movement of South Africa declares its stand with the workers and peasants of South Africa and stresses the imperative necessity for the independence of the struggle.

It points out the false premise which prompts the leaders of the African National Congress (who are outside the country and divorced from the rank and file) to continue organising "international pressure" against the apartheid (Nationalist) regime and appealing to the United Nations to step in. From the outset it exposed the role of the United Nations, dominated as it is by United States imperialism. The Unity Movement of South Africa counterposes to the "democratic revolution" now being proclaimed by ANC leaders outside South Africa, the socialist revolution which only the peasants and workers of South Africa can achieve.

With the founding of the African People's Democratic Union of Southern Africa (APDUSA), the chief political body affiliated to the Unity Movement in 1961, it confirmed the proletarian character of the struggle. The Presidential Address to the first national conference of the APDUSA is in effect a manifesto declaring the permanent revolution.

Now a selection from the extensive literature of the Unity Movement can never be a satisfactory method of conveying the development of the struggle in all its ramifications. However, as a beginning, we focus mainly on the speeches and writings of I.B.Tabata, President of the Unity Movement of South Africa, because they are typical of a leadership which acted in the traditions of scientific socialism. By typical we mean that in his actions and ideas we are able to see the political essence of the Movement he represents. He is one of a corporate leadership, the emphasis being not on individual leaders but on principles. Tabata was a founding member of the All-African Convention and one of the young militants who led an attack on the opportunist leaders, exposing their tie-up with the liberals, thus paving the way for the regeneration of the Convention and the founding of the Unity Movement. As President of its political affiliate, the African People's Democratic Union of Southern Africa since its inception in 1961-62, he has identified the independent struggle of the oppressed workers and peasants as the only way to the liberation of South Africa. His influence amongst the African peasantry was demonstrated as far back as 1948 when he was arrested on a charge of incitement at the time of peasant resistance to the governments land schemes. Pondoland peasants attended his trial in force. In 1956 he was the first African leader to have a five-year ban and confinement imposed on him.

By 1963, as a new fascist law, the 90-Day Detention Bill, was being rushed through Parliament and meantime the police were constantly dogging his movements, the leadership decided that he, together with N. Honono, President of the All African Convention and Miss J Gool, a staunch fighter in the Movement since the thirties, and by this time under a five year ban, should establish a base in an adjacent territory. Tabata first effected the escape of Honono, who was under house-arrest in the Transkei. Already in 1960 Honono had been kept six months in solitary confinement while the police tried in vain to extract from him an admission that the Pondoland peasants had been in consultation with the leadership of the All-African Convention.

As the police-net tightened on the South African borders, Tabata and his two companions were instructed – as the only members of the Unity Movement executive outside the country – to make their way somehow to Dar-es-Salaam in order to place before the Liberation Committee of the recently formed Organisation of African Unity (OAU) the appeal of the Unity Movement and the All-African Convention for recognition and aid in pursuing the armed struggle in South Africa. They had been unable to attend the first meeting of the Liberation Committee, and recognition was refused. We shall not here go into the reasons for this strange refusal.

The seven lean years of exile have compelled Tabata to grapple with the problems of liberation in the perspective of the African Continent. Thus in his speeches and in the pages of APDUSA, which the group in exile publishes from time to time, he urgently analyses the machinations of imperialism in its continued stranglehold on Africa and probes the ambiguous world role of the present Soviet bureaucracy, which, if it is not guilty of complicity, yet in its foreign policy of "peaceful coexistence" must pursue the logic of betrayal of the workers of the world.

It is as a Marxist that Tabata has made a particular contribution to the liberatory movement and has always been concerned with educating young cadres to ensure the continuity of a principled struggle. As he once expressed it to his young kinsman, Nelson Mandela, who was a member of the Congress Youth League: "Opportunism is the worst disease that can infect any organisation. It is the canker that has taken the greatest toll of all our organisations up to the present day". Tabata has constantly battled – and not only with the impatient activist youth – against a common attitude of contempt or distrust of political theory as an academic luxury unnecessary to the conduct of the struggle.

This contempt for the necessity for a scientific understanding of the historical forces in society and the method of struggle, he maintains, plays into the hands of the enemy. Political illiteracy even amongst intellectuals is a tradition that is as carefully nurtured throughout the capitalist-dominated world as under the present Soviet bureaucracy, and for the same reasons. When Tabata urges the necessity for a revolutionary leadership, the political training of the youth and the use of the proper ideological tools – which is summed up in his injunction: "Whatever action we take must bring us nearer to our goal" – it is because of his acute awareness that in a century of socialist struggles throughout Europe and the colonial world the workers have been betrayed not once but many times through their lack of a clear understanding of their political interests and their precise objectives.

It was at the last open and public conference of the Unity Movement held in Edendale, Natal, 1962, that he accurately expressed the function of a revolutionary vanguard. The Verwoerd Government was then stepping up its repressive measures to stamp out resistance in the Black population. It was all the more necessary for the leadership to clarify its stand. Tabata stated:

"For the first time in South African history we are seeing society as a whole thrown into motion, and not because of international events only but because of the pressures from within .... As I said, they (the imperialists) are afraid of revolution, because if a revolution happens in South Africa and it goes beyond the bounds of capitalism, it means the loss of the African continent to Imperialism. The important thing to understand is that an essential pre-requisite for drastic change in any society is that it must be set in motion, and when it is set in motion it is the party or movement that is clearest about the historical process that, in the final analysis, will get the ear of the population. It is for this reason that you see us sticklers for theory. We must stress the need, before everything else, to be clear about our objectives. It is of paramount importance not to allow the population to be taken along other lines that are worthless to them."

(Here he referred once more to the danger of being diverted into the anti-apartheid struggle simply to unseat the White Nationalists.) And again:

"We must know our long-term as well as our immediate objectives – the changing of the whole social order." (From a speech on Bantu Education, 1953).

FOCUS ON PEASANT STRUGGLES

Already in the late thirties the All-African Convention, under the influence of the young militants, had sent organisers amongst the peasants in the Transkei (Cape Province), the largest of the Reserves. (Its population today is about one and three quarter million.) In 1945 a so-called Rehabilitation Scheme focussed anew the burning question of land-hunger.

The Scheme was designed to smoke Africans faster out of the Reserves into the gold mines by depriving them further of cattle and arable plots and was applied simultaneously with tighter urban control through the extension of the pass laws to Africans in the Cape Province. That same year Tabata addressed meetings of the peasants in the Transkei, linking the new Scheme with the whole Native policy of the Government. After a further campaign in the urban areas, addressing both African and Coloured workers, the All-African Convention published the pamphlet The Rehabilitation Scheme, A New Fraud, summarising and extending its exposure of the Smuts Government in its post-war schemes affecting both workers and peasants, and all sections of the Blacks.

For the next fifteen years the Rehabilitation Scheme became the pivot of the peasant struggle. Breaking out first in sporadic outbursts, it grew in momentum as it spread from village to village in the Transkei and the Ciskei (Cape Province) till it reached a climax in the Pondoland revolt of 1960. Resistance to the Scheme built up in Zululand, Natal Province, where organisers carried the policy of the All-African Convention; a spontaneous revolt in Witzieshoek, in the northern province of the Orange Free State, was ruthlessly crushed.

But by the late fifties peasant resistance assumed new dimensions with their revolt, not only against the Rehabilitation Scheme, but against Bantu Authorities, that is, chiefs invested with increased powers of oppression, and the debased Bantu Education over which the illiterate chiefs had been given control. Added to this the compulsory carrying of the hated passes imposed for the first time on African women − a further function carried out by the chiefs − excited their fiery wrath against these Government stooges. When the women become militant, let the oppressors beware. As resistance on these several levels mounted in the areas of Zeerust and Sekhukhuniland in the Northern Transvaal, the Government instituted a reign of terror with the invasion of villages by police armed with Sten guns, the mass trials of men and women, the banishment of peasant leaders, the burning of the peasants' homes and crops, and the flight of many people into the arid regions of Bechuanaland across the border.

The task of the Unity Movement was to bring political consciousness into the peasant struggles and provide political directives towards unifying them. But it was only after a long and bitter intensification of the struggle that the peasants first of all in the Transkei accepted the full implications of the slogan; Land and Liberty.

Convention cadres encouraged them in the formation of peasant committees which acted independently of the council of chiefs and white Native Commissioners. These democratic peasant bodies affiliated to the federal organisation, the All-African Convention, sending delegates to its conferences and there discussing their problems with peasants from other parts of the country. They attended such conferences in spite of rigorous pass laws, police spies and victimisation.

It was significant of their growing militancy that when the All-African Convention in a Statement: Along the New Road, called for a boycott of bogus segregated elections of White "Native Representatives", the Transkei peasants threw themselves into the struggle and set the pace for the cities, where the boycott became an issue affecting every African organisation. The strike of

African miners in the Transvaal in 1946 demonstrated the close links between town and country, owing to the flowing back and forth of migrant labour. The boycott struggle in turn reinforced the peasant resistance to the Rehabilitation Scheme in the Transkei.

In both struggles they were up against the same collaborators: the chiefs, members of the Native Representative Council, together with white Native commissioners and liberal candidates as "Native representatives". Then in 1948, a year of intense activity on the part of the collaborators to break the boycott of elections, I.B.Tabata as a Convention representative was arrested and tried for incitement after addressing the peasants in Pondoland. As a result of the trial news that enforcement of the Scheme was not legally valid travelled by grassroots and resistance spread to other areas.

The unfolding dynamic of resistance took another step. Owing to the success of the boycott of elections, the liberals and their protégés, the members of the Native Representative Council, lost face with the people, and therefore their usefulness. The Verwoerd (Nationalist) Government got rid of both by abolishing the white Native Representatives as well as the Native Representative Council (on which served leaders of the African National Congress). The bridges of collaboration were crumbling and Verwoerd had to resort to stronger repressive measures.

Now he launched his master-scheme to intensify the process of turning the Reserves into a reservoir of slave labour by means of the Bantu Authorities Act and the Bantu Education Act. With this, to use a familiar phrase, he became a catalyst of history. More oppressive powers to the chiefs (Bantu Authorities) meant the final demolishing of chieftainship. The peasants defied the Bantu Authorities, revolted against Bantu Education and more violently resisted the Rehabilitation Scheme. When Verwoerd threatened to close schools in those areas where the peasants refused to slaughter their cattle under the Scheme, the peasants took the point and burned down Bantu Schools.

Meantime, into the mounting stream of resistance came a hitherto passive sector of the African population, the teachers. The Cape African Teachers' Association (CATA), after affiliating with the Convention and identifying the teachers' struggle for equality with that of the workers and peasants, rejected Bantu Education. In this they were supported by the Coloured Teachers in the Teachers' League of South Africa, a national body itself affiliated to the Unity Movement. A nucleus of CATA teachers provided Convention cadres in the

Transkei and the Ciskei and played an important part in organising the peasantry into the national movement. Addressing these cadres, Tabata said: "We have to call forth all the resources of liberation latent in society. For this task we must carry political education to the masses .... The schemes of the Government in the Bantu Authorities and Bantu Education Acts can be utilised to bring home our policy of non-collaboration. The boycott of committees under both Acts puts our policy into action and helps to clarify its meaning. More than this, the boycott of these committees by the African people in many areas carries the population into the broad stream of political struggle."

The CATA received the full force of Government attack; it was the first African organisation to be outlawed; hundreds of teachers were thrown out of the profession and hounded by the police. Extracts from *Education For Barbarism*, published by the independent Prometheus Press, give some idea of the sheer barbarity of racial repression under Bantu Education. By establishing the African People's Democratic Union of Southern Africa (APDUSA) as its political wing in 1961, the Unity Movement recognised at once the acute social crisis of fascism and the fact that the oppressed, acting according to the new ideas of independent struggle, were throwing off the shackles of their slave mentality. The slow but cumulative discontent and resistance demonstrated by the several sectors of the population had prepared the way for a new development. Naturally under fascist pressures, the organisations of the Blacks were in a state of upheaval; intellectuals were deserting and, as always, had to attack in self-justification. It was precisely in this situation that the Constitution of the APDUSA gave clear expression to the role of the workers and peasants in the liberatory struggle. In the Presidential Address to the first national conference of the APDUSA, 1962, the socialist goal was unmistakably made manifest.

This was a political directive of paramount importance at the very time when Verwoerd sought to terrorise the Blacks into submission, while the agents of imperialism, through their control over the leadership of the African National Congress, sought to split their ranks and thus avert the explosion they most feared.

It is true that in all this, temporary success has gone to the Verwoerd regime. Yet the rapid growth of the APDUSA in the sixties, particularly amongst the peasantry, bears witness to a fundamental growth of political consciousness in the vanguard of the movement. The essential task of the APDUSA is to bring the separate struggles into a single organisational channel thus preparing the way for the involvement of the whole population in the protracted struggle for liberation. The peasants themselves take up the slogan: We build a nation. As we state elsewhere, under conditions of a police State, the detention of leaders, jail, torture or exile, the process is not and cannot be complete. But it points unmistakably to the revolutionary road. It is this situation which explains the strenuous efforts by imperialism and its agents to abort the struggle and deflect it from its true course. Its control of the main channels of propaganda and publicity constitutes a part of this continuing effort outside the country.

THE REVOLUTIONARY PERSPECTIVE

This brings us back to the initial concept of the class struggle on which the leadership of the Unity Movement based its strategy. This concept has a vital bearing on the next phase of the struggle in South Africa. In its *Preamble to the Ten-Point Programme*, the Unity Movement specifically included an invitation to white organisations (see *The Awakening Of A People*, p.79). Again, in leading a discussion on the necessity for the trade unions to be within the national liberatory movement, Dr GH Gool, Chairman of the National Anti-CAD, said: "To the white workers the Non-European Unity Movement poses the straightforward question: either with the oppressor against the Non-European – and ultimately against themselves – or with the oppressed Non- Europeans for the liberation of all workers and for the liberation of society as a whole." (Minutes, 4th Unity Movement Conference, 1945).

To pose the class struggle as the basic struggle in South Africa is to see it as part of the struggle against capitalism as a world system. That is, the real allies of the oppressed workers of the colonial and semi-colonial world are the workers of the metropolitan countries exploited by capitalism. To put it another way, it is a class war and not a race war between Black and White. Today the gloom prophets of a race war engulfing the world are manifold. And who are these prophets of doom? It is they who stoke the fires of racialism, who commit genocide in Vietnam, who are haunted by the spectre of the liberated workers of the world. To speak, then, of the inevitability of a race war in South Africa is to fail to recognise the class nature of the struggle and the dynamic of that struggle.

There is much talk in these days about guerrilla warfare. It is not, however, the guerrilla's gun that decides the issue but the winning over of the population, the involvement of the whole population in a liberatory struggle. In South Africa a vital factor is the vulnerability of its whole economy, the dependence not only of the gold mines but of every branch of its industrial complex on black labour.

At first the brunt of the struggle must be borne by the blacks, who comprise the bulk of the labour force. In this situation great importance attaches to the role of the landless African peasantry, the mass of migrant labourers who work on the mines and the white farms. But the very nature of a revolutionary situation disrupts the whole economic machine. The objective effects of such an enormous upheaval are such that a section of the white workers, becoming aware of a new power, will discover their true allies and desert the ruling-class camp.

It is in this way that the dynamic of the class struggle will assert itself. In South Africa, where an advanced industrialism approximates more than anywhere in Africa to that of Europe, a successful revolution must depend on the co-operation of the white workers with the black.

This is the revolutionary perspective of a struggle for the socialist goal in South Africa, and for a socialist Africa as the only means whereby the continent can begin to solve its problems. More than this, the Unity Movement with this perspective expresses solidarity with the struggle for international socialism.

Dora Taylor
September 1969

CHAPTER ONE:

The revolutionary road for South Africa

A Unity Movement pamphlet, published in exile, 1969
(Partisan Press, England)

THE UNITY MOVEMENT OF SOUTH AFRICA

Now that our newsletter APDUSA (organ of The African People's Democratic Union of Southern Africa) is becoming more widely known, we have been receiving enquiries from many parts of the world concerning the Unity Movement of South Africa. All the enquiries can be summed up as follows:

What is the Unity Movement of South Africa?

What is its policy and programme?

For whom does it speak?

What is its position in relation to the struggle for liberation in South Africa and how does it propose to solve the basic problems of that country?

We have therefore decided to issue a special Statement to meet in part these many enquiries. We say 'in part' because a proper elucidation of these questions would require a book. We recognise the urgent necessity today to clarify the complex situation in South Africa about which a great deal of political confusion has been engendered.

While this Statement is not intended to be a thesis, it is none-the-less important to give a brief outline of the objective situation within which the Unity Movement of South Africa has sprung up. It is impossible to grasp the full significance of the activities of the Unity Movement without knowing the milieu within which it has to operate and the problems confronting the oppressed people of South Africa.

The peculiarities of the South African situation are many and varied and some of them are of sufficient importance to warrant a variation in the classical formulae with which socialists are familiar.

From the point of view of the white minority, South Africa is an independent state and a highly industrialised one at that. It is by far the most advanced in the continent of Africa. Indeed in this respect it might be said that it is comparable to European states.

From the point of view of the black majority (four fifths of the population) South Africa is a colony, a slave colony, with all the barbarous oppression and exploitation that this connotes.

The 1910 Act which created the Union of South Africa — what is today known as the Republic of South Africa — was an Apartheid Act. In those days it was called segregation. It decreed that no black man shall have a franchise. And every succeeding Act, by whatever government in power, relentlessly pursued the logic of this apartheid law in every sphere of life, political, economic and social, so that today every black man is a pariah in the country of his birth. A black man has no say whatever, directly or indirectly, on who is elected to Parliament. He hasn't even a formal vote. By statutory definition an African is not a worker. That is, he is by law excluded from the classification of an employee, despite the fact that the whole economy to a large extent depends on his labour, and more especially the vital industries, mining and agriculture. He is bereft of all the rights of a worker; he cannot form trade unions and for him to strike is a criminal offence. (**Africans comprise more than three fourths of the non-white population. Ed.**)

The Urban Areas Act robs the African of the right to sell his labour-power to the highest bidder, in that he is forbidden to enter an urban area without a permit to seek work from a specific employer. This means that Africans are recruited in the Reserves as labourers who can be allotted in the requisite numbers to the various concerns of the white man.

According to new regulations (April, 1968) under the Bantu Administration Act, the fascistic Nationalist Government requires every African, whether born in the town or in the country, to be registered with a specially created tribal labour bureau under the control of the chiefs in the Reserves. Even schoolboys do not escape the operation of this draconian law which creates ever-expanding reservoirs of cheap black labour.

If a man working in town loses his job or wishes to change his employment, he has to go back to a tribal village which is allotted to him. (In many cases he himself has never seen this village but his ancestors were born there.) And he cannot get back to the town in order to work except through the channel of the tribal labour bureau. Speaking in Parliament, a government spokesman made it quite plain that the new regulations are designed to close every loophole to stop industrialists from circumventing the law. The purpose of the Act is to turn the whole African population into migrant labourers, extending it to include those who have lived all their lives in the city locations (segregated areas).

Every African will come under the blanket term 'work-seeker', and as such he will be requisitioned from the common labour pool to serve in the white areas. The regulations provide that the maximum period for such contracted labour shall be one year, or three hundred and sixty shifts, whichever is the shorter. This entrenches the migratory labour system with all its devastating effects on the individual: the destruction of family life, the separation of men from their wives and of children from their parents, the herding of men into compounds or barracks surrounded with barbed wire.

The principle of turning a whole population into shuttlecocks to be tossed hither and thither according to the demands of white employers has been enshrined in the statute book. This is what is called apartheid in practice. The inhumanity of this system staggers the imagination and arouses revulsion in every decent human being throughout the world. And rightly so.

Under the Group Areas Act, designed to segregate the population and settle them into their separate racial pens, the whole of South Africa was turned into a white Group Area, with little enclaves totalling less than thirteen percent of the land area allocated to the blacks. These enclaves dotted throughout the country are strategically placed so as to serve as reservoirs of labour for the white man, for gold, diamond and coal mining, for secondary industry, for agriculture and the rest.

With one stroke of the pen all black people were declared foreigners in the country of their birth, and like all foreigners they have no right to live anywhere in South Africa except in their particular segregated pens.

It is abundantly clear that it is a physical impossibility to crowd fifteen million people, i.e. four fifths of the population, into thirteen percent of the land. The fascist lawmakers know this all too well. It was never their intention to drive the Africans back into the Reserves to settle there. For this would mean the collapse of the whole economy of the country.

What, then, is behind this seemingly senseless, sadistic, indeed one could say crazy law? Their purpose is to uproot a whole population, render them homeless, rightless and without any means of independent livelihood.

Wherever they happen to be living outside their segregated enclaves, they must live by permit. The very few who had properties no longer live in them as of right. Their title deeds are worth no more than the piece of paper they are written on. Once uprooted and deprived of rights of tenure, the whole black population is thrown into a state of complete insecurity in the fullest sense of the word. Then a whole spate of oppressive laws is let loose on them. They come within the compass of the elaborate system of laws that has been evolved for the control and regimentation of labour, for super-exploitation. (For a full exposition of this system of inter-related laws, see I B Tabata's pamphlet *The Rehabilitation Scheme: A New Fraud*, published by the All-African Convention, 1945.)

To put into operation this gigantic scheme that affects the entire black population an army of officials is required, and the savagery of the laws finds its way from top to bottom, with all the brutality of a dehumanised automaton. The pass system is an essential part of this regimentation.

No African can move without a pass, and he will be granted a permit or pass to go only where labour is required in the white area. This is why the greatest number of criminal convictions of Africans under any single Act is for infringements of the pass laws. But the actual operation of a law has its own logic, bringing about untold sufferings to the mass of the people. It is impossible to imagine in human terms the devastating disruptive effect of the system of laws designed for the super-exploitation of a people. This is apartheid in practice.

Apartheid – a word that triggers off all the emotions associated with the horrors of Hitler's concentration camps; a word that makes the Afrikaner (Boer) Nationalist Government stink like a polecat amongst the peoples of the world. Imperialism, in its internal quarrels with its boss-boys, the Afrikaner die-hards, has itself mounted a whole propaganda campaign in its press, holding up to execration the abominable deeds perpetrated in the name of apartheid.

But what the same press does not tell the world – indeed is careful to conceal from it – is that imperialism itself is the true originator of the vile system it so eloquently castigates. We have only to recall a statement by that arch-imperialist Cecil Rhodes, one time Premier of the British Cape Colony and the man who gave his name to Rhodesia where Ian Smith now struts in authority. When introducing what he called 'a Native Bill for Africa' in 1894, he said, 'My idea is that the natives should be kept in these native reserves and not mixed with the white men at all.' (*The Role of the Missionaries in Conquest*, by Nosipho Majeke, 1952.)

What is this if not apartheid? In order to be quite sure that there was no mistaking his intentions as the spokesman for British imperialism he declared, 'I prefer to call a spade a spade. Let us boldly say: in the past we have made mistakes about native representation. We intend now to change all that .... We are going to be lords of this people and keep them in a subject position .... They should not have the franchise because we don't want them on an equality with us .... These are my politics on native affairs and these are the politics of South Africa .... We must adopt a system of despotism, such as works so well in India, in our relations with the barbarians of South Africa.' (Ibid.)

This policy was called segregation. But Verwoerd himself would have found it difficult to express his policy of apartheid any differently. Let us quote Rhodes once more, 'It must be brought home to them (the Africans) that in the future nine tenths of them will have to spend their lives in daily labour, in physical work, in manual labour.' (Ibid.)

All this was dictated by the needs of the recently discovered diamond and gold mines for a vast source of cheap black labour. It was the British mining companies that instituted the migratory labour system and demanded the introduction of the pass system that accompanies it. As will be seen from the above, the Verwoerd-Vorster régime of the Afrikaner Nationalists has introduced no new principle. It has simply pursued to their logical conclusion, and with a diabolical thoroughness, the policies laid down by British imperialism.

Why, then, did Verwoerd and Vorster after him find it necessary to castigate and even imprison the spokesmen of British imperialism in the persons of the white liberals in South Africa? This brings us to the second peculiarity in the South African situation, which adds another dimension to its complexity. Whoever fails to grasp this point will find himself entrapped in the toils of imperialist machinations. More than this, he will be unable to formulate a consistent policy to guide the liberatory struggle through the maze of conflicting interests and political crosscurrents on to a vantage ground from which to wage the struggle that will bring nearer the socialist goal.

The white minority in South Africa, which alone enjoys democratic rights, is divided into two main groups of different origins. They are the Afrikaans-speaking descendants of the Dutch Boers who came to South Africa three hundred years ago, and the English who took occupation of the Cape Colony at the beginning of the nineteenth century, and at the turn of the twentieth century conquered the two northern Boer Republics. The Boers, who now call themselves Afrikaners, regard themselves as the indigenous people, claiming priority even over the blacks of Africa, and viewing the English as foreign conquerors. The emotional attitudes, the hatred against the English associated with defeat, were reinforced by the fact that they represented two different economies. The demands of a unified economy under capitalism brooked neither Boer feudalism nor African tribalism.

It is true that the English wooed the Boers after conquest, making them co-partners for the more thorough exploitation of the black man. But the die-hards among the Boers continued to fan the fires of hatred even after they had embraced the capitalist system. Regarding themselves as the indigenous people, they saw themselves as Nationalists leading a struggle against the imperialist oppressor. Two years after the Act of Union creating South Africa as a single state we find Hertzog, leader of the Afrikaner Nationalist Party, (note the designation 'Nationalist') declaring that 'the two white peoples must be left free to develop along their own lines in two streams, and that the Union should be ruled only by pure Afrikaners.' (Eric Walker, *A History of South Africa*, 1928.) And again, on the occasion of the rebellion in South Africa of the die-hard Boers during the First World War, Walker lists some of their motives as 'the longing to regain their lost independence; a desire to avenge themselves on Great Britain for their sufferings during the Boer War .... and the feeling that the Afrikaners were an oppressed people, oppressed by all the social, political and economic forces .... associated with the name of Britain.' (*Ibid.*)

To this day the economy of South Africa is heavily dominated by British investments and increasingly joined by United States capital. About seventy-nine percent of all economic activity in the country is in the hands of the English-speaking section, which is closely associated with Britain economically, culturally and politically. But the Afrikaners happen to be numerically more than the English-speaking section, and it is this fact that the politicians utilised to put themselves in power. They dubbed the English as a foreign race, uitlanders, and proceeded to whip up racial passions against them, resuscitating all the hatreds of the Boer War with a view to moulding the Afrikaners as a separate race, a separate nation, divinely destined to rule their god-given country. From this it can be seen that the struggle of the die-hard Afrikaners was from the start, from their point of view, a nationalist struggle led by the rising bourgeoisie against the foreigners. They declared themselves most vociferously as anti-imperialists. The one-time honoured General Botha, one of their leaders in the Boer War, who became the first Prime Minister of the Union of South Africa, and General Smuts who succeeded him, were both denounced as pro-imperialist stooges and traitors to the Volk (people). There was a split in the Afrikaner camp. The rich farmers and the moneyed section threw in their lot with big business, and joined hands with the local English-speaking representatives of British finance capital.

The existence of the aggressively chauvinistic and racist Afrikaner element which claimed to be indigenous while violently antagonistic to the indigenous Africans, presented in the early days a thorny political problem to the different socialist groups in South Africa. Many a split took place over what attitude should be adopted towards Afrikaner white nationalism. The problem, from a theoretical point of view, was made more difficult by the fact that at one time there was not even an aspiring native bourgeoisie among the Africans and no national organisation ready to vocalise the concept of nationalism and initiate a struggle on the basis of that concept.

A tragicomic aspect of this dilemma was exemplified in the fact that in the 1920s the South African Labour Party formed a coalition government with the Afrikaner Nationalist Party, the same party that was later to be led by Verwoerd followed by Vorster. The results were disastrous for the vast majority of the workers, namely the Africans.

On another level, amongst the revolutionary socialists, there was a split over the same question. One section argued that the Afrikaner Nationalists were anti-imperialists and in addition they constituted the rising native bourgeoisie. Therefore it was the duty of the revolutionists to support them. This grotesque courtship, however, was harshly and abruptly terminated when, with the outbreak of the second imperialist world war, the Afrikaners backed Hitler in a big way, and continued to be his most ardent worshippers even after his defeat. It is not surprising that these so-called revolutionaries vanished into oblivion.

A second group of what might be called the ultra-leftists rejected not only the Afrikaners, bourgeoisie and workers alike, but the whole of the white population in South Africa, arguing that they were all exploiters, while at the same time they refrained from organising the oppressed black masses, on the ground that it was not the duty of revolutionaries to form nationalist organisations or to encourage their formation. This, they argued, was the task of a native bourgeoisie, and since this class had not crystallised among the blacks, they limited their activities to discussion clubs. This group, too, having choked itself to death in its own verbiage, vanished unwept from the political arena.

It was in the midst of this atmosphere of intensive debate that, in 1935, a political crisis broke out and galvanised into action practically the whole of the African population. It was the notorious Slave Bills introduced by the Hertzog-Smuts coalition government that took away the last remaining voting rights of the Africans in the Cape Province and shattered all hopes of a development towards a franchise for the blacks. At the same time it robbed the Africans of the right to buy land outside the Reserves. In the guise of granting them more land, for which the Africans had already been clamouring, the so-called Land and Trust Act by some ruse robbed them of the right to the land which some of them already occupied. Thus it carried a step further the ruthless policy of landlessness and therefore the more intensive regimentation of African labour.

The publication of the Bills first stunned the African population, but as the implications became clear, a bitter anger seized them, penetrating every layer to the remotest corners of the country. The intellectuals and the vocal sections, the incipient petit-bourgeoisie, received a stunning blow with the finality of the clauses that closed the door to their long-cherished dreams of a franchise that would give them a privileged position. The workers saw the tightening of the net that consolidated the system for the regimentation of labour. The land-hungry peasants saw that, far from the Act giving them the promised extra land, their plight was going to be immeasurably worsened. They were doomed to starvation in their ever-shrinking, arid plots of land. Even the most backward section, the chiefs who were by now being resuscitated for administrative purposes, were alarmed at the wrath of the people they were supposed to control.

Land was the core of the deep discontents of the peasantry throughout the countryside. It was the prime factor that brought them into collision with all the local government agents in every village. From every part of the country, from every section, spontaneous protests came flooding in. It was in this situation that a nation-wide conference of all African organisations was called in December 1935. It was the biggest of its kind in the history of the African people. Over one hundred and fifty organisations were represented by more than five hundred delegates. The conference unanimously decided to reject the Bills in toto. At the same time it decided to establish the All-African Convention as a federal body that would be the mouthpiece of the African section of the oppressed people of South Africa.

The force of this political crisis catapulted the socialist groups from academic debate into action. A new situation had arisen. Every revolutionary had either to participate or be forever reduced to nullity. But the important point at issue was: what kind of participation? This was the crux of the matter. And this was to be determined by the overall outlook of each group, that is, their assessment of the objective situation in South Africa, their ultimate aims and the kind of solution they proposed to the problems presented by the historic epoch.

The Communist Party of South Africa, ever reformist in outlook, conceived the struggle as divided mechanistically into categories and stages. The first stage was for equality between white and black, in other words for bourgeois democracy. When the oppressed became absorbed into this system they would learn to organise themselves for a class struggle. In short, theirs was a reformist policy of gradualism which determined their strategy and tactics. In practice the activity of the Communist Party in those organisations which it controlled was confined to bringing pressure on the Government to grant concessions, centring all their agitation on isolated issues.

Their work in the trade union field was pure economism. Even at a time when the fascist Government had outlawed African trade unions and atomised the rest of the workers into separate racial trade unions, white, coloured and Indian, the Communist Party still concentrated the major part of its activity on building those racial trade unions whose slogan was 'no politics in the trade union movement'. It never seemed to occur to them that they were in effect accepting the myth of the inferiority of the black man and the apartheid policy, and in this regard they were quite indistinguishable from that particular species, the South African white liberal who, in the conditions of that country, is the spokesman of international finance capital.

That group which was later to constitute the leadership of the Unity Movement conceived of the struggle very differently. It saw the crisis of 1935 as bound up with the mounting crisis of world capitalism. With a sixth of the world having been wrenched out of the orbit of capitalism after the First World War, imperialism was faced with the necessity of a still more intensive exploitation of the regions under its domination. After a thorough analysis of the objective situation in South African society economic, political and social, this group came to the conclusion that the problems of the oppressed could not be solved within the framework of the capitalist system. It would require nothing short of a revolutionary socialist overturn. Even the bourgeois democratic demands for the oppressed black masses could not be achieved except under the dictatorship of the proletariat assisted by the peasants.

In this situation, the vast army of migrant labourers, who are in essence a landless peasantry, will play a significant role. It is the leadership of the proletariat in the conduct of the struggle for democratic rights that will ensure the continuity of the revolution uninterruptedly to its socialist goal.

This concept envisaged a continuous revolution with the one stage merging dialectically into the next, in other words, the permanent revolution. This was the overall strategy when this group entered the field of action within the national movement. It implies several things, the most important being, first, a recognition of the fact that in our epoch the national bourgeoisie no longer has a progressive role to play. This is particularly so in the conditions of South Africa, where the so-called national bourgeoisie – the white Afrikaner nationalists – is itself a conqueror and is virulently racialistic towards the indigenous oppressed population. Secondly, it implies that, with the attainment of the democratic stage, there will be no long protracted period between it and the next stage, and that, with the seizure of power, the proletariat must immediately put the socialist tasks on the agenda of the day.

Between the formulation of the strategy, however, and the achievement of the goal, all the interim is fraught not only with the manifold tactical difficulties of gearing the population into action along a particular course, but with the pitfalls and hazards of fighting battles on many fronts, fighting the internal as well as the external enemies. This in truth has been the history of the Unity Movement for the last quarter of a century. Marxism alone, used as an instrument of analysis and guide to action, can encompass all the problems, all the hidden snares and impediments inherent in this situation. Only the weapon of Marxism can cut a clear path through the ideological jungle with which imperialism so skilfully trammels up the unwary. We have mentioned that the All-African Convention was born in a time of crisis. At such times of general ferment the population is receptive to ideas. The problem was how to maintain the new-found African unity and how to broaden it; at the same time how to introduce new ideas that would permeate in the shortest possible period every stratum of the oppressed population and gear them to meet not only the immediate crisis but to set them on the revolutionary road of principled struggle consistent with the whole strategy referred to above.

For the first few years the battle of ideas took place inside the All-

African Convention itself. Young militant leaders clashed with the old leaders who by tradition were under the tutelage of the white liberals. It was the young militants who for the first time insisted on the necessity of having a clearly defined programme and policy as the basis of the struggle. The Ten-Point Programme was adopted. It was known as the 'minimum programme'. It was a demand for full democratic rights for all in South Africa. It was calculated to meet the aspirations of the intellectuals and the aspiring petit-bourgeoisie who felt acutely the national oppression; at the same time it voiced the needs of the poor and landless peasantry, as well as the demands of the rightless workers. Basically the programme was designed to unite two main currents, the agrarian and the national.

Having formulated the programme, the young militants who were now in the leadership of the African federal body, the All-African Convention, turned their attention to the question of broadening the unity to include all the oppressed nationalities in South Africa who for three hundred years have been kept in separate and antagonistic racial pens. The All-African Convention opened negotiations with a federal organisation of coloured people, known as the Anti-CAD (Anti-Coloured Affairs Department) and the South African Indian Congress. The latter body, being under the control of the merchant class, refused to accept the uncompromising policy and programme which demanded full equality, and argued that they were committed to a policy of compromise. In this they were acting true to form, confirming that the present-day rising bourgeoisie can no longer play a progressive role. They instinctively felt that the programme of the Unity Movement, while it was democratic in form, nevertheless, taken together with its uncompromising policy of non-collaboration, is in fact a revolutionary programme. It is essentially directed not to bourgeois democracy, which answers the interests of the merchant class, but must of necessity pass over into socialist democracy. Of this, more later. The federal bodies of the African and coloured sections went ahead to found the Non- European Unity Movement, now known as the Unity Movement of South Africa, and proceeded to go over the heads of the Indian merchant-class leadership to draw in the Indian workers in the towns and sugar plantations, as well as the youth, organised under the Anti-Segregation Council. It adopted the Ten-Point Programme as a minimum programme, together with the policy of noncollaboration with the oppressor.

NON-COLLABORATION

The minimum programme, the Ten-Point Programme of the Unity Movement, taken by itself, can be regarded simply as a bourgeois nationalist programme, though point seven, which deals with the land question, already envisages a development beyond formal democracy. But when taken together with the policy of non-collaboration, with which the programme is inseparably bound, it takes on a different connotation. It is for this reason that the leadership of the Unity Movement in all its writings, all its propaganda and agitation, always links its policy and programme together.

This is of vital importance to the understanding of the dynamics of the struggle, the approach, and the mechanics of it. To fail to understand the concept of non-collaboration in the given conditions of South Africa is to fail to grasp its significance and its potency. Unfortunately, even amongst revolutionaries there are very few who seem to comprehend its full import. Those who operate in the milieu of the highly industrialised countries are very conscious of the importance of the trade union movement. Their starting point is the recognition that a trade union is a reformist organisation which accepts the capitalist system as given and immutable.

These are the confines in which its struggle is conducted. That is why it never goes beyond the demands of a penny increase, shorter hours, better conditions of work, etc. In short, economic demands. Left to themselves, the workers will not go beyond the struggle for pure economic benefits. It is the task of the revolutionaries who work in the trade unions to broaden their vision.

For this they need a theory that illuminates to the workers the true nature of the system that exploits them as a class, and enables them to realise the necessity to destroy the exploitive system itself. In order to do this the revolutionary engages in the day-to-day struggle of the workers, including purely economic strikes. Many workers' strikes have in themselves no political significance, but they are none-the-less necessary not only for the more obvious immediate aims, but for a much more important reason, namely, that the workers begin to discover their own power. The militants utilise such strikes to heighten the workers' class consciousness in preparation for the day when the militants within the working-class movement will themselves use their collective might for political demands which will lead to the overturn of the system. A trade union is the most elementary, we might even say primitive form of organisation arising out of the conditions of social production at a given stage, namely, capitalism. He would be an ultra-leftist indulging in utopianism of the crudest kind who would turn his back on the trade unions on the ground that they are backward and reactionary. He must take cognisance of the actual conditions of existence pertaining to the stage of development in society, and most of all the dominant ideas which are invariably those of the ruling class.

Now the questions we have to ask are: What kind of organisations existed in South Africa when the Unity Movement evolved its policy of non-collaboration? What was the function of those organisations and above all what were the dominant ideas prevalent amongst the oppressed at that time? As we pointed out earlier, the arch-imperialist Cecil Rhodes enunciated what he called the Native policy for all successive governments, which in effect meant throwing the whole African population out of the body politic. During the wars of conquest it had been the prime aim of the invader to destroy chieftainship, because the chiefs were the rallying point of military resistance. Capitalism itself had to shatter tribalism. The normal consequence of this should have been to absorb the population into the capitalist system, with all that that implied: new social relations, new organisational forms and participation in the economic and political life as citizens of the country. But the white rulers had other schemes for the black man whom they considered as nothing but a beast of burden. Having thrown the Africans out of the body politic, Rhodes himself proceeded to devise special means for governing and controlling them.

A remarkable man was this Rhodes in his elemental savagery which expresses itself in his turns of thought and the very crudity of his language. Once on beholding a large gathering of Africans in their village he exclaimed, 'What a source of labour!', and when introducing his Glen Grey Bill, 'Now I say, the natives are children .... They have human minds and I would like them to devote themselves wholly to local matters that surround and appeal to them. I would like them to tax themselves ....'. This was the Act that created the notorious Bunga system, that is, village councils mainly composed of illiterate chiefs who were now being built up as paid stooges of the Government. These Bungas, acting under the chairmanship of the local white 'Native Commissioners', dominated the lives of all the people in the villages. It was through them that the many Acts of Parliament passed against the Africans were transmitted. It must be understood here that the white Minister for Native Affairs governed a whole people by proclamations issued in the name of the Governor-General, who, for this purpose, had the title of 'Supreme Chief of all Natives.' These, too, were transmitted through the Bungas, which with the utmost zeal saw to it that they were obeyed to the letter.

In addition to this, any piece of dirty legislation which was too inhuman even for the rulers to blacken the Statute Book, was left to the Bungas to enact. It fell to the Bungas to impose the local taxes under which the population groaned, that drove a starving people to seek work in the mines and on the hated white farms where their conditions were those of serfs. It was their duty also to supply forced unpaid labour for road-making so that the white Commissioner's car could go for inspections to the remotest villages.

As industry expanded by leaps and bounds with the exploitation of a vast black labour force, the Bunga system was extended to the urban areas where the African workers were ghettoed in special 'locations' outside the cities. Here they were called Advisory Councils. From the point of view of the oppressors, these institutions worked so well that they later created a Supreme Bunga, with the grandiloquent name of the Native Representative Council to 'represent' the total African population in town and country. This sat under the chairmanship of the white Secretary of Native Affairs, ably assisted by selected white Native Commissioners. Many African intellectuals vied with one another for positions on these bogus institutions created for a 'child race'. The leading politicians of the old school, protégés of the white liberals, regarded it as a great honour to be raised to this bad eminence, lording it over the mass of the people.

All the political activity of the Africans was restricted within these narrow confines: the Bungas, which prevented them from claiming direct representation in the provincial council where the whites alone sat; the Advisory Boards, which likewise headed them off from seeking direct representation in municipal councils; and finally the 'Supreme Bunga', the Native Representative Council, which blocked the minds of the people from demanding direct representation in the seat of government itself – Parliament. Thus we see that these segregated institutions created for an 'inferior people' were used not only as a machinery for oppression and exploitation but as an instrument for mental enslavement, perpetuating the myth of the inferiority of the black man.

It was within the setting of these conditions that the policy of non-collaboration was born and marked a turning-point in the history of the oppressed. The devastating effect of these longstanding conditions on the mind can be readily understood. To put it in the words of *The Awakening of a*

People (I B Tabata, 1950), "Although on paper it may seem a simple thing for a people to recognise themselves as equal to other human beings, yet if we visualise the generations of oppression, the sheer weight on mind and body of a system of slavery armed with all the machinery of the state, all the legal and ideological weapons designed to obliterate from their minds the very capacity to think of themselves as human beings; if we visualise the steady insidious effect of the conditions of their existence, the brutalising squalor and deprivation which of themselves engender the feeling of inferiority – if we take all these things into consideration we begin to understand the leap which the people took at this time."

This is the soil out of which sprang the policy of non-collaboration. The leadership of the Unity Movement was faced with the task of purging the minds of the oppressed of what we call slave mentality and directing their activities towards meaningful political channels, thus releasing the latent energies of a whole people to engage in a struggle that has a significant bearing on their life, a struggle that is intelligible to them, quickened as it is by their imperative needs. Such a policy with its great potentialities could not but arouse the alarm and excite the enmity of the ruling-class and its agents within the folds of the oppressed. For the first time in the history of South Africa both the imperialist and the Afrikaner press let loose a flood of abuse directed on two main prongs of the new development. It concentrated its attack on the organisational structure and on the new ideas. And no wonder. For these related aspects of the development signified the beginning of a serious challenge to white domination, which in turn would spell the doom of capitalism itself.

The federal structure of the All-African Convention, bringing together all the African organisations, was now extended to a larger federation, the Unity Movement, embracing organisations of all sections of the oppressed, African, coloured and Indian. This form of organisation representing a cross section of the oppressed, cuts across not only the lingering tribal affiliations but also those racial barriers so carefully nurtured by the oppressors in the timehonoured policy of divide-and-rule. This form of organisation, uniting a whole people, cleared the way for a national outlook. The new outlook expressed in the programme and in the policy of noncollaboration confirmed the enemy's worst fears and galvanised them into action.

The liberals and the Communist Party of South Africa pulled out of the federation the African National Congress, over which they had considerable influence and indeed control. Once out of the federation, the African National Congress was used as a tool in the attempt to destroy the unity of the people and swing the population back to the old policy of collaboration with the oppressor. Its leaders declared war on the policy of non-collaboration, and the local representatives of imperialism put their powerful press at their disposal. The press of the Communist Party of South Africa vied with the press of finance capital in their voluminous vilification of the policy of non-collaboration, while at the same time they praised the leaders of the African National Congress to the skies for their statesmanship, moderation and realism. They accused the leadership of the Unity Movement of adopting a negative policy and advocating inaction. Its advocacy of the boycott of elections to the inferior apartheid institutions was held up as an example of what they damned as inaction. This was political dishonesty calculated to create the maximum confusion. The real issue was not action versus inaction, but what kind of action.

All their outcry against the boycott was a cloak to conceal their own commitment to collaboration with the Government. For to operate these segregated institutions for any reason whatsoever was to accept the inferiority of the black man and to involve the population in working the machinery of their own oppression.

The policy of non-collaboration, far from advocating inaction and abstention, was, on the contrary, in the given conditions of South Africa, an injunction to engage in political action of the highest order. When the leadership of the Unity Movement put this policy before the people, it was compelled to explain its full meaning and significance. To do this, it had to unfold the nature of the system that oppressed and exploited them and the methods used to maintain it. The leadership had to bring home to the masses how they themselves were being deceived into assisting in the operation of the machinery of their own oppression, and convince them that without their participation it would be impossible to maintain the present oppressive structure.

Here was an opportunity for the Unity Movement to illuminate the whole range of the political, economic and social set-up in South Africa. In the economic sphere it placed the people in the very centre as the prime producers of the country's wealth and all its vaunted progress, while they themselves received in turn the very dregs, the offal of civilisation. In the midst of splendour which they themselves create, the blacks live in hovels, segregated like lepers. Their infant mortality rate is one of the highest in the world. All this because they are bereft of political rights. They have no say in the government of the country of their birth, no say in the planning and the distribution of the wealth they produce.

The policy of non-collaboration caught the imagination of the people. As ever-increasing layers of the population began to understand the meaning of this new policy, they threw themselves with vigour into political activity. Every new law and every issue was seen by them as part of the sum total of an inter-related system for their exploitation. The struggle began to take on a new meaning. With a growing knowledge of their own position, they threw off their dependence on the ideas of the ruling class and struck out on an independent road of struggle.

This liberation of the mind released the energies of the people. It was now no longer a question of seeking palliatives, of begging for the 'improvement' of this or that institution. It was a total rejection of the whole system. They had turned their back on the 'establishment'. Any official or anyone connected with the government or its institutions was suspect in their eyes. It must be understood of course, that the population had no clearly defined conception of the kind of society they wanted. But they knew what they did not want.

The leadership of the Unity Movement, sensing the changing mood of the people, increasingly involved itself in their day-to-day struggles, using every issue, whether in the countryside amongst the peasantry or among the workers in the town, in order to broaden their political consciousness. Their first targets were those hated institutions, the Bungas in the villages and the Advisory Boards in the urban areas, and on a national scale the bogus Native Representative Council.

Since these were important pillars of the administrative system, the rulers took alarm at the new turn of events. When the people boycotted the elections to these segregated institutions and isolated the quislings, bringing them into contempt, this meant the breaking down of the channels of control. With their success in jamming the administrative machinery in one village after another, they became aware of their power. This was a big undertaking which called forth the involvement of the whole population in ever-widening areas throughout the Union of South Africa. Everywhere the question was posed: the new road of non-collaboration or the old road of collaboration.

Or to put it another way: with the people against the Government, or with the Government against the people. There was a deep cleavage in which all the oppressed became involved, village by village and town by town. Every organisation had to declare itself on this vital question. As time went on a political polarisation took place. The majority of the masses threw in their lot with the new road and those organisations whose leaders were committed to collaboration began to lose their following. The African National Congress found itself in this plight. All the attempts of the imperialist press to bolster up its leaders were of no avail.

A new phenomenon took place. As the people turned their back on the Bunga, they began to create their own village committees and elected their own spokesmen to present their demands to the government officials. The Government replied with machine-guns. Much to the amazement of the rulers, these brutal reprisals no longer deterred the people but rather hardened them in their resistance. Peasants' organisations sprang up in all the provinces, so that today the biggest single organisations in the country are those of the peasants.

The immediate cause of the phenomenal growth of these organisations was the need for self-defence. They had learned from bitter experience that it was the easiest thing for the white army to surround a village, mow down the people and burn their crops.

In this way they saw the futility of an isolated struggle and responded to the new slogan of the Unity Movement: We build a Nation. Most of the peasants' organisations and certainly all the biggest ones threw in their lot with the Unity Movement and affiliated to it. Individual peasant leaders at the same time joined the African People's Democratic Union of Southern Africa (APDUSA), which is the most highly developed political organisation affiliated to the Unity Movement.

The imperialist wing of the South African herrenvolk raised the alarm and put all the blame for this state of affairs on the apartheid policy of the Nationalist Government. They advocated a relaxation of some of the more stringent laws to allow at least the black intellectuals some measure of privilege. The fascistic wing of the herrenvolk rejected any such suggestions and relied on the use of force to crush the rising movement. The liberals, the local representatives of finance capital, tried every means to oust the Afrikaner Nationalists from power. They even utilised their black protégés to stoke up trouble in the form of one-day strikes and carefully controlled acts of sabotage with the express purpose of frightening the white electorate into dislodging the Afrikaner Government.

In its turn the Government hit back by summarily arresting the liberals, the Communist Party leaders and their black protégés. As would be expected, even in this instance there was a differentiation. The blacks, who were being used by the wily liberals, received the most vicious treatment, some of them being hanged and others receiving life sentences.

The tragedy of it is that some of those African leaders were brave and honest men who sincerely believed that they were making sacrifices in the struggle for the freedom of their fellow men. True enough, their concept of freedom was a neo-colonialist regime and this is why they were acceptable to the far-sighted representatives of imperialism in South Africa. It never occurred to them that they were caught up in an internal quarrel between two sets of vultures struggling for power.

The enormity of the crime committed by the liberals and the Communist Party against the oppressed people of South Africa is to be seen in their role outside South Africa. They deliberately conceal the real struggle for liberation with the express purpose of smothering it, while at the same time they mount a vast anti-apartheid campaign to win the support of well-meaning people all over the world.

For what? In fact Africa and the peoples of the world have been subjected to a huge confidence trick. In terms of the South African set-up, anti-apartheid means anti-Afrikaner Nationalist Government. It means the return to power of the English speaking sections. It means the entrenchment of imperialism in South Africa and all that that connotes for the exploitation of the mass of the black population.

To suit the prevailing climate outside, some of them even don the cloak of anti-imperialism. But again, in the terms of South Africa, what does this mean? Verwoerd himself and all his diehard cohorts in the Afrikaner Nationalist Party proclaim themselves as sworn anti-imperialists.

This is another deception to win the sympathies of the more progressive forces in the world, particularly the socialist oriented countries. In a highly industrialised country like South Africa, to prate about an anti-imperialist struggle which is not at the same time directed to the overthrow of capitalism, is to perpetrate a gross political fraud.

The unpalatable fact that faces the liberals and the Communist Party of South Africa is that the only force that is committed to and is capable of conducting a consistent struggle for the liberation of the oppressed and exploited workers and peasants in South Africa consists of that group of organisations united under the banner of the Unity Movement of South Africa.

The programme and policy are clear. They serve as a guide through the various stages of the struggle, a guide to the revolutionary road of armed struggle, the only road that leads to the socialist goal.

CHAPTER TWO:
The policy of apartheid

I THE PROBLEM OF SLAVE MENTALITY

Editor's Note: In a speech introducing a discussion on the national situation at a conference in 1954 of the All-African Convention (a federal organisation founded in 1943), Tabata said, 'We had set ourselves a target — to weld the whole population into a unit in order to engage in a struggle for freedom. The first need therefore was to create an independent, national organisation free from herrenvolk influence. But in order to do this we first had to fight the battle of the mind. We had to break the intellectual slavery of the black man.'

Ten years later, in a letter written in exile to President Kwame Nkrumah, he stated, 'From the outset two things became clear to us. Firstly, that our people suffered from a slave mentality which was a barrier to all progress. Slaves cannot conduct a protracted struggle against their masters until they begin to see themselves as human beings. In our approach to this problem we had to show them that without their consent and participation it was not possible for the masterrace to keep them in bondage, and that they, particularly the black intellectuals, were the necessary cogs in this machinery for their own oppression. It was out of this that arose our policy of non-collaboration with the oppressor.'

Pursuing the same problem in a letter to a Minister of State in 1967, he wrote, 'We had formulated our method of struggle and organisation and put it into practice. In a comparatively few years we witnessed a change of political climate on a national scale. The whole population of the oppressed changed its political posture from a prostrate one to an upright one, from that of abject slaves to human beings ready to struggle for their rights. This could only be done by involving the people in limited battles which we presented to them as part of a war. In this way they began to discover their own power as a united people.'

Tabata was profoundly concerned with rooting out what he called the paralysing disease of slave mentality, which permeated the whole of the oppressed population, including the more sophisticated elements. I may add that this phenomenon is by no means limited to South Africa and those who have suffered colonial oppression in other continents. It is a blight that still rests on the mass of the working class in highly industrialised countries in Europe and the United States. Tabata dealt with it in different ways and on different levels.

For example, addressing a selected group of cadres on 'The State', in 1948, he said, 'There is today a dire need to return to the fundamentals of Marxism. Chief amongst them is the problem of the relation of the State to the revolutionary movement.

Capitalism, or shall I say, imperialism on a world scale has reached its apex, its limit of development. It now serves as a check on further progress. It can only produce explosion and convulsion which threaten to destroy the very foundations of civilisation. The objective situation is ripe, rotten ripe, for the destruction of capitalism and the ushering in of socialism. But the subjective factor is sadly lagging behind.

There is a tragic lack of a strong revolutionary leadership, able to grapple with problems posed by history today. The whole capitalist world is an arsenal; each country is armed to the teeth. The state machinery of each country has developed into a monster towering above society and threatening to destroy it. Any time now a spark may set the world into a conflagration. And yet the forces of the Left are still floundering in a sea of confusion. They are still steeped in social-chauvinism and opportunism, adventurism and petty-bourgeois superstitions and reverence for the State. They have become worshippers of bourgeois democracy. They stand in awe before this huge colossus, the State, which they regard as immutable, having been created with "divine" sanction.'

Now when engaging with the population at meetings Tabata had a particular method of illuminating a political point or thought by means of a homely and apparently naïve illustration.

This was the other side of his political style of address. He invented tales and animal stories in a tradition familiar to the peasant, or made up an incident that would speak to the city worker. Unfortunately, like many of his speeches throughout the country, few of these inventions of the moment have survived in the written word, though the peasants would retell them with salty additions of their own. He has commented that his audience would at first give an almost embarrassed laugh as they listened to his story, but then their eyes would gleam with something very different from laughter as the point came home.

It was on the day when the government press splashed the news that Verwoerd (Prime Minister) had declared that the Transkeian Territories were to be an 'independent' Bantustan (Reserve for Africans), with Chief Kaiser Matanzima as head of its 'parliament', that Tabata was moved to compose a savage lampoon. It was entitled A Baboons' Parliament, and was published, in February 1962, in the independent press of the Movement, Ilizwi Lesizwe, Vol. 1, No. 4. Ever since the appearance of this satire the African people refer to the Bantustan parliament as 'The Baboons' Parliament'. The story follows.

A BABOONS' PARLIAMENT

Now it has become quite clear that the herrenvolk have the most profound contempt for their creatures (the chiefs). Indeed it would seem that they have a justifiable basis for their contempt. Verwoerd proposes to give his chiefs a toy to play with. Matanzima grasps it with both hands and gleefully displays it to his people. He dances around, telling the people how they are going to draw up a constitution for their toy parliament. The people look on in amazement and consternation at this spectacle. They see before them the re-enactment of the famous story of 'The Baboons' Parliament'.

This story relates how there was once a wise farmer with large tracts of land where he grew mealies, pumpkins and fruit trees. He kept a few domesticated baboons for his pleasure. He used to dress them up in clothes, train them to sit at table, use cups and saucers. He taught them never to eat food that was natural to baboons but to feed on offal of wild animals. At reaping time the farmer was plagued by large troops of wild baboons which invaded his lands, causing great devastation to his crops.

THE MASTER PLAN

He thought of a plan to use his baboons in order to save his crops. He spoke to them about self-government and even took them to see a human parliament in session. 'Here,' he said, 'is where the humans make the laws which must be obeyed by every human being.' The domesticated baboons sitting in the gallery, somewhat uncomfortable in their ties and collars, were nevertheless highly impressed.

The wise farmer told his creatures that he was now going to liberate them. He would let them free to go back to the other baboons in the forest. But he warned them in grave tones, 'You must remember that you are now civilised baboons. A great responsibility devolves on you as leaders to uplift the other baboons, train them to accept the laws. You must have a parliament of baboons with baboon laws to be obeyed by all baboons. I will help you to draft a baboon constitution and you must ensure that these laws are strictly obeyed. To ensure respect for the pomp and circumstance of the law I shall give you some of my clothes to be worn by the baboon parliamentarians.' So saying, he handed them a bundle of cast-offs.

THE CHOSEN FEW

The gratitude and joy of the baboons was immeasurable. Prancing about and chattering as they made their preparations to go, it seemed to them that this was the dawn of a new era for baboondom. They rounded up all the troops in the various forests and announced their plans. On the appointed day they assembled at a clearing in the forest. Proudly the domesticated baboons distributed the tattered cast-off clothes amongst a few chosen males who were to become the Members of Parliament. A great deal of time was spent on discussing the finer points of the niceties of dress. Some of the baboons insisted that it was more artistic to wear their jackets back to front. Amongst them were the sophisticated ones who had once come into close contact with the human species. They declared that these clothes were cast-offs and unfit to wear. They expressed their indignation in no uncertain terms, pointing to the various holes in the rags.

Undaunted, the domesticated ones, however, pointed out that these holes would come in handy, since they, the baboons, unlike humans, had tails which had to be accommodated.

This hurdle over, the parliamentarians settled down to discuss the importance of the baboon constitution and laws. The domesticated ones were now in their element. They whipped out from their back pockets – or was it under pockets? – a prepared constitution all complete with special laws to control the rest of baboonkind.

The laws prescribed that the baboon was now free to roam in the forests they already occupied. It was a freedom charter giving them their own parliament and stressing above all obedience to all baboon laws on pain of death if necessary. All power was given to the new Members of Parliament. They could act as legislators, judges and juries, policemen, prosecutors and hangmen.

The regulations framed under these laws were most interesting. The baboons were allowed to eat anything that grew wild in the forest. They were strictly forbidden to eat fruit, vegetables or anything whatsoever that was cultivated by man. If they wanted meat they had to learn to eat, besides scorpions and the like, only the offal of wild rabbits which are a pest to the crops of humans. They were forbidden to leave the forests without permits, and these were granted only to those who intended to hunt rabbits on the farms.

Thus the wise farmer instituted the first baboon parliament. Forever after that, he had the richest harvest, free from marauding baboons. He learnt afterwards that his liberated baboons enforced his baboon constitution and laws with a ruthlessness possible only in baboonland.

THE DOG STORY

(from a speech to a peasant audience)

There was a time when the dog was a proud animal roving in the forests. He lived his life like all other wild animals hunting for food and free to roam at will. Then along came this creature called Man, captured him and domesticated him. The first thing that Man did with him was to wipe out all memory of his past existence in the forest. Man enslaved his mind, until the poor thing began to think that he could not exist without his master. For his food he relied on his master. For protection from the elements, from the cold and the rain, he looked to his master.

Now this creature called Man is the most physically helpless of all animals. He has not the strength to fight the lion or other beasts of prey. He has not the speed to catch the smaller animals. He depends on his dog to do these things. This once proud animal, the dog, is now used to catch other animals for Man to eat. And what does he get for his service? The master throws him the bones and the offal, while he himself enjoys all the choice meat. And the poor thing is perfectly satisfied with all this.

Why? Because Man has enslaved his mind. He has destroyed in him all the attributes of doghood and replaced it with a slave mentality.

Now, my countrymen, all of you here own dogs. But when the white rulers employ the same methods to divide us and subjugate us, we do not recognise what is happening. Let us put the matter plainly. Who has built up the civilisation of this country? It is our black hands. It is these black hands that dig the gold out of the bowels of the earth, the gold that creates the wealth that only the rich white man enjoys. These black hands make the roads, build the railways, load and unload the ships at the docks laden with merchandise. The same black hands till the fields, and gather in the grain that fills their granaries to bursting-point. The very houses, the mansions of the rich, are built by these black hands. And what do we get for all our labour? They throw us only offal to eat and hovels to live in – the very dregs of the civilisation which we ourselves create.

What has happened to us? Just as man breeds certain dogs to catch other animals, so has the white ruler turned some of us into his dogs, the chiefs and the quisling intellectuals, to keep the rest of us as chattel slaves. For as long as we submit to the leadership of those white man's dogs so long shall we remain in bondage.

A STORY FOR THE CEBINDEVUS OR – SLAVE MENTALITY

This was written in October 1947 as a reply to a certain Mr Cebindevu, who had published an article condemning the boycott by Africans of separate (segregated) elections under the Native Representation Act. The peasants of the Transkei boycotted the white liberal candidate as their representative. Note the pun on the name Cebindevu, which happens to mean 'The shearer of beards'. In the story it becomes Cebimbovu. Ed.

A certain Mr Cebindevu, in an article entitled 'Transkei's Folly in Election Boycott', took it upon himself to chastise what he regards as his erring brothers in the Transkei. Like all breeds of servile devotees, Mr Cebindevu is imbued with more enthusiasm than reason. His whole article is devoid of any rational argument. He merely condemns the boycott decision as 'folly' and scolds the Transkei people for presuming to put any blame on the white candidate for his action.

It is a waste of breath to argue with these irrational enthusiasts. What, however, is of importance to us is to recognise the basis for this attitude of mind, which is none other than that old disease – slave mentality. Where argument is of no avail, perhaps a little story will be the most effective means of driving our point home even into the minds of the Cebindevus.

The scene is in the island of San Domingo, a French slave colony in the West Indies, more than a hundred and fifty years ago. When our story opens all was quiet on the plantation of a large French landowner called Monsieur Bou. Among his slaves he had a special favourite who went by the name of Cebimbovu (Shearer of moustaches). This slave got his name because his job was to see to it that all the slaves removed all trace of beard from their faces, for the master did not want the slaves to have any mark that signified their manhood, and by removing their beards he hoped to defy nature itself. This act of shearing the hair from the slave's face signified the cutting off of his very right to manhood. It was a badge of shame and the outward brand of the overlordship of the oppressor.

Now in the large, well-filled kitchen of Monsieur Bou, worked Cebimbovu's wife. She was a small, anxious woman whose body carried all the signs of ceaseless toil and the bearing of many children. She had a perpetually anxious look on her face, because she was tormented by the cries of her children who were always hungry for food. As they grovelled in the dry earth round the miserable pondokkie which was their home, it was difficult to believe that they were human children, because their stick-like arms and their swollen bellies gave them a grotesque appearance.

At last she could not stand it any longer. Her master's larder was filled with good things to eat, while her children starved. The law of her master forbade her to touch his property. But there was a still stronger law which she must obey − the love of a mother for her children. Her timid soul that had so long accepted her fate, suddenly became bold. Desperation gave her courage. For her children's sake she resolved to steal from her master, just a little sugar here and a little bread there. He would not miss it.

But one day the lynx eye of her mistress detected the theft and stormed and beat Cebimbovu's wife and then went to tell her husband, Monsieur Bou. Without a word he went to call Cebimbovu. He told him that that 'slut of his' was guilty of theft and must be punished for it. The master curtly commanded his slave to fetch a rein and bring his wife to the big shed. Cebimbovu obeyed. Then the master rapped out another order, 'Tie her to the wagon-wheel', he said. 'Tie her firmly.' And Cebimbovu obeyed.

The master said, 'Now let her back feel the bite of this lash. That'll teach her not to touch my property again.' And Cebimbovu obediently lifted up the whip and brought it down sharply across his wife's back. 'Harder,' shouted the master. Cebimbovu obeyed. 'Faster,' roared the master again. The slave's arm, obeying like an automaton, went up, down, up, down, savagely, each crack of the whip searing his wife's flesh, till the blood began to soak through the thin garment hanging in shreds on her back. Cebimbovu panted with his exertions but did not cease till his wife hung fainting on the wheel. With great satisfaction the master turned on his heel and went indoors to sleep.

Left alone with his wife, Cebimbovu untied her body from the wheel, gathered her into his arms and carried her to their shack. At last a sigh escaped from her parched lips and consciousness came painfully back to her tortured body. 'Water,' she gasped, her voice scarcely above a whisper. He quickly brought her the water and as she put her lips to the cup, Cebimbovu began to scold her. 'Why do you do such wicked things?' he said. 'Why did you anger the master so? Don't you know he is the kindest master and the most upright gentleman in the whole district?'

The woman, now fully conscious, was dumbfounded at his words. Her eyes burned with amazement and anger in her haggard face. But she could not speak. She felt it was useless to argue with him. For each spoke a language the other could not understand. For her, her first duty was to her children and she would do again what had nearly cost her her life. But he, her husband, thought and spoke the language of his master. How could she make him understand? In a flash of insight the woman saw her husband as she had never done before, and she pitied him, for she realised that he was afflicted with a terrible disease, though she could not name it – a disease called slave mentality.

The incident happened only a month before the whole slave population of San Domingo rose in revolt against the oppressors. A few months later the Negro slave, Toussaint L'Ouverture, became commander-in-chief of all the armies, of black and white soldiers, and Governor of the Island. He and many brave, militant spirits liberated not only themselves, but the Cebimbovus also, and thereafter proceeded to re-educate them and cure them of their affliction.

Today we say, 'Bravo' to the militants of the Transkei. 'On with the fight and do not allow the Cebindevus to deflect you from your goal.'

THE CONCEPTION OF EQUALITY
From *The Awakening of a People* – Chapter 9

When the All-African Convention declared the policy of the rejection of trusteeship and asserted the claim to full equality, few realised the far-reaching effects it would have upon the people. First on their minds, on their outlook, and thence on their struggles. Although on paper it may seem a simple thing for a people to recognise themselves as equal to other human beings, yet if we visualise the generations of oppression, the sheer weight on mind and body of a system of slavery armed with all the machinery of the state, all the legal and ideological weapons designed to obliterate from their minds the very capacity to think of themselves as human beings; if we visualise the steadily insidious effect of the conditions of their existence, the brutalising squalor and deprivation which of themselves engender the feeling of inferiority – if we take all those things into consideration we begin to understand the leap which the people took at this time. We begin to have some idea of the magnitude of this conception of equality.

It enabled them to throw off their dependence on the ideas of the enemy-class. It made it possible for them to assess the various groups in society, their policies and their class interests, and the motivations of their actions. In this way they were able to cut across the current ideas imposed on society by the ruling-class for its own interests and self-preservation. They could now strike out on an independent path. That is why they were able to choose their true allies in the struggle, those who had the same disabilities and therefore the same political aspirations as themselves. This liberation of the mind released the latent energies of the people.

At the moment the struggle is still in its first tentative stages. Nevertheless the basis has been laid and the broad general lines have been established. It was no longer a question of palliatives, of 'improving' this or that separate institution for the black man. It was nothing short of full equality, political, social, economic.

II   TEACHERS JOIN THE STRUGGLE

From *The Awakening of a People* – Chapter 9

The teachers, who constitute the greatest single unit of the vocal section among the African people, had up to now either been lukewarm or had been too timid to join in the struggle as a body. Some of them, it is true, had participated as members of other organisations of the people.

The attitude of the majority of them had been that of maintaining the professional sanctity of the Teachers' Organisation and preserving it from the taint of politics. But so much had the new spirit permeated the mass of the people that the teachers for the first time posed to themselves the question: What is the position of an African teacher in the given social set-up? And what is his function? For three years a battle was being waged within the Cape African Teachers' Association (CATA) representative of the whole of the Cape Province and the Transkei. It brought home to them the realisation of the fact that their organisation, though a few decades old, had no clear policy, because it had no clearly defined principles. Thus at the 1948 Conference of CATA the teachers discussed and adopted a Statement of Policy which was a culmination of the long drawnout struggle within the organisation itself. In its Preamble it stated:

'Our struggle is inseparable from the general struggle of the African people. Whether we like it or not .... the salaries of African teachers are based upon the wages in other fields of employment open to Africans .... In order not to upset the labour policy of the country a constant ratio must be maintained between the wages of the black labourer and the wages of the black teacher .... It is clear that our struggle is inextricably bound up with the struggle of the African labourer. Even our slogan 'Equal pay for equal work' is an old trade union slogan. It implies the recognition of merit irrespective of colour .... So anyone who makes this demand is fighting for the principle of full democratic rights. But we have already established the fact that it is futile to strive to obtain equality between white teacher and black teacher unless there is equality between white labourer and black labourer. In short .... to seek equality between white teacher and black teacher is to seek full social, economic and political equality between white and black in South Africa. Our slogan therefore implies that our struggle is the general political struggle for emancipation of the African. There can be no escape from that conclusion.'

Editor's Note: *A notable addition to the arsenal of ideas characteristic of the Movement is CATA's Memorandum on 'Native Education', drawn up in answer to a questionnaire which was sent out in1949 by a Government Commission on 'Native Education', in preparation for the imposition of the Nationalist Government's scheme of what is called Bantu Education. The CATA executive turned its Memorandum into a denunciation of all racialist policies in education challenging the Commission on the first and basic point of the questionnaire, namely, 'What do you consider should be the guiding principles and aims of Native Education?' The Memorandum declared war on the Government's policy of segregated and inferior education for Africans.*

CATA boycotted the Commission but published its Memorandum, calling on all sections of the oppressed population to support them:

'The government is attacking the non-whites on all fronts, politically, economically and socially. There is no better time for rallying together all the forces of the non-white organisations than now. What is threatening us is no longer a purely educational matter. It affects the whole fabric of African life and that of South Africa.' (Teachers' Vision, June 1949.)

The CATA executive requested I.B.Tabata, executive member of the All-African Convention, to draw up the Memorandum on its behalf.

FROM THE MEMORANDUM ON NATIVE EDUCATION

To answer adequately the extensive questionnaire on 'Native Education' submitted for our consideration by the Commission on 'Native Education' would require time and space which are not at our disposal. We propose, therefore, to confine ourselves to certain fundamentals, certain basic points which reflect our views on the all-important question of education.

We consider it relevant to our purpose to sum up the guiding principles of the present policy of the State towards what is known as 'Native Education'.

As far back as 1889 the Superintendent-General of Education formulated the duty of the State towards the education of the European (white) children as preparing them to maintain 'the unquestioned superiority and supremacy of the whites in this land'. Since Union, **(Act of Union, 1910, uniting British and Boers. Ed.)** this educational policy has been systematically put into practice. In other words, segregation has been the ruling principle in the educational system of the Union of South Africa.

And, since education and the social system are closely inter-related, segregation in education must be seen as an integral part of a whole political and social system designed to perpetuate the domination of the white section on the one hand, and the political and economic enslavement of all non-whites on the other. As stated in the *Report of the Inter-departmental Commission on Native Education* (1936):

'The education of the white child prepares him for life in a dominant society and the education of the black child for a subordinate society .... The limits (of Native Education) form part of the social and economic structure of the country'.

From the questionnaire it is abundantly evident that the Commission bases itself on this concept of 'Native Education'. The very formulation of the questions indicates the preconceived idea that there should be differentiation in education according to race. The very terminology, 'Native Education' is vitiated by racial discrimination and indeed has no meaning outside it.

OUR VIEWS ON EDUCATION

The first question brings us to the crux of the whole matter.

Question 1: "What do you consider should be the guiding principle and aims of 'Native Education'?"

In order to answer this question properly we must state our views on what should be the guiding principles and aims of education. They have frequently been formulated by educators all over the world. Briefly: A sound education aims to develop the individual to his fullest capacity, mentally and physically. It should enable him to take his place in the life of the community. It should make him capable of assuming the responsibilities of citizenship. It includes the development of a free spirit of scientific enquiry, the reverse of indoctrination and the regimentation of the mind. In any given State the aims of education must be the same for all its citizens, since there cannot be two or more kinds of citizenship within a State. Any such term, therefore, as 'Native Education' is untenable because it immediately violates the very principles of education. It is an absurdity from the point of view of true education.

We may be accused of refusing to face the facts of the special situation pertaining in South Africa. We maintain that, on the contrary, it is the authorities who, ostrich-like, bury their heads in the sand and stubbornly refuse to face the economic and social actualities, the dynamic of the living forces at work in South African society. Politicians are continually harping on 'the development of Natives along their own lines' .... The phrase is a conveniently pleasant way of covering up a deliberate policy of educational starvation designed to arrest the development of the under-privileged in order to perpetuate white domination.

It is clear that the existing policy is bound up with what is generally assumed to be the essential economic demands of the country, namely, cheap Native labour. The Report of the Native Affairs Commission, 1940, states:

'The life of the gold-mining industry, the economic flywheel of all our economic activities, depends on the continuance of cheap native labour .... Any attempt to alter the existing economic structure by drastic action would bring it to ruin.'

Cheap 'Native' labour and illiteracy go hand in hand. But it is common knowledge that if South Africa is to maintain its position in the civilised world, its whole economy will have to undergo a radical change .... There is a great shortage of skilled workers in the country and to have skilled workers the State must provide at least elementary education for the whole population .... We can only conclude that the whites, who hold all the political power, are actuated by a fear complex. This complex seems to be responsible for policies which cut right across the best economic interests of South Africa.

The present 'guiding principles and aims of Native education' are destructive in every way, not only for the individual but also for the State in terms of the colossal wastage in human and material resources. For the African they are particularly abhorrent because they are calculated to keep him in a state of perpetual subjection and because in their consequences they will exact an immeasurable toll of human life and happiness. They are responsible for the material and spiritual deprivation of a whole people.

WE DEMAND FULL CITIZENSHIP

We repeat that the fundamental guiding principle in education should be to equip every individual to take his place in society according to his capabilities and make his contribution to it as a fully responsible citizen. All the inhabitants of the Union of South Africa should receive the same facilities for education. All the children, irrespective of race, colour or creed, should be regarded as its future citizens. Knowledge is the heritage of all mankind.

The above exposition of our fundamental views makes it unnecessary to answer the other questions in detail. Most of them are already answered by implication.

Question 2: "Is it correct to regard the Native as a separate and independent race?"

No. In no sense is the African independent or separate from the rest of the Union. To regard him as separate and independent is to fly in the face of economic realities and necessities.

To legislate for him as if he were separate simply means subjecting him to repressive segregatory laws which exclude him from the body politic while he is an integral and indispensable part of the economy of the Union. No race can be regarded as separate and independent from the society of which it is a part and which is based on a unified economy within a single State.

Question 3: "What do you understand by the 'racial characteristics' of the Native?"

We do not accept the concept of 'racial characteristics' if it implies the assumption that any race has inferior mental capacities to another. Neither do we accept the assumption that the African should receive a different, separate education supposed to be suited to assumed racial differences. The concept of racial differences has been prostituted to the political aims of white domination. It is only when the term 'racial characteristics' is used in a physiological sense that it is valid. But this can have no bearing on education.

Question 4: "What are the special qualities and aptitudes of the Native?"

The African has no 'special' qualities and aptitudes peculiar to himself and different from other human beings. As a member of the human race he shows the same varieties of intelligence, capabilities and aptitudes common to all.

Question 5: "In what way has the social heritage of the Native been determined by the characteristics referred to above?"

This question is not clear. In the first place, the social characteristics of people are determined by their environment, and not vice versa. If, however, the allusion is to the old tribal system of the Africans before the advent of Europeans in this country, we would like to point out that this no longer exists. It is true that the Government still persists in fostering artificially a 'tribal system' which at the present day has no basis in fact. Economic forces in the country have completely broken down the whole basis of the tribal system. The demands for African labour in the towns, on the farms and on the mines have made it impossible for any tribe to remain intact. We may add that the drift to the towns has not been confined to the Africans but has been a general movement of the whole population as a result of the growing industrialisation of the country. What does exist, however, is a very large peasant population, the majority of whom are Africans.

What appears, therefore, to be a special characteristic of the majority of the Africans is nothing but the 'characteristics' common to all peasant populations throughout the world.

Question 6: "What do you consider the most important changes at present taking place in the social conditions of the Native?"

This has been partly answered under Question 5. But in order to emphasise our point, we would like to draw attention to the fact that from time to time various Native Commissioners have complained that the word of the chief has no longer an authority over his people, and that the younger generation in particular no longer considers itself bound by tribal customs and tribal moral codes. This fact simply reflects the vast economic developments which are transforming the whole country and which bring into play forces which inevitably bind the whole community into a single economic unit. The African population is fast becoming part of the industrial machinery of the country.

Only thus far do we consider ourselves called upon to answer the questionnaire on 'Native Education'. Questions 7-16, which were obviously meant for those informants who believe in a policy of differentiation in education according to race, deserve no special treatment in our memorandum, for they are directly or impliedly answered in our preamble, in our treatment of Questions 1-6 and particularly in our exposition of 'the guiding principles and aims of education'.

April 16th, 1949. (End of Memo)

Editor's Note: **Under the Bantu Education Act, education for Africans was transferred to the** notorious Native Affairs Department which controls labour requirements for the mines and white farms. The Cape African Teachers' Association (CATA) called on the teachers of all four provinces to reject Bantu Education. The CATA was denounced even from the pulpit. The Education Department threatened the teachers, prohibiting the holding of the CATA conference, but the militants were not to be intimidated. Delegations from the Teachers' League of South Africa (representing coloured teachers), the Transvaal Indian and Coloured Teachers' Association, and the Natal Indian Teachers' Society attended. The atmosphere of Conference was charged with the knowledge that the teachers had thrown down the gauntlet and faced expulsion. This militancy was reflected in every speech.

A Memorandum submitted by the All-African Convention and the Unity Movement to the Liberation Committee of the Organisation of African Unity (OAU) in December 1963, states:

In every district throughout the Transkei there existed a branch of the CATA (Cape African Teachers' Association). The membership of these branches acted as cadres of the All-African Convention in the villages, carrying out the policy of organising the peasantry into the national body .... Everywhere the peasant leaders of the resistance were being exiled and thousands were put in jail. The first exiles were peasant members of the All-African Convention in the Glen Grey District (Cape). Thereafter the Government turned its attack on the All-African Convention itself.

The CATA was outlawed. By this time the Convention had linked together the struggle against the Rehabilitation Scheme with the struggle against the debased Bantu Education. All members of the Executive of the Cape African Teachers' Association were summarily dismissed from the profession and later hundreds of teachers, members of the CATA, lost their jobs. In this way the Teachers' Association was the first African organisation to be outlawed.

III BANTU EDUCATION IN SOUTH AFRICA

Abridged from Education for Barbarism (Durban, Prometheus Press, 1959)

Editor's Note: The Prometheus Press was a new branch of the struggling independent Press of the Movement. The fascist Government soon made it impossible for it to continue. Verwoerd, with the Bantu Authorities and Bantu Education Acts, was trying to turn back the clock of history by enlisting the aid of the chiefs in maintaining virtually martial law in the Reserves.

Education for Barbarism does more than document the vicious operation of the Bantu Education Act on African teachers, students and children. It is a penetrating study of the social origins of the policy of 'Christian-National Education', on the basis of which the

Afrikaner Nationalists indoctrinate whites as well as blacks. The ingredients of Calvinism and Nazi ideology evident in it are nicely differentiated. Tabata makes clear how the absurd anachronism of Bantu Education is doomed to fail. The resistance of the African peasants to the chiefs and to Bantu Education reinforced their resistance to the Rehabilitation Scheme, which deprived them still further of land and cattle. Like all the literature of the Unity Movement, this book is banned in South Africa.

From *Education for Barbarism*, Chapter 1

In any society, ancient or modern, it is the duty of the older generation to prepare the young to take their place in the economic, intellectual and social life of the community. In modern times this duty falls largely to the State. It provides a system of education in keeping with the highly complex activities of man in an industrial age. Any system of education, therefore, is concerned not only with the teaching of certain skills and professions, but with inculcating certain ideas which are basic to the society and necessary for its perpetuation. Education is carefully designed and organised so that the children imbibe these moral, cultural and intellectual attitudes that are the essence of that society.

When politicians, however, want to juggle with the social order, they make for the system and content of education. Hitler threw to the winds the rich legacy of education in Germany that had been steeped in the culture of centuries and prided itself on its modern scientific approach. Instead, he introduced barbaric ideas based on superstition and race fanaticism. In the name of race superiority, education was debased and scientific theory prostituted. Fascism and intellectual freedom are mortal enemies. Barbarism and superstition cannot tolerate free enquiry and the scientific approach to problems. Thus, in Germany the monstrous machinery of fascism was geared to maintain a myth and educational institutions were employed to drug the mind of the German youth.

In South Africa, where the ruling minority, the herrenvolk, feel impelled to arrest the natural processes of development in an industrial age, in so far as the non-whites are concerned, they have similarly seized upon education as the instrument for carrying out their purposes.

The apostles of apartheid have fathered a new monstrosity called Bantu Education, by means of which they aim to arrest the development of the African people, who comprise nearly three quarters of the population. It has its counterpart in 'Coloured Education' for the coloured people of South

Africa. They want to recreate for the subject races a social order belonging to the pre-industrial age.

It is in this light that the elaborate schemes of the Nationalist Government for establishing Bantu Education must be viewed. It falls to Dr Verwoerd as Minister of Native Affairs to resurrect a dead tribalism for the African people. And all this for the purpose of ensuring the continuance of baasskap (bossdom – white domination) and preserving the racial myth of white superiority. In Dr Verwoerd's scheme of things, Bantu Education becomes a means of artificially resuscitating an outmoded tribalism. Both the system and the content of education must be transformed to suit the purpose of the rulers. In outlining his policy on Bantu Education, Dr Verwoerd states, 'My Department's policy (i.e. the Department of Native Affairs) is that education should stand with both feet in the Reserves .... The basis of the provision and organisations of education in a Bantu Community should, where possible, be the tribal organisation.'

And again, 'There is no place for him (the African) in the European (white) community above the level of certain forms of labour .... Until now he has been subjected to a school system which drew him away from his own community and misled him by showing him the green pastures of European (white) society in which he was not allowed to graze.' (*Bantu Education: Policy for the Immediate Future*; p.23, 1954). What is significant is the way he links Bantu Education with his concept of a 'Bantu Community'. To understand the full import of the plans for Bantu Education, we must examine the nature of the Bantu Community envisaged by Dr Verwoerd. But before doing so, let us briefly indicate the position of education as he found it.

'NATIVE EDUCATION'

When the Union of South Africa was formed in 1910 by the Act of Union, the Colour Bar against the black population, which had always been practised, was embodied in the very constitution of the land. Every succeeding Government, of whatever political protestations, made it its duty to pass laws to maintain white domination. While utilised as a cheap labour force, the non-whites were thrown out of the body politic and a policy of social segregation was strictly adhered to.

As part of this policy, a system of education known as 'Native Education' was evolved for the Africans. Thus the rulers utilised education to maintain their dominant position. In practice this meant inferior education for every section of the non-whites but most of all for the Africans.

There is free and compulsory education for the white child only. The figures indicating State expenditure for white and African children respectively, eloquently sum up the position. As quoted in Parliament (1949) the cost per head for the white child was £50; for the African child it was £7. The position is even worse when we consider that the £7 was only for the few African children actually in schools. The vast proportion receive no education at all. As Dr Verwoerd himself stated, 'Only 40% of children of school-going age are in school. Of these nearly half are found in the sub-standards.' These figures reveal not only educational starvation but also the economic destitution of a whole people. For it is well-known that African parents will make sacrifices to enable their children to attend school. The most backward of them, the illiterate peasants, will sell their few remaining stock so that their children can learn at least to read and write.

At this stage, however, a trickle of non-white students managed to reach the professions, holding the same qualifications as any other qualified people in the country. Now it was precisely this section that constituted a menace in the eyes of Dr Verwoerd and his fellow apostles of apartheid. Such men and women were dangerous. A number of them became teachers. This development was completely at variance with Dr Verwoerd's idea of South African society. Listen to the way in which he describes it.

'A considerable number of those (Africans) who were trained in this way have been absorbed again in the educational machine, which has created a vicious cycle.' A choice phrase! – Vicious cycle! He goes on to condemn educated Africans as 'the class which has learnt to believe that it is above its own people and feels that its spiritual, economic and political home is among the civilized community of South Africa, i.e. the Europeans.' (Bantu Education).

Such statements, which must seem shocking to the ears of every civilised person throughout the world, do not issue from the lips of an illiterate man. They are the considered opinions of a man who has taken stock of the developments in South Africa in every field of human activity and has come to the conclusion that it is heading for a crisis. White domination is seriously threatened. The safeguards that have so far been taken to make South Africa a white man's paradise are no longer adequate and the situation calls for drastic measures.

From: *Education for Barbarism*, Chapter 2: Plans for a Bantu Community
Bantu Authorities

Dr Verwoerd keeps putting into juxtaposition what he calls the Bantu community with the white community and Bantu society with white society, as if the people of South Africa constituted two entirely separate entities. All his plans have this idea as their starting-point. To bring this about, he pushed through Parliament two laws that supplement each other: the Bantu Education Act, which is designed to fit the African into a separate Bantu Community, and the Bantu Authorities Act, which aims to create this Bantu Community.

The Bantu Authorities Act is a remarkable Act. Its aim is to re-establish tribalism in the midst of industrialism. The whole African population at present living in what are known as the Native Reserves (comprising about 12% of the total land area) is to be uprooted, reshuffled and re-settled according to their ethnic groupings. Every village will be turned into a Bantu Community, with a government-appointed chief and councillors constituting a Bantu Authority. (Government here means the Native Affairs Department, with the Minister of Native Affairs as its head.)

In the towns, where the Africans have to live in segregated locations, they will also be reshuffled according to their old clans and tribes, each with a government-appointed chief at its head. It does not even occur to the makers of apartheid in South Africa how ludicrous the idea of chieftainship is, particularly in the old towns, where many Africans do not even know the language of the tribe to which their forebears belonged.

But all that the rulers are concerned with is the splitting up of the Africans; for they are mortally afraid of African unity, and still more of the coming together of non-whites. These chiefs have the power to regulate and regiment the lives of every African man, woman and child. A proclamation in the Government Gazette has recently been published, giving them unheard-of powers over the people. These illiterate representatives of a barbarous age can order any person in their area to obey perhaps some old tribal law or perform some archaic rites. The same proclamation enables the chief to compel any person or group of people to carry out any public work without pay. Overnight, the whole African population found themselves bereft of the most elementary human rights, and this simply by a proclamation in a Government Gazette.

The chiefs constitute a glorified police force, and more, with powers to search, arrest, prosecute, convict and even order corporal punishment on an adult man. The chiefs are to be enlisted in the Government Rehabilitation Scheme (so-called) and order the people to reduce their stock. Under the Pass laws, it is their duty to order the women to apply for their book of passes and see to it that they carry it about on their persons. (There are already many instances where the women are refusing and being dragged off to prison in hundreds.)

The latest Resettlement Schemes involve the rearrangement of villages, often the shifting of whole villages from one place to another. All these people who depend on stock for a livelihood, but who have no arable lands, have to be thrown out of their homes and forced to sell their stock. Together with their families they have to be dumped in camps, where they will live by selling their labour. This is what the restoration of chieftainship really means. Now we begin to have a picture of Dr Verwoerd's ideal of a 'Bantu Community'.

What he aims to create is a completely rightless, voteless, defenceless community, segregated from 'European society' and completely dominated by the chiefs who are employed and paid by him. But we would be very much mistaken if we assumed that this Bantu Community (or 'Bantustan') will be allowed to develop into an independent nation. The community will be without any means of independent livelihood and serve only as a reservoir of cheap labour for the mines, the white farms and industry. An elaborate machinery has already been established to control the sending out of labourers in the required quotas.

In other words the Africans must use their hands and muscles to carry out menial tasks in the Union's industrial machine. But their life, their modes of thinking, their social forms of living must be in an artificially created stage of barbarism.

BANTU EDUCATION IS THE KEY

This brings us to the second part of Dr Verwoerd's far-reaching schemes, namely, Bantu Education, which is to wrench the African from the progress of the civilisation of mankind and condition him for life in a backward tribalised community. In other words, it is education for barbarism. A machinery of state worked out to the minutest detail is already set in motion to create an intellectual gas chamber for the children of a whole people. **(The author illustrates how the apartheid policy also covers all vocational training in skills or professions, such as nursing and in the building trade. Ed.)**

What emerges from these new laws is the determination of the rulers to arrest the natural development of the non-whites. There must be no loophole left unclosed in any sphere. Mr Maree MP, Chairman of the Permanent Commission of Native Affairs, summed up the situation during the debate on the Bantu Education Bill:

'Today we have come to the crossroads, as far as South Africa is concerned. We have arrived at the historic day when we sincerely hope that education will be directed along another course, a new course, where the fundamental idea will be that functionally the Native must fill a role in the community different to that of the Europeans, and in the second place, that the Native has a different cultural background from the European, and in the third place, that the Native must fit into his own type of community, a different type of community to that of the white man. Therefore the fundamental idea in Bantu Education must be that he should be taught to develop along his own lines in all social and economic aspects.' (*Hansard*, Vol.10, 1953)

From *Education for Barbarism*, Chapter 4 — Bantu Education: An Instrument for Serfdom

Under the Boerenasie (Boer Nation) Republic the non-whites will be reduced to utter helotry. In preparation for this, the schools are no longer centres of education, but of indoctrination for the docile acceptance of this position. Dr Verwoerd himself, in introducing the Bantu Education Bill, has said, 'Above all, good race relations cannot exist when education is given under the control of people who create wrong expectations on the part of the Native, if such people believe in a policy of equality .... It is therefore necessary that Native education should be controlled in such a way that it should be in accord with the policy of the State.' (*Hansard* No.10, 1953).

The invoking of a dead tribalism and of Bantu Communities wherein 'education will find its fullest expression' is cynical political claptrap. The plain fact is that 'Bantu education' is intended to rob the African of education, cut him off from the mainstream of modern culture and shut him into a spiritual and intellectual ghetto. If we look into the management of the school, the curricula and the calculated debasement of the teacher, we find ample confirmation that the scheme before us is a huge conspiracy, first against the Africans and eventually against the whole non-white population of South Africa.

Their plans for reducing the numerically small section of the non-whites (the coloured and the Indians) to the same position of helotry are still at the earlier stages. But it is already clear that they are working out the same pattern for them as for the Africans. Having first removed the coloured and the Indian people from the Parliamentary Voters' Roll, the Government proceeded to create a special department of State known as the Coloured Affairs Department (CAC) which means lifting the coloured people out of the body politic and treating them as a separate entity in accordance with the Nationalist policy of apartheid.

The CAD is the counterpart of the NAD (Native Affairs Department) which was instituted for Africans. Following the (DeVos Malan) Commission on coloured education, the Government intimated its intention to transfer education for the coloured and Indians from the Department of Education to the political department, the CAD. It thus becomes an instrument for fitting the coloured people into a separate community as Bantu education prepares the African people for a tribalised community. Bantu education presages what is in store for the coloured and Indian people. In the fully developed plans for the Africans they can see an image of their future state of complete bondage. **(These plans have been carried out in the sixties. Ed.)**

The control of education for Africans was transferred to the Native Affairs Department (NAD). This is the Department that is charged with the artificial retribalisation of a whole people and the setting up of Bantu Authorities. It deals with the supply of cheap African labour to the mines, the farms, and industry; it deals with agriculture, the compulsory culling and dipping of cattle, the collection of poll-tax and the enforcement of pass-laws. Dr Verwoerd makes it plain that education is in the service of these activities:

'A community, for example, will not be able to claim advantages of education and at the same time ignore or even oppose guidance in regard to the care of the soil.' (Bantu Education). This has meant that when the people in a village refused to reduce the number of their stock under the culling regulations, their school was closed down.

The local management of the schools is handed over to tribal school committees and school boards who work under the tribal authorities, with a chief at the head. It is these people (often illiterate) who not only direct and supervise the schools but employ and dismiss the teachers. The curriculum likewise is fundamentally altered. The old text-books on science, history and even languages are declared taboo. New ones considered suitable for Bantu schools are being written by servants of the Native Affairs Department. A furious and lucrative industry has been set up.

Hack writers are manufacturing books for Bantu schools. It is easily understood that existing libraries must come under the axe. The library of an old established college collected over a period of more than a century was put up for public auction. The minds of young innocents must be protected from 'dangerous' ideas. Such an act of vandalism ought to revolt even the weak-kneed apologists of the system, that breed nurtured in the Let's-give-it-a-trial school of thought.

THE AFRICAN TEACHER

The debasement of education for Africans is further illustrated in the attitude towards the teachers and the savage conditions of their employment under Bantu education. Those who were trained under the old system, more especially the University graduates, are regarded as highly dangerous in the new set-up. They have to be replaced as soon as possible. 'In the meantime,' says Dr Verwoerd, 'the Department will take over complete control of teacher training schools.'

Obviously a special creature, a Bantuised teacher is necessary for Bantu education. Meantime the old undesirable teacher, whose services are required in the interim, is being broken in. He is being humiliated and hedged around with obnoxious regulations. He is completely deprived of professional status. In the case of the farm schools, of which there are many, the whole of the teacher's time – 24 hours a day – belongs to the farm owner, who now also owns the school and may act as its manager. It is he who employs the teacher. It is also laid down in the regulations that a teacher cannot claim his annual salary increments as a right.

The debasement of the teacher is something to outrage those who are accustomed to think of teaching as an honourable profession. He is not only robbed of status but of security of tenure and the proper practice of his calling. The Act provides for the imprisonment of any teacher who breaks any of the regulations.

The truth is that since Bantu Education was instituted, a reign of terror has been let loose on the teachers. Members of the CID (police) have swooped on the schools, interrogated teachers in front of their pupils and searched them. Some of the finest teachers with long records of distinguished service have been summarily dismissed without any charge or trial. The only reason given was that they were unsuitable under Bantu Education.

At the outset the Native Affairs Department saw to it that the executive members of the Cape African Teachers' Association, which was established nearly a quarter of a century ago, were thrown out of the profession. They had dared to protest against Bantu Education. Not content with the dismissal of these teachers, the NAD, which, as we pointed out, controls every aspect of African life, pursued them relentlessly wherever they tried to get any other employment. Utilising the iniquitous pass system, it has hounded them out of the reserves where they had established their home, and also out of the towns where they went to look for a job. Men were separated from their wives and families and deprived of the means of supporting them. Hundreds of teachers have been dismissed as the Bantuised trainee comes on the market.

A Nazi-like regimentation governs these young trainees, as it does the whole schooling from top to bottom. They are carefully screened, selected, and indoctrinated before they are let loose on the children. Regimentation is indeed the essence of the system. It must be remembered that no one may run a school or conduct classes for African children without the Minister's permission, on pain of a fine or imprisonment. This permission is granted only if the Minister is satisfied that nothing but Bantu Education is being provided. To give but one example, a retired African teacher of sixty, who had gathered a number of African children together, chiefly to keep them from the danger of the streets, was arrested and fined £75, or seven months. What a monstrous system is this that makes a criminal of a man who was manifestly actuated by his sense of responsibility as a teacher towards the children of the community.

TRIBAL 'UNIVERSITIES'

For the pitifully few who squeeze through the examination bottlenecks to the university stage, the prospect is a bleak one. The Government is at present forging the final links in the chain of Bantuised education. It is not surprising that, once they had conceived the idea of Bantu Education they had to cap it with the invention of that educational monstrosity, tribal universities. What is surprising, however, is that they should find it necessary to pass a law forbidding the existing universities to allow non-whites to enter them. (Here we may mention that the so-called 'Open' universities, of which there are only two, permit non-whites only into a limited number of faculties and without participation in the social amenities of the university.) Legal exclusion seems unnecessary.

For Bantuised education carefully incapacitates the African student from reaching the required standard for entering a university. But then, far from the Afrikaner really believing in his own myth about the mental inferiority of the African, his actions would suggest that he sees himself as contending with a superman. Hence the mountain of oppressive laws and his obsession with erecting every possible barrier against the non-whites. The Bill purports to close the existing white universities to all non-whites and to provide for the establishment of segregated universities which will not only separate black from white but African from Indian and coloured.

The universities for Africans will be further divided into Zulu, Xhosa and Sotho universities, in other words, tribal universities. These have to be established in the rural areas in the midst of the respective tribal groupings. In the familiar phrase, they must 'have their roots in the spirit and being of Bantu society' – and what that means we already know. The existing non-white College of Fort Hare, which is affiliated to Rhodes University, is to be placed under the Native Affairs Department. It will now be limited to Africans only and later to members of the Xhosa tribe only. In truth, race-baiting in South Africa would seem to have reached the heights of madness.

Likewise, the young Medical School for Non-Whites, an already segregated institution but attached to Natal University, is to be wrenched away from it. The training of black doctors, who are going to serve 'Bantu communities', must not be in any way associated with the training of white doctors. As it is, non-white trainees may not touch, or even see, a white corpse, let alone examine the living body. **(The writer depicts the regimentation of professor and student alike in tribal colleges. Ed.)**

The whole scheme is bad enough on paper, but its sinister nature emerges more fully when we view it in practice. What stands out with appalling clarity is that the more progressive section of the non-whites, the educated section, is delivered into the hands of the most backward elements of the population. For the purposes of local management, power is put into the hands of the chiefs, the illiterate representatives of a barbarous age. The teacher, completely deprived of all those rights vested in his position, including the legal right of tenure of his office, is thereby placed at their mercy. Such a situation opens the door wide to corruption, bribery, nepotism and other malpractices.

IV CHRISTIAN-NATIONAL EDUCATION – ORIGINS

From *Education for Barbarism*, Chapter 3

This concept of the 'proper' education for the subject races is an offshoot of what the Afrikaners call Christian-National Education. In 1948, the year in which the Nationalist Party came to power, the Institute of Christian-National Education published a definitive Statement of its policy:

'It is a Policy .... that can now stand as a guiding principle in our cultural struggle which has now also definitely become an educational struggle .... Our culture must be brought into the schools .... Our Afrikaans schools must be the places where our children are soaked and nourished in the Christian-National, spiritual and cultural "stuff" of our nation'.

This means a thorough indoctrination in a fanatic belief in the 'Boerenasie' (Boer nation) and its culture. Afrikaans children must be 'soaked and nourished' in the creed of the Dutch Reformed Church. The active, spiritual force of this brand of Calvinism can only be understood in the light of the history of Afrikanerdom, in its isolationism, its aggressive exclusiveness, its rigid imperviousness to outside influence. In a word, Afrikaans culture is a culture that has become ingrown. Thus they find it possible to declare in their Statement of policy:

'We want no admixture of language, of culture, of religion or of race.'

It will be necessary briefly to indicate the history that lies behind such a declaration. The Afrikaner people of South Africa think of themselves as the descendants of those Dutch immigrants who came to the Cape of Good Hope in the latter part of the 17th century, further reinforced by the Huguenots, the religious refugees who left France after the revocation of the Edict of Nantes in 1685. To this day they insist on calling themselves Europeans and continually reiterate their claim to be the only defenders of Christian European civilisation in South Africa.

In order to appreciate the mainspring of their intellectual and emotional attitudes, it is important to consider at what historical period these emigrants left Europe and severed their connections with it. It was that period before the vast and rapid expansion of material forces, before that gigantic development of capitalism which was to transform social, political and economic institutions and the ideologies and philosophies that accompanied it. Situated in the southern-most corner of the 'dark continent', they were shut off from the strong current of rational thought on man, nature and society, which gained impetus in the 18th century and radiated through the countries of Western Europe. They missed that age of criticism and enquiry that was to question everything hitherto regarded as sacred and immutable; they missed that age of scepticism which submitted ideas and established institutions to the scrutiny of reason, when all values, the nature of society and man's position in the universe had to be re-assessed. In a word, the forbears of the present-day Afrikaner did not come into contact with the keen ideological struggles of the Age of Enlightenment in Europe – the Age of Reason, as it has been called – when dogmatism and bigotry had to give way to progressive thought. It is true this movement was already under way, but the emigrants were untouched by it: for they did not belong to that class which deals in ideas. Moreover, while that element which represented the French Huguenots sought religious freedom, they were imbued with the bigotry of the most rigid of the Protestant creeds, Calvinism.

The epoch-making discoveries of science, the work of such men as Copernicus in the 16th century, Galileo and Kepler in the early 17th century and the crowning achievement of Newton, with his formulation of the laws of universal gravitation, had already paved the way for material advances and strongly influenced the new philosophical concepts of the Age of Reason, as expressed by the French philosopher, Descartes, and by the English philosophers, Hobbes, Locke and others. At the threshold of this era Francis Bacon had said 'knowledge is power' – a fitting motto to that age which was to see such an expansion of material forces, the vast commercial enterprises of capitalism in the New World and in Asia, the industrial revolution and at the same time the evolution of revolutionary ideas. Locke in the 18th century formulated the philosophy of liberalism, which represented the expanding forces of capitalism and became the ideological weapon of the rising bourgeoisie. While in the political field it upheld parliamentary democracy, in the religious sphere it favoured religious toleration. In France during the pre-revolutionary era the intellectual revolt against feudalism and the entrenched despotism of Church and State found varied expression, in the works of Voltaire, Diderot, Rousseau and others. Diderot's Encyclopaedia, the work of twenty years, in which he gathered together the new ideas and the new knowledge of his age, was a great monument to the spirit of free enquiry. The philosophers enthroned Reason and not only placed man at the centre of the universe but formulated the idea of the equality of man.

We are not unmindful, of course, of the untold suffering, the terrible toll of human life that followed in the wake of developing capitalism both in the metropolitan countries and in the colonial world. But what we are concerned with here is that intellectual awakening, the development in the womb of society of humanistic ideas, ideas that restored man's self-respect and human dignity by liberating the spirit from the thraldom of the Dark Ages, when superstitious fear and the fatalistic concept of original sin had degraded him, warping and enchaining the mind.

CALVINISM

But at the time when the new ideas of humanism were struggling to be born, Calvinism in Europe excelled itself in establishing a new religious tyranny and utilised the whole machinery of its despotism to control thought and conduct. Here we do not intend to dwell on the complex influence of Calvinism in Europe and how it became modified according to the political environment and the social class in which it took root. **(Passage on Calvinism abridged. Ed.)**

This is the religious creed which the ancestors of the Afrikaners carried with them to Southern Africa. The narrow religious dogma of Calvinism provided the very sinews and moral fibre of their outlook. And to the present day they continue to draw their spiritual and moral sustenance from it. In the conditions of isolation in Southern Africa, where they found themselves surrounded by people even more backward than themselves, the effect was to reinforce these traits of rigidity, narrowness of outlook and intolerance characteristic of their creed.

When Capitalism, expanding to the far-flung corners of the world, reached the shores of Southern Africa, bringing with it its powerful agents of liberalism, new ideas of government and in fact all the equipment of its age, both material and ideological, with which it had felled feudalism in Europe, then the Afrikaner people trekked northwards to escape from a civilisation that was foreign to them and from ideas that were bringing disruption to their fixed way of life. In the 19th century they undertook the 'Great Trek', which to them was the second Exodus. They saw themselves as the Elect, the Chosen people of God. **(The writer proceeds to characterise Christian-National Education as being steeped in the spirit of Calvinism, which in South Africa was embodied in the Dutch Reformed Church. Ed.)**

NAZI IDEOLOGY

It would be misleading, however, to take this Christian-National Education policy at its face value pure and simple. It has far more sinister ramifications. As we have said earlier, when politicians want to juggle with the social order they make for the system and content of education. Your present-day Afrikaner Nationalist – thanks to his defeat in the Boer war which hastened the development – is himself a capitalist standing four-square on the heights of a fully developed capitalism. In fact he is confronted with the problems of capitalism in crisis, and it is in an attempt to solve these that he falls back on formulae that others have already evolved. While leaning heavily on the efficacy of religious training, he has found inspiration in the Nazi ideology which was formulated in the thirties to meet the crisis of capitalism in Germany – and this, regardless of the disasters that later engulfed the German people. It is a well-known fact that the Afrikaner Nationalists have looked up to German fascism as their ideal and have closely modelled themselves on it.

In Germany the Nazis evolved a system of education with a double purpose. First of all it had to transform the whole way of life from democracy to fascism. All the processes of thought that are traditionally associated with democracy: freedom of thought, of speech and association, free democratic elections, had to be systematically broken down and destroyed. In their place a new ideology, a new attitude to life necessary for the establishment of the Fascist State, had to be built up. The principle of the sacred State with its Führer was installed. National Socialistic education was the instrument for carrying out this plan and it was organised and employed with diabolical thoroughness in the training of all children from pre-school age to manhood and womanhood. This was the internal aspect of the Nazi plan.

In its wider aspect, the whole German population had to be organised for a future war .... The parallel between National Socialistic education in Nazi Germany and the Christian National education formulated by the Afrikaner Nationalists is all too painfully close. Just as the Nazis had to re-organise the whole German population and indoctrinate it with ideas of fascism, so the Afrikaner Nationalist conceived the idea of Christian National education in preparation for establishing the South African Fascist State under a Boerenasie republic.

In this scheme of things it is obvious that education for the non-whites must be clearly differentiated. While the white youth must be filled with ideas of race superiority and power, together with worship of the Boerenasie and obedience to the Leader (Führer), the non-whites on the other hand must be trained for abject serfdom.

It is this combination of sanctimonious Calvinism with the most diabolical inventions of German fascism that makes Christian-National Education, as applied to the blacks of South Africa, so completely vicious.

V   BANTU EDUCATION MUST FAIL

From: *Education for Barbarism*, Chapter 5

The People Reject It

There is not a single section of the African population to whom Bantu Education is acceptable. None see it as bestowing benefits of any kind. All of them, including those living in the most remote corners of the country, have rejected it. Everywhere the Government has had to rely on threats and intimidation. The people see Bantu Education as part and parcel of the imposition of Bantu Authorities, enforced re-tribalisation, the pass system and the schemes for the forced removal of whole communities, and the so-called Stabilisation Scheme. All these are seen as measures for the rigid control of a people placed outside the body politic, measures that create pauperisation and ensure a regimented labour force. What the authorities themselves say about the benefits of Bantu Education is irrelevant. The people, who experience the objective effects of all the schemes, draw their own conclusions. It is for this reason that they are fighting a desperate battle against all of them, including Bantu Education. A number of incidents involving violence show how in the minds of the people these schemes are linked together. Indeed, the Government itself links them together.

The course of events in Sekhukhuniland, in Northern Transvaal, over the last few years illustrates the kind of thing that is happening in the country. In November 1954, Dr Verwoerd himself, accompanied by a number of senior officials of the Native Affairs Department, had addressed the people, urging them to accept the Bantu Authorities and Bantu Education. Upon the introduction of the Bantu Education system an Anglican mission school was taken over by the NAD. But the people were dismayed when it was demoted from secondary to primary grade.

Simultaneously they were compelled to reduce their stock, pay grazing fees and increased rentals for arable lots, all under the 'Betterment Scheme'. Strongly resentful of these measures, they decided to reject the Bantu Authorities. Thereupon a number of their leading spokesmen were banished. Tension in the whole region mounted. At the end of 1957 armed police in a procession of cars and pick-up vans invaded the villages. A further batch of leaders was deported. In February 1958, a Government proclamation was gazetted, giving the Minister of Native Affairs the right to 'seal off' any area by prohibiting the entry or exit of Africans without a written permit from the Native Commissioner. This carried a maximum fine of £300 or three years, or both. In addition, the car used to convey such persons might be confiscated. It also prohibits anyone in the area from making a statement, verbal or written, which, in the opinion of the authorities, interferes with Government action in the given area. The same heavy penalty is prescribed.

A week after the proclamation was gazetted it was applied to Sekhukhuniland. The regulations imposed an obligation on all people over eighteen, living in the area, to report anyone who entered without permission. Failure to report carried a penalty of £100 or six months imprisonment, or both. In April the authorities closed down a primary school and the pupils were not allowed to attend any other school. Incensed and outraged by all this, the people refused to send their children to Bantu Education Schools. The situation in Sekhukhuniland is one of mounting tragedy. Invasions by the police armed with Sten-guns are the order of the day. And now at the time of writing (1958) there is a mass trial of two hundred villagers. They are being charged with 'murder, arson and incitement to riot'.

This pattern of events is becoming all too familiar in South Africa. The people of Zeerust have already suffered their 'Sekhukhuniland'. There the trouble centred round the refusal of the African women in the villages to carry passes. There, too, there were mass arrests and deportations. Resistance was significantly accompanied by the refusal of the people to send their children to Bantu schools. At other places, where the Government is using strong-arm methods to impose Bantu Authorities, the people have burned down Bantu Education Schools. To those who know how much the Africans are prepared to sacrifice in order to educate their children, such an act dramatically brings home their deep resentment of Bantu Education. Those flames that destroy the schools must for them symbolise their consuming desire to rid themselves of this monstrosity.

No one is left in doubt as to the total rejection of Bantu Education by the people. Even those intellectuals who had succumbed to coercion and assisted in working it are dismayed at the position in which they find themselves today. Thus there is no section left to defend it. Even the illiterate Government chiefs do not pretend that it is of benefit to the people; it is something that has to be carried out like the culling of their cattle – because the Government wants it. It is obvious, then, that a system of education that is so completely unacceptable to the people, a system that has to bolster itself up with police pick-up vans and Sten guns, mass arrests and deportations, is doomed to fail.

AN ABSURD ANACHRONISM

The prognosis of the failure of the Verwoerdian scheme rests not only on a consideration of the subjective factor, the African's rejection of it, but also on an examination of the objective situation in South Africa. The whole concept of Bantu Education flies in the face of the economic, cultural and political forces at work in society. The old tribal economy of the African people, as well as the feudal economy of the Afrikaners, were long since wiped off the face of the land and replaced by an industrial economy. The gold mines use the most up-to-date machinery in the world today.

Since the second world war secondary industry has grown by such leaps and bounds, considerably outstripping both mining and agriculture, that it makes by far the largest contribution to the national income. In spite of all the severe legal impediments to urbanisation, the non-whites constitute the largest force and are an essential element of the industrial machine of the country.

This inescapable fact has dictated a change that is rapidly taking place in their mode of living, with all its hardships, and in their habits of thought. The operation of an industrial machine is itself a potent means of education of a kind necessary to the society that is no longer tribal or feudal. The hand that moves the lever is very different from the hand that wielded the hunter's club or the plough.

For the worker the machine and the factory dictate a new set of relationships and attitudes, and outside the factory also, a new set of social and economic needs. In this industrial setting education for tribalism has no place and no meaning. It is an absurd anachronism.

Capitalism has not simply changed the habits of the tribalist and the feudalist. It has created a new man. The powerful forces of production have transformed society, creating a social order essential for their operation, and determining the nature of social, political and economic institutions. The educational system, too, must fit into this social order, since it prepares the individual to take his place in such a society and make his contribution to it. The content of education must be the same for all. For in this economic unit with its multifarious activities each member must be armed with the necessary equipment to play his part to his utmost capacity. Industry and commerce by their very nature shatter the tribal order with its separate little entities; it binds the population together into a single economic unit, while at the same time it creates its own internal divisions, namely, class divisions.

These have nothing to do with tribal or ethnic groupings. In fact they cut across such relationships. Anyone, then, who attempts to foster tribal education today, with the purpose of turning history backwards and creating an outmoded social system, is attempting the impossible. Bantu Education schemes are the pipe-dreams of those politicians who, like the ostrich, persist in burying their heads in the sand and stubbornly refuse to face economic and social realities.

The dynamics of the forces at work in South African society must inevitably demolish those fantasies. The colossal wastage of such a policy is not to be reckoned simply in terms of the overall inefficiency in the organisation of industrial activity, but in the immeasurable cost in human suffering, misery and death. Herrenvolkism, it seems, would hang itself and South African society as a whole on the altar of race superiority.

South Africa cannot much longer afford to indulge in the luxury of hare-brained schemes of retribalisation and education for barbarism in defiance of the demands of a modern industrial economy. Nor is it Bantu Education alone that will have to go. The Augean stables of the whole educational system require drastic cleansing. Christian-National education, intended for white children, is itself so encrusted with anachronisms and outmoded ways of thought that it is unable to equip even the privileged whites for the demands of today. Yet for further progress, universal education is the *sine qua non*. It is essential to adapt the content and purpose of education to the system of which it is an integral part.

In the rapidly changing world of today the outlook of the feudal racialist is an anachronistic as the tribal outlook was in relation to the ideas of enlightenment that accompanied expanding capitalism in the eighteenth century.

A NEW RENAISSANCE

Once more mankind stands on the threshold of spectacular developments, that must embrace the whole world. Today distant continents have become next-door neighbours; nations have become more and more inter-dependent economically and in other ways. With the vast network of swift communications, the giant jet planes, radio and television, the world grows smaller and smaller.

All these things make it impossible to stand apart from the mainstream of human progress. There are no longer any dark continents for the feudalist to take refuge in; no laagers (stockade of ox wagons) behind which he can barricade himself. There are no high walls so impregnable that ideas cannot penetrate them. Mankind is on the eve of the second Industrial Revolution, a revolution that is more far-reaching in its scope than the first, and will transform the face of the earth. At present the world is gripped in that state of disease and turmoil which has always marked periods of transition.

Automation is the key to this vast transformation. The electronic computer has opened up possibilities in industrial techniques hitherto undreamed of. Automation is not simply a quantitative improvement in mechanisation, which up to now has been regarded as the last word in the development of industry. It is a new factor. In its effects it must produce a qualitative change, both in the industrial process and its organisation, and in society as a whole. Just as capitalism disrupted the whole mode of life under feudalism, so will the new industrial revolution bring about radical changes in the way of present-day life and modes of thought.

From this soil must spring a new cultural renaissance. And we are already witnessing its first stirrings. It is not, like the earlier Renaissance in Europe, a rebirth limited to a single continent. It is a world phenomenon. Signs of this rebirth are manifest throughout Asia and Africa, too. The foundations of a new culture are being laid.

Just as the idea of universities, those centres for acquiring and spreading universal knowledge, came into being during the early stages of the first renaissance, so now questions of education, both in the East and the West, have become all-important. Undeveloped countries are concentrating on educating their people and the fight against illiteracy is given pride of place. The new generations cannot afford to be steeped in ignorance. Everywhere the demands of the new era are for more and ever better education. 'Knowledge is power' has become the slogan of all the backward nations.

While automation opens up vast possibilities of development, it must not be supposed that it will usher in the new heaven and the new earth. The first industrial revolution brought immense wealth, but at the same time it created many unexpected social problems. It swept large numbers of people off the countryside and drew them into the cauldron of industrial activity. It produced all the evils associated with early capitalism in Europe: child-labour, long working hours, low wages, the disease and squalor of crowded cities. And in its wake came bloody wars.

Faced with new problems, man devised methods of dealing with them. Social and political institutions, as well as economic organisations, came into being to meet the new situation. The first cycle is coming to an end and the next and higher stage of the spiral is opening up. If automation is to achieve its purpose and fulfil its productive potential, it will create more wealth in goods than man has hitherto conceived of. But instead of drawing an ever-increasing number of men and women into employment in industry, it will replace not only manual labour in all its repetitive operations but also clerical staff, reducing to a minimum the armies of book-keepers, accountants and managers. It is enough to state only this aspect of the matter to imagine some of the problems that will arise.

Questions that present themselves immediately are: what will happen to the millions of workers who would become redundant in industry, and where will markets be found for the superabundance of goods? It is not our task here to pursue this aspect of the subject, but there is no doubt that automation will bring disruption to the present way of life. Once more man will be called upon to solve the problems brought about by progress. And one thing is certain, in the process man himself will change both in his modes of living and of thought.

It will be the function of education to prepare men and women with increased capacity both for greater skills and for creative leisure. In all this a new man will emerge, capable of tackling the problems of society. And a new cultural renaissance will accompany this development. Man must increasingly unravel the secrets of nature, conquer its forces and harness them to his needs. All this will involve a prolonged and hazardous climb, a climb fraught with difficulties and social convulsions.

One does not need to visualise the end, it is in the nature of man always to pursue a further goal. The magnitude of the task is itself a challenge to the indomitable spirit of man.

At present science is, in the main, harnessed to the chariot of war and the genius of man is employed for the most barbaric purposes. The discovery of the limitless power of atomic energy is turned to the creation of diabolical instruments of devastation and destruction. The ways of progress are devious and growth is painful; the mechanical inventions of man have outstripped his social evolution and moral values. But there will come a time when war will have been banished from his affairs and these same inventions will be harnessed for the benefit of humanity. His energies will be liberated for the task of exploring fields of conquest.

Viewed from such heights, how small must seem the fanatic devotees of apartheid, how narrow their vision, how puerile and ineffectual their schemes for re-tribalisation and education for barbarism. It is hard to believe that, while the world is astir with change and new forces are making themselves felt throughout Asia and the rest of Africa, the rulers of South Africa can stubbornly keep their gaze fixed on the past. Do they think, Canute-like, that they can hold back the tide of human progress at a word of lordly command?

Confident as we are that the Verwoerdian policies must fail, we do not for one moment minimise their dire effects in the present. No one can take refuge in facile hopes or contemplate with equanimity the fate of a whole people doomed to frustration and penury, a people to whom every channel of development is closed and whose children are excluded from the knowledge and culture of a modern state. The whole concept of apartheid is an insult to human dignity.

Apartheid, with all its miserable brood, its Group Areas, its Immorality Acts, its Pass Laws, its Bantu Authorities, its Bantu Education and Coloured Education schemes – all this is an outrage to human intelligence.

It is our belief that the people of South Africa, both white and non-white, will one day jerk themselves out of their complacent smugness, and their prostration, wake up to their responsibilities and seek to wipe out from the book of history this chapter of degradation, misery and moral destitution.

VI   LET US RALLY
A Call to the Conference of The All-African Convention, November 1958

A VAST CONCENTRATION CAMP

Parliament has met once more. It is a herrenvolk parliament, whose primary occupation seems to be piling up more and more burdensome laws one after the other against the black people of this land. It is as if the herrenvolk were under the irresistible compulsion of an obsession. The sum total of their laws presents a grim picture of a whole country being turned into one vast concentration camp. Each new set of laws adds fresh stakes and barbed wire to a huge network designed to fence in a whole people.

The people against whom these laws are passed have no voice in the herrenvolk Parliament, no say in the making of the laws. If the laws have the effect of producing hardship and starvation, the weakening of the resistance to disease and increasing infant mortality to a fantastic rate; if, in a word a whole people is being impaled on the barbed wire of these laws, theirs only is to obey and die. They are not allowed to discuss the laws, not even in their villages; for they are not permitted to hold meetings. Prisoners in jail have the nominal right to express their grievances against prison conditions. But a black man in this country is not allowed to voice a protest freely.

Freedom of speech, of association and meeting are denied him. A whole black population exists in an atmosphere of permanent martial law.

In a land that has been turned into a huge prison camp, no one has a place he can call his home, either in town or country. Those of us who are working in the towns are like rock-lizards, with no security of any kind. No security of job, for the Minister may say he must no longer do that kind of work and find reasons for putting him out of the urban area. Neither has he any security of residence. For he and all the other Africans in the location (ghetto) may at any time be bundled on to lorries and shifted to another location far from their place of work. Each day he does not know if he will sleep with his family that night. For he is constantly in danger of being caught in the dragnet of the innumerable police raids. Even as he goes to bed in the night, he does not know if the next morning will find him with his family. Night raids have become the daily bread of the location dweller. He lives in a perpetual state of harassment and dread, dread of the police who may at any moment pounce on him in terms of one or the other of the many laws passed against him. He has a continual sense of scurrying to and fro. Like the rock-lizard whose natural habitat has been inundated by a flood, he cannot find even the narrowest crevice where the claws of the law may not reach into.

A black man in town is not permitted the security of a home of his own. He can never own the house he lives in. If he was born in the country, he cannot as of right return to his village and build himself a home. The only thing any black man is sure of is that one day he will be permitted a hole six feet beneath the earth for his dead body to lie in a segregated cemetery.

Those in the country, in the so-called 'Native Reserves,' fare no better. There, too, they have no home they can call their own. They occupy their poverty-stricken houses at the mercy of the various Native Commissioners and the Minister of Native Affairs, who, under the Rehabilitation Scheme, or Stabilisation Scheme as it is now called, can shift whole villages without granting any compensation for the demolished houses or assistance towards building new ones.

Even the cattle and sheep that are registered in their name are on loan, so to speak; for it is the stock-inspector or the magistrate who has full authority over them. He may tell the 'owner' what stock to keep, where it must graze, and when. If a man slaughters his ox, he has to report to the master. He may not buy cattle or sheep, no matter how much he needs them to provide for his children. He may be ordered to get rid of all his stock at any time. The people who have arable lands registered in their names may not plough what they choose.

The magistrate decides what each man shall plough in any season; he gives permission to people to start ploughing. If anyone ploughed before, or fails to start at the time stipulated by the magistrate, he is guilty of an offence. The peasant is a hut-prisoner in his own home. And if any individual should voice a protest, he may be banished as a trouble-maker or an protester.

Our children, too, are growing up in the atmosphere of a concentration camp. They must get a special kind of education, 'Bantu Education,' to prepare them to be docile inmates when they grow up. From a tender age they must be taught that they are something different from other humans; they are outside the pale of ordinary human society. In fact, what happens in schools today under the Native Affairs Department almost passes belief. No mother who has a child at any of the boarding schools can have a sound night's sleep for worrying about what is happening to him. For at any moment a child may walk in with his bundle to say he has been expelled, or a message may come that he has been arrested with the other children at school. It has become a common occurrence for the police to be in and out of the schools on matters of ordinary school discipline.

In this prison camp, all prisoners must have their badge and number. At any time any policeman or any official of the Native Affairs Department can stop a black man in the street or wake him up at dead of night to demand his pass.

Our women, too, are subject to the same indignities of the pass system and police search. Even young children attending schools are liable to be arrested if by some chance they leave their passes at home or drop them at play. As if the backs of the people were not already bending under the yoke of oppression, the herrenvolk now propose to pass a law for new taxation of the blacks to pay for running this prison-camp. The old taxes are to be increased – the poll-tax and the hut-tax payable whether a man is employed or not.

Our women, too, will now have to pay taxes. Those women who entered domestic service to support their aged and pensionless parents and to send their children to school, are now to be milked of part of their meagre earnings – all this to pay for an army of petty officials. How costly is this thing 'apartheid'!

FUNCTION OF CHIEFS

The corner-stone of the herrenvolk apartheid plans is the Bantu Authorities Act and the Bantu Education Act. The former seeks to re-organise a whole people, splitting them up into tribalised segments, each with an appointed chief at its head. These so-called chiefs are to be used as hangmen of the black people of the nation. The newly gazetted regulations defining the duties of chiefs show clearly what their function is to be. They are to constitute a glorified police force with powers to search, arrest, prosecute, convict and even order corporal punishment on grown-up men. They are to spy on people's lives, report to the magistrate what people are saying amongst themselves, what meetings have been held, what strangers have been seen in any village, where they sleep at night and what they do. These services will be cheap at the price. And what they lack in pay will be made up for in the elevated name of chief. They are to be enlisted in the carrying out of the Rehabilitation Scheme; they are to order people to get rid of their cattle. They are to order the women to apply for their book of passes and to carry it about on their persons. The latest scheme is to re-arrange the villages. The new plans under the Stabilisation Scheme are that all people who have no arable lands registered in their names will have to get rid of all their stock.

They themselves are to be shifted from their villages and dumped in new camps where they will live by selling their labour. They will have to buy all their foods, milk and meat. No one will be allowed to keep a single beast in these new village camps. The chiefs will have to enforce these violent measures. This is what re-tribalisation means. This is what restoration of chieftainship means.

The second corner-stone of the herrenvolk apartheid plans, the Bantu Education Act, seeks to stifle the mind and kill it. Our children are to be denied all education. Their minds are to be filled with the trash that belongs to a barbaric age. Special books are being written by government servants for use in Bantu schools, all with the purpose of enslaving their minds. All the books that open up a world of knowledge are taken away from our schools and our children are being denied the benefits of human culture, which is the heritage of men and women of all races. Our children are denied the very fruits of a civilisation which we ourselves are helping to create. For without our labour there could have been no civilisation in this country.

These two Acts, then, the Bantu Authorities Act and the Bantu Education Act, are the main pillars of the apartheid policy. They are the most dangerous and the most vicious Acts ever conceived by any herrenvolk mind in South Africa. They are all the more pernicious in their deadly effects on the African population, because their effects are not at once perceived by all.

They are like a slow poison that a man takes daily without knowing it. Slowly and steadily it seeps into his body, but it is only when it has penetrated right through his system and destroyed his innards – only then does it show itself outwardly in his finger-nails, his tongue and his gums. But by that time the man is a corpse.

It is these death-dealing Acts that the chiefs have to put into operation. It is their appointed task to see that the Bantu Authorities are established and that the Bantu Education functions as planned. The chiefs and headmen are to police the schools, which are to be put under their charge. They are to spy on the teachers to see that they dole out the poison to our children every day. The appointed school boards and school committees all over the country are to help them in this task.

To make sure that no children escape, chiefs are to be created even in the urban areas, in the locations. This is what the restoration of chieftainship means, together with its Bantu Education.

What is it all about? What is it all for? Is it that the herrenvolk hate us, and would like to destroy the black population out of spite?

No, they do not hate us. Neither would they like to destroy that which produces their wealth. It is their desire to keep us as mere instruments of toil and beasts of burden in their insatiable greed for wealth and more wealth, which we must create in abundance for them. It is this that makes them pass inhuman laws against us.

To achieve this, they devise barbarous laws to stunt the development of our minds, shut our mouths and blind our eyes. They would prevent us from seeing beyond the walls of our concentration camp. For great things are happening outside.

The oppressed throughout the world are throwing off the yoke of oppression. Our black brothers, too, in other parts of Africa, are struggling for their rights. They want to be in Parliament themselves, where the laws are made. It is the natural right of all men and women, except imbeciles, to be in Parliament and have a say in the government of their country. It is because we lack this most important right that it is possible for them to pass these inhuman laws against us.

The question we must ask ourselves is: What are we Africans and the other non-white oppressed doing about it? For they, too, have fared no better. The coloured people, having been robbed of their last remaining voting rights, are now being hounded into locations, with no longer the right to buy land where they choose.

The Indians, too, under the provisions of the Group Areas Act, are being robbed of their properties worth millions of pounds. They are to be thrown out of the towns which they have worked hard to develop, and are to be sent into the bushes, where they must live as paupers. They, too, like ourselves, must go and work for the herrenvolk for a pittance. What, then, are we all doing about it?

ISOLATED STRUGGLES

We hear of the isolated struggles here and there throughout the country. We hear of the women in Zeerust in the Transvaal facing imprisonment because they refused to be photographed for the book of passes. Elsewhere in the same district both men and women were arrested because they rejected the Bantu Authorities Act. There were the 3,000 African women of Pietersburg (Transvaal) who refused to accept the book of passes.

We hear of the people of Peddie (Cape), Zululand (Natal) and the various districts of the Transkei, rejecting the Bantu Authorities Act and opposing the Rehabilitation Scheme. We hear about the teachers facing dismissal in the struggle against Bantu Education. We hear about the magnificent struggle of the people of Alexandra and other locations in Johannesburg and Pretoria, and their almost superhuman spirit of endurance during the bus boycott. But all these are isolated episodes. While they reveal a common desire and a determination to resist oppression, and while the people learn from these experiences, yet we must understand that they cannot succeed by themselves in bringing us near our goal.

For they are spasmodic and unconnected efforts; they dissipate our energies. Such isolated struggles must end in failure, which in turn leads to despair and a sense of frustration. It is true that these isolated struggles have seriously alarmed the herrenvolk; so seriously that in some instances they have temporarily stayed their hand. This must not lull us into thinking that we have scored a victory. The herrenvolk pauses only to play for time and to think out more effective methods. They will come back – as they must – with greater ruthlessness to carry out their plans.

WE MUST LIBERATE OURSELVES

We must learn to see the struggle as a whole, and while tackling the single issues, we should at the same time keep our eyes fixed on the goal and direct our energies towards it. It must be concerted and sustained effort, which alone can give the people the necessary strength and power to put an end to oppression. No one will come from outside to help us. The international situation may create conditions favourable to our struggle, but we have to do the job ourselves. All the oppressed people, in whatever part of the country they are, should see themselves as part of one vast army of the oppressed and centralise and co-ordinate their struggles. Each organisation, however small, should see that it links up with other organisations in the All-African Convention. It is this body that federates and gathers together all the African organisations in town and country.

There are many amongst us who pose as our friends, who say they are going to help us liberate ourselves. But what do they do? With us, they shout loudly in protest. But they do not allow us to come together. They keep us divided. Indeed they do everything in their power to split our ranks.

They see to it that some organisations of the Africans refuse to join those of their brothers in the All-African Convention. They throw dust in the eyes of our brothers, pretending that they are going to lead them to salvation. What kind of help is this, that weakens our struggle by splitting our organisations and keeping them divided? At one time the African National Congress was with us in the Convention. It helped to found the Convention.

But with whom is it today? At one time the Ministers' Associations were with us. But with whom are they collaborating today? If the liberals were our true friends, would they not have seen to it that all the African organisations went back to where they belong, to the All-African Convention, with its Ten-Point Programme? – that body which was established to stake the claim for full equality for all people in South Africa; that body which has refused to be hoodwinked and diverted from its clear path in the search for freedom; that body which gathers together all the African organisations and unites them with the organisations of other oppressed Non-European people in the Non-European Unity Movement.

The task before us is an extremely hard one; the road is arduous and the obstacles are great. We can never reach our goal by each one travelling in a different path. There is no short cut to liberation. We must bend all our efforts in a united, concerted struggle. At every turn there will be those who will seek to disrupt our unity. For there is nothing the herrenvolk fears so much as the coming together of all the oppressed. Let us say again that every African man and woman, wherever they are, in town or country, in the cities, dorps (small towns) and villages, should see to it that their local organisation is linked up with the All-African Convention, which leads to the greater unity of all non-whites of South Africa in the Unity Movement. This is the road, the only road, that leads us out of the vast prison camp. This is the road that leads us to equality and freedom for all.

CHAPTER THREE:
The political situation and perspectives

I POLITICAL PROGRAMME OF UNITY

Editor's Note: A number of contemporary documents and speeches amplify in close-up, as it were, the evidence of a quickening political tempo generated during the second world war and expressed in the formation of the Unity Movement of South Africa. Its directives, which have been summed up in The Revolutionary Road For South Africa, *marked a turning-point in the struggles of the people. There is a sharp break with the past, a rejection of trusteeship and segregation; the claim to full equality for all; the formation of a principled policy and programme on the basis of which the Unity Movement went into action. In the present chapter we catch the spirit of the time in some of these documents.*

The All-African Convention took the first step in launching the Non-European Unity Movement, now known as the Unity Movement of South Africa. Its first Unity Manifesto, 'Calling All Africans', was issued in June 1943 by the Western Province Committee, of which Tabata was chairman. Here, 'Africans' designated all non-whites. A month later the central executive of the AAC issued a 'Clarion Call'. It declared, 'There is only one way open for us, to fight for our rights as citizens of our country. The white rulers of South Africa will never voluntarily give us our freedom and our rights.'

This Clarion Call contained an eleven-point programme which became the Ten-Point Programme of the Unity Movement. In a challenging statement — Along The New Road — the All-African Convention rejected the whole segregatory machinery of the bogus elections under the Native Representation Act and called on all members of the Native Representative Council, which was manned by leaders of the African National Congress, to resign forthwith. It exposed the sham of the Atlantic Charter drawn up by the imperialists, pointing out that General Smuts (Prime Minister of South Africa), who reached freedom abroad, was waging war on the rights of all non-whites at home.

It was under the chairmanship of Dr G H Gool, a young militant of the thirties, that the National Anti-CAD, a body federating coloured organisations, at once responded to the Convention's call for unity. Delegates representing the two federal bodies held a Preliminary Conference of the Non-European Unity Movement in December 1943, at which the Ten-Point Programme, containing the minimum demands of people seeking democratic rights, was laid down as the basis of a principled struggle. This is a historic document. (See

Appendix 1) Point 8 of the Preamble to the Declaration of Unity recognised the necessity for a battle on two fronts, against the oppressors and against the opportunists who co-operate with the government.

'Our fight against segregation (i.e. the government machinery of racial oppression) must be directed against the segregationists within as well as without.' Point 9 of the Preamble refutes the lie, frequently directed against the Unity Movement, that it is anti-white. It states, 'As the purpose of this unity is to fight against segregation, discrimination and oppression of every kind and to fight for equality and freedom for all, such a Unity Movement cannot and must not for a moment be considered as directed against the Europeans (an anti-European front). It is an anti-segregation front. Therefore all those European organisations and societies which are genuinely willing to fight segregation — as distinct from those who profess to be against segregation but in reality are only instruments of the ruling class — are welcome in this anti-segregation movement.

THE TEN-POINT PROGRAMME

The ten demands of the Ten-Point Programme sum up all that the masses lack in a capitalist system where economic exploitation is reinforced by racial oppression. There is thus a dynamic unity in the concept of this Programme as the basis of a co-ordinated struggle of all sections to throw off the yoke of an inter-related system of oppression. 'The Government plans for the whole and each scheme is part of a single comprehensive plan. It is precisely this circumstance that imposes on us the necessity to view our struggle on a national scale .... You cannot lift that oppression from one section and leave the other straining under its yoke. You cannot hope to liberate one section without at the same time liberating all.' (The Rehabilitation Scheme: A New Fraud.)

The dynamic nature of the Ten-Point Programme is elsewhere elaborated: 'The problem of liberation in South Africa, as we saw it, was how to bring together the national struggle (against racial oppression) and the agrarian struggle of the mass of the African peasantry for land, into one gigantic stream; how to mobilise the whole oppressed population into an irresistible fighting force to throw off the yoke of oppression; how to work out a policy and formulate a programme expressing the aspirations of all sections. This problem was resolved with the formulation of the Ten-Point Programme of the All-African Convention and adopted by the Unity Movement, together with our policy of non-collaboration with the oppressor, that is, the refusal of the non-whites to operate the segregatory machinery for their own oppression .... The demand for full democratic rights for all men and women — defined as a minimum programme — included also a demand for land for the peasantry. In the given conditions of South Africa this was a revolutionary programme involving the complete re-organisation of the whole structure of society.'

For the historical record it is necessary to be quite clear about the fundamental difference between this Ten-Point Programme of the Unity Movement and the 'Bill of Rights' which was drawn up at an ad hoc Convention called by Dr Xuma, President of the African National Congress after he had not only swept aside a decision by a joint committee representing the All-African Convention and the African National Congress that the latter should rejoin the federal body — the All-African Convention, but had also ignored the AAC call for the unity of all sections. It is significant that the chief signatories of the Congress 'Bill of Rights' were the collaborators who were actually operating the segregatory Native Representative Council. More than this, this 'Bill of Rights' subsequently became the 'Freedom Charter' of the Congress Alliance, which was a liberal/CP front designed to counter the dangerous influence of the Unity Movement with its ideas of complete independence from ruling class parties.

The truth is that the Congress 'Bill of Rights' stemmed from a position diametrically opposed to that of the All-African Convention and the Unity Movement. It contained those nebulous demands for rights extolled in the name of democracy, but calculated to conceal the aim to establish the dictatorship of the few, that is, of the bourgeoisie over the vast majority of the toiling masses, the workers and peasants. The Ten-Point Programme, on the other hand, together with the policy of non-collaboration with the oppressor, a crucial test for the collaborators, recognised that the democratic demands of the blacks could be achieved in one way only, the revolutionary overthrow of the existing system. In other words, it pointed to the socialist goal.

The campaign for unity, then, which was carried jointly throughout the country by the All-African Convention and the National Anti-CAD brought a hundred and fifty organisations to the first national conference of the Unity Movement held in January 1945. Of this body, the Rev Z R Mahabane, who had given many years to the struggle, was made chairman, while Dr G H Gool, one of the forward-looking revolutionaries, was made vice-chairman. Rejecting the idea of making any humble appeal for justice for the blacks at the imperialist Peace Conference (1945) — such as Dr Xuma invoked in his preface to the Congress 'Bill of Rights' — the Unity Movement issued a Declaration to the Nations of the World, addressing itself not to Governments but to the oppressed peoples. This was printed in five languages spoken within the country and was sent far afield to other countries. It is of interest to note that the Pan-African Congress held in Manchester, England, in October 1945, made this Declaration the core of their discussions on South Africa and requested permission to reproduce the document in England and the United States. The veteran W E B du Bois presided at this conference and the young Kwame Nkrumah, the future President of Ghana, was also present.

Here we quote in part from: The Manifesto of The All-African Convention (November 1945). This manifesto was issued in November 1944, in preparation for the first National Conference of the Unity Movement, January 1945, known as the Third Unity Conference. The international nature of the struggle against imperialism is the keynote of the opening of this third manifesto for unity.

The world is immersed in a deep and painful struggle. It is suffering from the most acute birth pangs, the birth of a new era. The working class and the masses of oppressed people throughout the world are striving with determination to smash and throw off the shackles of slavery that bind them. The imperialists aroused the latent forces of the masses, whipping them out of their deep lethargy. And naturally it was for the purpose of tying them to their own imperialist war chariot. But the workers and oppressed peoples throughout five years of bitter war and all that it entails, have been learning a number of things and are learning with still greater rapidity as the war draws nearer an end, or rather as the defeat of Germany is almost an accomplished fact.

Firstly, they have learned that the so-called 'defeat of fascism' may mean replacing German fascism with British, American or French fascism. They have learned that the 'freedom' for which they have sacrificed their very lives may mean freedom for the financiers and industrialists of the allied imperialists to exploit not only the colonial slaves in distant countries but also their own workers.

Most important, the workers and oppressed peoples throughout the world have learned through harsh experience to see things as they are and to think independently for themselves.

And still more, they have learned to know their own power. It is a power that demands true freedom and real democracy. The war has rudely shaken the people out of their sleep of blind endurance, pulled the scales from their eyes and compelled them not only to realise their own strength but to see through all the tricks and subterfuges used by the ruling class to keep in perpetual bondage.

The oppressed non-whites of South Africa are not lagging behind in this process of awakening or this ability to see clearly and to think independently for themselves. Up till now the ruling class has done all the thinking for the non-whites, who have accepted their masters' opinions as infallible. White supremacy in South Africa, for instance, has been accepted as a divine law; the policy of 'divide and rule' has worked inevitably as if it had been a law of nature and not simply a weapon in the hands of the ruling class for the greater deception and the more complete enslavement of the people.

Now this new clarity on the part of the non-whites threatens white supremacy, which is the cornerstone of their whole policy. But the ruling class is fully aware of the process that is taking place. The fascist forces all over South Africa are rearing their ugly heads. The extreme Nationalists are whipping up a mass hysteria in preparation for launching pogroms against us, as Nazi Germany did against the Jews. The Smuts government, while making feeble protestations against this blatant fascist propaganda, is in reality busy making fascist laws against the non-whites.

It was in this last session of Parliament that the Amendment to the Urban Areas Act was passed. This Act not only extended the vicious system of the Pass Law to the Cape Province, but actually threw the African back to pre-feudal days, robbing the urban African of the right to possess property. This same government brought the Pegging Act against the Indians, denying them the elementary right to own property where they please. It was this same government that created the Coloured Advisory Council as the first step towards robbing the coloured people of their semi-franchise and reducing them to the same status as the other non-white groups. All these measures are part of the preparation for the complete enslavement of the non-whites, and bringing them under the heel of Fascism.

But war has awakened the latent forces of the people for liberation. It is no longer possible for the government to deceive them with false promises. It is no longer possible for the ruling class to impose upon them the lie of race superiority. The non-whites are rallying in self-defence. When the government imposed the CAC on the coloured people, they countered by uniting round the Anti-CAD Movement which spread wherever the coloured man was to be found. The leadership laid bare every trick used to hoodwink the coloured people into accepting this new link in the chain of their oppression. They brought to the people the realisation that the oppression of the coloured man is inseparably bound up with that of the other non-white sections, and their fight, therefore, is the same as theirs. The coloured people are in one section of the whole non-white army in the fight against oppression. The majority section, the Africans, have begun to move in line with the rest. The strike waves on the Witwatersrand, **(mining region in Transvaal Province – Ed.)** the disturbances and discontent among the peasants, are unmistakable signs of this new ferment.

This ferment has found political expression in the decisions taken at the last conference of the All-African Convention (December 1943). It decided to reject the old road of passivity and compromise and embark on the new road of leadership. It rejected the myth of white supremacy with its resulting policy of trusteeship. It decided to embark on a policy of non-collaboration with the government in its application of the slave laws passed against the Africans. It rejected the government policy of 'divide and rule' and embarked on a policy of establishing the Unity of all Non-White oppressed. Through these decisions the AAC expresses the very essence of the aspirations of the unvocal masses as a whole. The coloured people in the National Anti-CAD have readily accepted the call to Unity. The Indian masses, too, though hampered by their official leadership, have shown signs of the same spirit. These decisions are laying the foundations of a new movement with infinite possibilities for fulfilling the aspirations of the people. They are opening up a new era in the struggle for liberation.

THE BUILDING OF UNITY

Extracts from a summary of a speech delivered by Tabata at the first all-in National Unity Movement Conference, January 1945.

It is my task to introduce the discussion on the Building of Unity. Judging from what took place yesterday there is going to be a good deal of discussion. Today we are faced with one of the most contentious problems of Conference. Yesterday Conference accepted a new policy, a new outlook, but it is no use accepting this new policy unless we are prepared to put it into practice. We have to create channels, we have to create a vehicle through which to carry this policy to the masses. It is the nature of this vehicle, the organisational form of the Unity Movement, that we are now called upon to discuss.

Controversy will be inevitable. In a big conference of this nature there will be differences of opinion, which must be expected, for the people represented belong to many different schools of political thought. We shall anticipate a few of these.

Editor's Note: Tabata deals at length with the ultra-Lefts who 'are inclined to skip stages and fail to realise that it is necessary to take cognisance of the different stages of development of a people and their struggle'; with the young hot-heads who want to abolish all existing organisations and form one unitary national organisation that would sweep away oppression overnight; and with the conservatives who do not want this particular Unity, fearing that this federal body will swallow their own organisations.

There are those (he continued) who really do not want Unity. You may ask: how can a non-white in South Africa not want Unity? Last night a member of Conference mentioned that amongst the Indians there is already crystallised a bourgeois class. While he mentioned this, he failed to draw the proper conclusions from it. This class is afraid of the Unity Movement because it is a threat to its own economic position. This is the Indian merchant class.

Now it is important to know who are with us and who are not with us, so I propose to say something more on this subject. When we speak of the South African Indian Congress (SAIC), we do not speak of the Indian people. The SAIC is in the control of the Indian merchant class. Why have we not been able to draw in this class? Because our aspirations are totally different from theirs. For us, Unity is a means to our liberation.

That is why we want to put it on a sound programmatic basis. But for them, the Indian merchant class, Unity is a weapon with which to threaten the Government, something to be used for striking a bargain with the Government, for gaining concessions for themselves. They, like all bourgeoisie, are mortally afraid of the working class. They are fully class-conscious and clear-sighted; their vision is not blurred by the colonial issue; they transcend the demarcation of colour, see the real class issue and take up their position alongside their class-brothers.

The time is past when we could have a bourgeoisie that is progressive and revolutionary; at a crucial moment they will turn against the working class. This holds true of the bourgeoisie throughout the world. No section must be allowed to use the Unity Movement as a pawn in the game for its own benefit. The Ten-Point Programme shuts out all possibility of bargaining. But what about the Indian people, who still belong to the Indian Congress? We want them. We will not rest until the Indian workers and peasants are working alongside of us. I must here remind delegates that this Conference does not in itself constitute Unity, but marks the beginning of a long struggle for Unity. We are prepared to try and get in all those elements whose interests are with us. We shall go out and fight along with them, but only on the basis of the Ten-Point Programme.

We must next consider the problem of how to carry out the programme we agreed upon yesterday. After three hundred years we have only now adopted the Ten-Point Programme, only now decided to change our whole outlook. The decisions made yesterday have still to be taken to the country and still to be understood, for it takes time for an idea to become part and parcel of a human being. We must view the whole struggle in motion. We cannot skip stages in development.

We must realise that, so well have we imbibed the ideas of the ruling class that our segregationist outlook has not been and cannot be overthrown overnight. In order to create a vehicle which will carry our new outlook, we must know what we have at hand, namely, various national bodies. Let us not create a new body at every Conference. What we have to do is to give a new function to the existing federal organisations, namely co-operation and co-ordination of their activities. In this way they will become more powerful.

I suggest that the Conference shall agree to the creation of a Central Unity Executive Committee which shall be made up of representatives of the three federal organisations representing the three racial groups – African, coloured and Indian. This Committee must rest on, and draw sustenance from the federal bodies, which in turn we must strengthen, so that they may take root amongst the people. Already the Anti-CAD, for example, has formed local committees all over the country, and all coloured organisations in a locality are represented in these committees. The Convention is also building up local committees whose primary task is to work among the Africans so that not a single organisation is left out of the committee. In the same way the Unity Movement must find roots among the people by creating a new function for those local committees.

Supposing a measure is passed by the Government against any one section of the non-whites, then not only the local committee of that section will take up the struggle, but also the local committees of the other two sections shall be asked to join in the fight. This co-ordinating function rests with the Local Co-ordinating Unity Committee.

What I have been trying to describe has already been demonstrated in Cape Town, the only place in which the Anti-CAD Local Committee and the All-African Convention (Western Province) Local Committee exist side by side. When the Government raised the bogey of the 'influx of Natives' and painted a lurid picture of Africans pouring into towns to take the bread out of the mouths of the coloured people, the Government propaganda machine was set in motion amongst the coloured people to stir up feelings against the Africans. The scare went so far that the European Ratepayers' Association invited the coloured people to come along with them to discuss this 'influx'. But the AAC Committee (WP) and the Anti-CAD Committee united in a campaign to expose this piece of propaganda. They pointed out to the people that it was an attempt to nip the Unity Movement in the bud; they broke up the meeting and defeated the attempt to stir up race hatred between the coloured and the Africans. There is one thing that the Government does not like to see and will do everything in its power to break, and that is the Unity of all non-whites. In the example I have quoted we see that Unity was not only preached in leaflets and from platforms, but coloured and Africans came together in action. Here was Unity in practice. The theory and the practice, that is, the actual struggle on the basis of the Ten-Point Programme, will teach the people to forget their racial groups and think only in terms of their common oppression.

But it must be clearly understood that these Local Co-ordinating Unity Committees are not there merely for defence, i.e. to wait until Government passes some new measure against one or other section of the non-whites. There are many laws which have already been passed against us which we have to fight. The Local Co-ordinating Unity Committees are going to organise the people, draw the community into the struggle, prepare the masses for a concerted onslaught against oppression and rally them in the fight for liberation.

Editor's Note: Under the question of the building of unity, the Unity Movement had to consider the whole problem of the trade unions and the necessity for the non-white workers to see the trade union struggle as a political one. It stressed the paramount importance of the trade unions to belong to the national body and to fight from within it. The following passage from The Awakening of a People, Chapter 2, sums up the approach of the Unity Movement to this all-important problem.

TRADES UNIONS – A POLITICAL PROBLEM

The present-day African trade unions are the natural successors to the ICU (Industrial and Commercial Workers' Union). They represent the present stage of the development of the African people who have now become fully conversant with the relationships in the industrial set-up. They have become an essential element of the capitalist system and share its outlook and modes of thinking.

It is our firm belief that the main reason why the African trade unions today are moribund is precisely that they have persistently kept aloof from the political struggle of the oppressed peoples of South Africa.

The desire of the African workers to defend themselves against exploitation had given rise in 1919 to a clumsy, undefined, all-embracing structure, the ICU. This attempt corresponded to the undefined nature of their own position as members of an oppressed people (mainly landless peasantry) harnessed to the industrial machine of the new society. Yet, willy-nilly, the very nature of the industrial forces, with the relationships involved, directed them to the necessity of forming an organisation for the purpose of defending themselves against their employers. The realisation by the African people that they were doubly oppressed – as workers and as members of an oppressed race – was a fundamental one. And the formation of the ICU had given expression to this basic fact. But to this day the problem of the dual nature of oppression has not been tackled in the proper way, in spite of the fact that the Africans evolved trade unions. It is precisely the dual nature of oppression which the trade unions today have lost sight of. The trade unions have become preoccupied with their specialised tasks and completely ignored the general political struggles of the African people as a whole.

Yet it is essential to realise that at this stage the political struggle and the trade union struggle are inextricably bound together. Racial oppression is a part of economic exploitation and reinforces it. Stripped of every vestige of political rights, the oppressed people of South Africa cannot fight exploitation in all its forms. Without political power outside the trade unions, they are helpless. In fact, political and industrial laws – the Colour Bar Act, the Apprenticeship Act, etc. – tie a rope round the necks of all non-whites. Furthermore, they drive a wedge between the white and the non-white workers with the result that they are blinded to their common interests.

In other words, without political equality it will never be possible to speak of working-class unity, and without working-class unity it will never be possible to fight exploitation.

Since, therefore, he is denied even the rights of a worker, the very act of forming a Trade Union is for the African a political one. So that he cannot do other than participate in the political struggle. To put it another way, the Trade Union question in South Africa presents itself primarily as a national (political) question and only secondarily as a class question. The second cannot be solved independently of the first.

It is clear from what has been said that the present Trade Union leaders are not capable of measuring up to the tasks facing the Trade Unions amongst the oppressed non-whites today. They have first of all to orientate themselves to the idea that their struggle is part of a national struggle. Even in their approach to the specific problems of low wages, segregation in industry, the 'uncivilised labour' policy, the exclusion of Africans from unemployment benefits, their exclusion from the provisions of the Industrial Conciliation Act, they have to realise that all these are essentially political questions. They are the warp and woof of the national struggle of the racially oppressed non-whites.

The present attitude of the Trade Union leaders of divorcing the Trade Unions from politics, dooms the Trade Union movement to futility. It is criminal for them to take up the slogan of the white bureaucrats, 'No politics in the Trade Unions'. Such a slogan is designed to render the non-whites defenceless before the oppressors. It is tantamount to a renunciation of the Trade Union movement among the non-whites. More than that, these henchmen and agents of the ruling class amongst the non-white workers are guilty of the greatest irresponsibility. For they are holding back the national liberatory movement itself. The only way to revitalise the now moribund trade union movement is to plant it squarely in the midst of the national struggle for liberation.

Editor's Note: It is of interest here to add to this chapter the political directives of the Unity Movement contained in its resolutions on international questions. At its second national conference it passed the following resolution:

This Conference of the Non-European Unity Movement held in Kimberley on the 19th and 20th December, 1945:

   — Expresses its unreserved support of the people of Indonesia, China, India and all the oppressed peoples of the Continents of Asia and Africa in their heroic struggle for independence and full democratic rights.

   — Supports the struggle of the people of India for their independence from British rule; supports the people of China in their fight against foreign Imperialism and native oppressions; greets the heroic and uncompromising battle waged by the militant people of Java and Indo-China for their national independence and fundamental human rights; condemns the brutal intervention of British, Dutch and French Imperialism; calls for the immediate withdrawal of all foreign troops, and for the democratic right of the people to decide their own destiny.

   — Sends fraternal greetings and declares its solidarity with all peoples in every country who are fighting for a world free from exploitation and tyranny. The thrust of the leadership towards a still wider Unity extending into the African continent is shown in the following unanimous resolution, 'That this Conference of the Unity Movement instructs the Executive to endeavour to contact the liberatory movements in all other States on the Continent of Africa with a view to establishing fraternal relationships as a step towards the eventual unification of the struggle for equality and full citizenship.'

At the next conference the following resolution protested the proposed incorporation of South West Africa (ex-German colony) into the Union of South Africa: 'The Non-European Unity Movement wishes to declare its emphatic opposition to the proposal to incorporate South West Africa as a fifth province of the Union.

'We are opposed to the inclusion on the principle and on the grounds that it will be detrimental to the people in the Protectorates (British: Basutoland, Swaziland, Bechuanaland, later declared 'independent.' Ed.) and to the Non-Europeans in the Union. For, however intolerable the conditions under which the people of South West Africa live, there can be no worse fate than their falling under the domination of the South African herrenvolk. As long as the Non-European population of South Africa is deprived of citizenship rights, the inclusion of any other provinces or Protectorates cannot but be a retrogressive step. Therefore we dissociate ourselves from all such territorial claims on the part of the rulers.'

II. THE BOYCOTT AS WEAPON OF STRUGGLE

Cape Town: All-African Convention Committee, Western Province, 1952

Editor's Note: The concerted attack by the enemies of the Movement who were alarmed by the response of the people to the use of the boycott weapon prompted Tabata to look into the whole question of this phenomenon of collaboration between a section of the intellectuals and the ruling class, and trace its historical roots in South African society. For it was one of the problems of liberation to open the eyes of the masses to the function of these collaborators. At the same time Tabata was battling to win the understanding of the young intellectuals and place a clear choice before them – either to follow in the footsteps of their elders or take their place alongside their people. The pamphlet is here slightly abridged.

Since the first days, in 1943-44, when the All-African Convention, the National Anti-CAD and the Non-European Unity Movement adopted the Boycott slogan, the enemies of the Movement have alternately sneered at it, pretended to adopt it in order more effectively to debase it and render it ineffectual, and, finally, they have misrepresented it to the people with the express purpose of making it appear meaningless and ridiculous.

This vicious attack upon one of the most potent weapons in the armoury of the people struggling for liberation came from the intellectuals. The most interesting feature in this 'struggle' of the intellectuals against the people's boycott weapon is that it has thrown into one camp elements of the most diversified political outlooks: intellectuals who proclaim themselves as internationalists: rabid African nationalists, or more simply, ardent tribalists; doctors and professors who mouth democratic phraseology but secretly harbour a nostalgic hankering for the return of the idyllic days of barbarism; Gandhi-ists, and now the latest adherents of Gandhi-ism called Dadoo-ists **(Dadoo was chairman of the S A Indian Congress. Ed.)** – all of them have formed a tacit united front in their self-appointed task of not only besmirching the people's boycott slogan and laughing it out of court, but rendering its application impossible. While all of them are opposed to the unity of all non-whites they are nevertheless united on this issue. Their common hostility to the people's weapon is so strong that it cuts across the artificially created racial barriers and brings them together.

This situation makes it necessary to explain the meaning of the boycott weapon, its effectiveness and its proper use. It is also incumbent on us to show why the intellectuals are mortally afraid of it. For their attitude towards it has its roots in the historical setting of the political and social structure of South Africa.

(The passage that follows at this point – 'Our struggle is not unique' – opens Chapter Four of this book. It is here omitted. Ed.)

THE NATURE OF SOUTH AFRICAN SOCIETY

We do not intend to give a detailed history of the past. It is necessary simply to indicate in broad outline the stages of conquest and the problems that arose at each stage. First the white invaders had to defeat the inhabitants and confiscate their land. This they did by force of arms, in a protracted fight lasting over two hundred years. This conquest was not effected without the assistance of the persuasive tongues of the missionaries, who gave able assistance to the conquerors by a judicious use of indoctrination at strategic times and places.

Having acquired possession of the land, the invaders had then to establish themselves and organise their way of life. Thus in the southern part of Africa there existed side by side two incompatible systems: tribalism and capitalism. (Actually there was a third, the feudalism of the Dutch, which was nearer to tribalism, and is of no consequence for our purpose.)

This new social system could develop only at the expense of the tribalism of the original inhabitants. Industry required a certain culture for its growth and this had to be provided by the local population. This involved not only forcing the inhabitants to supply all the labour required, but something much more than that. It meant creating a new market by creating new needs, new tastes, new desires on the part of the dispossessed tribalists. In short, it meant creating a new outlook and a new way of life. Tribalism had to be burst asunder and overthrown by a money economy.

Obviously, at this stage of conquest, where the two mutually incompatible systems are fighting it out, the military machine is ineffectual and has to recede into the background while other agencies come to the fore. Not that the use of brute force is ever completely superseded, but it is convenient at certain stages to sheathe the naked sword. Now was the time for the missionary to come forward with his secondary function; he had to educate the people, i.e. cultivate in them the new needs and desires which were necessary to industrialism. Mission schools were planted all over and as there were not enough white missionaries to go round, they had to train young Africans as teachers to carry their message among their own people.

These schools were centres of indoctrination acting as a disruptive force within the various tribes. Each black teacher presented himself before his pupils clad from head to foot in the products of the new industrial system and from his mouth issued forth those solemn injunctions which have since become so familiar to us: on humility (turning the other cheek to the hand that smote it); honesty (after you have been robbed of all you possessed); love thine enemy (provided you don't expect it to be reciprocated); faith and hope (provided you wait for your reward in the next world); and finally, the 'dignity of labour' (by which is meant only the most menial tasks, and that only when performed for the benefit of the white employer).

Of course our teacher had to teach also the rudiments of the three R's, in order to fit the prospective labourer for his task in the industrial machine.

PROBLEM OF GOVERNMENT

As capitalism won the battle over tribalism, as all of the non-whites were becoming encompassed by the new social system, the problem of government became more acute. Capitalism had taken over the territory, but the people had not yet been integrated into the system, which has its own logic in the regulation of relations between man and man. During the period of military conquest it had been a matter of prime importance to break the power of the chief, who was the rallying point of resistance. But the very efficiency with which the military machine had smashed the authority of the chiefs presented the whites with the problems of governing the people they had conquered. The lack of cohesion made government well-nigh impossible and anarchy threatened to become the order of the day.

The rulers were faced with a problem which was all the greater because they had decided to keep the power of government exclusively within their own hands. Between the white ruler and the ruled there existed a yawning gap. Obviously some channels of communication had to be established in order to maintain control. But the only centres of authority that the people knew were the chiefs and councils familiar to them in their tribal life. Failing the only sane policy – to the rulers, anathema – of integrating the people into the new system of government on an equal footing, they were left with only one alternative, namely, to create chiefs who would constitute the channels of contact they needed. This placed the rulers on the horns of a dilemma. For to resuscitate chieftainship was to run the danger of summoning up the memory of the heroic resistance of the recent past and provide the vanquished with a new rallying point.

POLICEMEN-CHIEFS

The dilemma was resolved by the creation of policemen-chiefs. Once more it was the missionaries who came forward to assist and evolve this diabolically clever idea. It was a hybrid conception partaking of tribalism and capitalism and deliberately calculated for the deception of the people, while at the same time it met the requirements of the rulers. The chiefs were to be paid a fixed wage by the Government. They were to be its paid servants and were to be responsible, not to the people, but to the Government, their master. Each policeman-chief was surrounded by a troupe of headmen, each of whom was responsible not to the policeman-chief, but to the Government. In this way the whole of the so-called Reserves was infested with an army of these Government creatures who vied with one another in serving their masters. In them the Government had a band of willing and efficient agents for controlling the African masses. All the laws and regulations which it pleased a tyrannical

Government to make, were energetically carried to the people through the channel of these agencies. The policemen-chiefs and headmen were the first effective instruments for the domination of the African people.

One has to imagine the situation at the time when this scheme was set afoot, to realise the Jesuitical cunning of it all. The people, while they were forced to live and work within the Colony (Cape), nevertheless remained aliens in the country of their birth. They had still to be broken in.

Wherever the people were, they were subjected to close surveillance. Every few square miles throughout the whole Colony had its inevitable headman who snooped and pried into their most intimate affairs. In such an atmosphere it is easy to imagine how the people could be dragooned into accepting any law or scheme imposed by the Government, even though it was obvious that it was diametrically opposed to their own interests.

INTELLECTUALS AS SECOND AGENTS

As the country developed, capitalism disrupted tribalism and swallowed up feudalism; industry grew and towns sprang up all over the country. The sons of the Dutch feudalists drifted into the cities and there either invested their capital in industry and commercial ventures or took up jobs as foremen and overseers. With all this expansion Africans in their thousands were absorbed as labourers for the various undertakings. Cheap labour was abundant; white farmers prospered; export trade in skins, hides and other agricultural produce increased many times over. Later diamonds were discovered, to be followed soon afterwards by the opening up of the gold mines.

These two discoveries revolutionised the life of the colonies in South Africa. It accelerated the land-grabbing and precipitated the Boer War. The sham of respecting territorial boundaries and the independence of small states was dropped. Britain had to organise a unified economy for the whole of Southern Africa; she had to establish a network of communications linking up the diamond and gold mines with the coastal towns. At the same time many subsidiary industries sprang up and thousands of miles of railways were built.

This colossal expansion could only be done by harnessing a vast army of the dispossessed. It could not be carried out without the cheap labour of the conquered non-whites. All this reinforced the disruption of tribalism and shattered the last remnants of the tribal unit. As the people became absorbed into the new system, the hold of the policemen-chiefs over them was necessarily loosened. Even the migrant labourer who returned home from time to time came back with a new outlook. He no longer accepted the old traditions that gave the chief power over him. During his sojourn in the mines, the towns and the white man's farms he had learned to fend for himself as an individual. He no longer thought in terms of the tribe, but of the welfare of himself and his family. Large numbers severed the tribal bonds and settled in towns and peri-urban areas, while new generations grew up without any knowledge of the tribal life. Once more a new problem of maintaining control over the African arose.

Obviously the policeman-chief could not cope with the new situation. His usefulness as a means of domination was becoming ineffectual since the younger generation had no room for him in their outlook. So a new method of control, a new instrument of domination, had to be found. The eyes of the rulers now turned seriously towards the African intellectuals. And who could be more suited than they for the desired purpose? Side by side with the tremendous expansion of industry and commerce, there was another development taking place in the field of education. A new 'class' had emerged, namely, the intelligentsia. This section of the population, though small in number, had begun to speak the language of the rulers. These intellectuals were regarded as knowing the ways and customs of the white man and able to find their way about in the intricacies of the new system. Thus the people looked up to them for guidance and reposed their faith in them. It was this circumstance that made the rulers turn to the intellectuals as a means of controlling the masses.

It is pertinent to ask: how did the old intellectuals come to play the role they did? This might be answered by another question: how did the first generation of intellectuals look upon themselves? From the early days when they were converted to Christianity they accepted the new system with all its modes of life, of social organisations and of thought. Capitalism was correctly seen by them as an advancement over tribalism. In it they saw a vista of progress opening up before them and from that time on they decided to do all they could to bring their people within the orbit of this new civilisation. They saw themselves as men with a mission. The missionaries had introduced them to the rudiments of education; they had learned to read and write; through books they were brought into contact with a new world, new realms of thought, new experiences, new possibilities of development.

In the eyes of the intellectuals, then, the missionary was educating them and helping them to bring their people into the civilisation which created all these things with the express purpose of enabling them to enjoy the fruits of such a civilisation. They were not to know all the complex forces at work in capitalism; forces that had produced the missionary himself and made him come to their country. They were not to know that the missionary himself was an instrument in the hands of the industrialists and merchants of Britain, of that process of colonial expansion that was undertaken for the benefit not of the inhabitants but of the mother country. He was allowed to come out and preach 'the rewards of the hereafter' only because such preachings were eminently suited to facilitating the task of the British soldiery.

If they knew none of these things, how were they to know that the three R's and the whole system of education given them by their 'benefactor' were not all for their benefit but were the requirements of an industrial system? Capitalism seemed to them like the promised land. So to this task of leading their people into the promised land they bent all their energies. This explains why the old intellectuals were ready to co-operate with the missionaries. Their co-operation was made all the easier because the authorities gave the educated Africans preferential treatment.

They were granted the franchise and were made, nominally at least, the equals of the whites. They were free from the burdensome pass-laws. Let it be said that the old intellectuals did not regard this as a bribe intended to be enjoyed by the few. They regarded it as an inherent right of all those who had accepted the new mode of life and they were spurred to work all the harder to bring their people to the same standard of education as themselves in order to qualify for those rights. Many of them made considerable personal sacrifices for the community, a circumstance that earned them the respect of their countrymen – who had every reason to be suspicious – and gained them the following of the masses. In a word, the old intellectuals regarded themselves as torch-bearers and not traitors.

It was because of the tangible benefits which they believed would accrue to the whole population, that the old African intelligentsia accepted the fateful pact which started a chain of collaboration with the missionaries, and later with the liberals – a collaboration that was to cost the non-whites of South Africa so many lives and bring in its trail untold suffering, humiliation and degradation.

As the system of capitalism unfolded, however, it became abundantly clear that the promises of salvation were a delusion and a snare. The educational system itself was not designed to liberate the people, but to enslave them.

Now a new crop of intellectuals sprang up, with a totally different outlook, and corruption set in. If the old African intellectuals who collaborated with the missionaries can be excused because they were unaware of the pitfalls involved, the same cannot be said of their successors. This new generation was fully aware that the few privileges they enjoyed were offered to them as bribes in order to separate them from their people. By this time a pattern of racial discrimination had clearly emerged and was crystallised in the so-called Act of Union, which glorifies herrenvolkism and extols racialism as the very foundation stone of the South African State.

All the Acts that reached the statute book thereafter were simply the working out of a clearly evolved plan. Year after year the African intellectuals could see unfolding before their very eyes a whole series of legislative measures that were grinding their people ever more ruthlessly and reducing them to a state of unmitigated servitude. The new generation of African intellectuals were self-seeking impostors who inherited the prestige and traded on the good name of their predecessors. They knew that the narrow margin of privilege that separated them from their more unfortunate brothers was granted them at the price of collaboration with the white agents of oppression. The whole process of reducing the black man to his present position would have been impossible without the help of these intellectuals. It was they who shackled the mind of the people and led them into bondage.

Before we elaborate on how this was done let us pause to answer an accusation often levelled at us: that the blacks are ungrateful to the whites for bringing them Western civilisation. In the first place the term is a mischievous catchword employed by the herrenvolk to exclude all but themselves from enjoying the fruits of civilisation. There is only human civilisation which is the sum total of knowledge and techniques slowly acquired by man in the course of his development through the ages. The ancient civilisations of Asia, in China, India, Babylonia, Assyria, Persia and North Africa, which flourished while the peoples of Europe were sunk in barbarism, laid the foundations of modern civilisation. The civilisation of Greece, which owed a great deal to those of Mesopotamia and North Africa, later spread to Rome and thence to the so-called 'Western' nations. Civilisation as we know it today is thus the property of mankind. As we, the blacks of South Africa, are part of humanity, we claim this civilisation as our natural heritage. We have every right to condemn the herrenvolk for denying us the full benefits of civilisation. It is an act of immorality to withhold the fruits of civilisation from the black section of the human race. Every day of our lives since the advent of capitalism in this country we have been creating civilisation. In every field of South African life a black man's labour is indispensable: from the production of food in the fields, the building of roads and railways, the loading and unloading of goods at the docks, the extraction of gold from the mines, to the manufacture of industrial products and their distribution; from the building of their towns, their very homes, to the tending and rearing of their children. How monstrous, then, is this idea of the black man's ingratitude!

To come back to the question of how the intellectuals were enlisted in reducing the people to slavery and maintaining domination over them.

First of all it must be clear that education played a very important part in this process. Insidiously in the schools the germ of inferiority was implanted in the mind of the black child. In the history books, for instance, his forbears were painted as loafers, thieves, scoundrels and cowards, until he learned to be ashamed of them. He was taught to 'know his place' in society; he had to see himself as 'different' and he had to 'develop along his own lines', so that by the time he grew up he was conditioned to accepting an inferior position, politically, economically and socially. And it was a black teacher who had to implant all this in his mind. **(Full section on policy of 'Native Education' omitted. Ed.)**

The effect of this special system of so-called 'Native Education' is not limited to creating a predisposition in the minds of those who have attended school. It is more far-reaching than this. It produces a section of intellectuals who become the human agency for the dissemination of those ideas of inferiority amongst the people – the section from which the leadership is drawn.

POLICEMEN-INTELLECTUALS

The pattern of South African society had fully emerged and segregation was being rigidly enforced in all spheres. Politically the non-whites were being reduced to a voiceless people; economically they were in a state of destitution and were by law relegated to the performance of unskilled labour; residentially they were being crowded into 'Reserves' and 'Locations'. The cleavage between black and white was complete. The breach was open. It was a situation that might well stir the people to revolt, and in fact there were sporadic disturbances. It was at this point that the intellectuals demonstrated their usefulness to the rulers. It was necessary to embark on a scheme for disarming the people intellectually. This was the more easily done because the mantle of leadership had fallen on the new generation of intellectuals who, as we said, were still trading on the prestige of their predecessors. The people looked up to them to lead them in the struggle.

The intellectuals were faced with a grave decision. They had a choice of two things: to place themselves at the head of their people and launch a struggle against the Government, or to side with the rulers against their own people. If they went with the people they would be denounced as radicals and unreasonable. They would earn the frown of their masters and lose their little rewards for services rendered, those marks of approbation and all those intangible favours that are so comforting to a 'good boy'. If on the other hand they openly joined the rulers they would lose their position as leaders of their people.

It was the liberals who came to their rescue and helped them out of their dilemma. As masters of diversionary tactics the liberals threw out the meaningless slogan 'Development along their own lines'. The African intellectuals seized upon this as a means of saving their own face. They turned the attention of the people away from the conflict and diverted their energies into useless channels. Now they were fully aware of the treachery of the slogan. What else could it mean but cutting the people off from the body politic and leading them down into serfdom?

But, alas, the people themselves did not know. To the vast majority of the illiterate masses groaning under the conditions of serfdom, 'development along our own lines' meant escaping from the clutches of the white man and taking the road that led to salvation. To the semi-literate, with their minds already prepared by the small dose of 'Native Education' they had received, the slogan pointed the road to a supposed independence from the yoke of the white man, to a Utopia of an independent Black State. It was only the small minority of intellectuals who were aware of its true meaning.

For them the prime motive was the desire to escape, as a privileged few, from the rigours of oppression. Although segregation spelt frustration and stagnation for the rest of their people, it offered the so-called elite the possibility of fat jobs – jobs that would only be open to them in segregated spheres. They had visions of themselves in the sphere of education, for instance, receiving professorships and inspectorships in 'Native' colleges and schools; in segregated areas they visualised themselves as running big businesses, freed from white competition; there would also be plenty of jobs for them as petty officials. In short, this small elite would be free, like their masters, to batten on the masses. It was the dangling of this miserable bribe before their eyes that set the intellectuals along the tortuous road of collaboration, the road that led the African people into a political desert.

From this time on, the intellectuals, locked in an unholy embrace with the white liberals, dragged the oppressed into futile ventures, and thus demonstrated their usefulness to the rulers.

The masses had been gathering their forces and a head-on collision was imminent, but the intellectuals stepped in and deflected them from their course. Henceforward, in pursuing this chimera of 'developing along our own lines', they were not simply following a road away from the true struggle but were actually engaged in forging the chains of their own enslavement.

When Rhodes (British imperialist) came out with his infamous Glen Grey Act in 1894, it was the intellectuals who now cajoled, now dragooned the African people into accepting the Bungas (advisory councils of chiefs), those toys of government for a child-race.

When this system was seen to work effectively, it was the intellectuals who were employed to carry it to the urban areas where Location 'Native Advisory Boards' were established to keep the urban Africans from clamouring for direct representation in city and town councils. When Hertzog and Smuts passed the notorious Slave Acts of 1936-37, it was the intellectuals, in collaboration with the white liberals, who turned the people from the course of struggle into the acceptance of the glorified Bunga, the Native Representative Council (NRC).

It was the intellectuals who proceeded to embroil them in working a complete system of dummy councils and dummy elections. And the more they pursued this policy of 'developing along our own lines', the more they entrenched in the minds of the oppressed the idea of the inferiority of the black man. In this sense it can be said that it was the intellectuals who policed and dragooned the African people into accepting a subordinate position in society.

To get an idea of the police-function of the intellectuals, we have only to visualise what takes place to this day. Dotted all over the country in the so-called 'Native Reserves' are the Resident 'Native' Commissioners' offices. They are the centres of administration. It is here that the people have to come for their allotments of land and get permission to buy cattle; it is from here that they have to get their passes to go and seek work; it is also here that they have to pay their taxes and the inevitable fines. In short, these offices are the centres of control over the lives of the people.

If you have the time to spare, if you have a heart of stone and nerves of steel, go one day and stand at the entrance of any of these offices. There you will see how these black pseudo-intellectuals behave towards their own people. There you will see the powerful combination of the policeman-chief and headman, and the policeman-intellectual at work.

All day long the impoverished peasants stream in to settle their many problems. The headman brings in from the villages men and women charged with breaking one or other of the many regulations. As they enter, the clerks and interpreters bark their orders. All day long you hear the voice of the white master issuing through the black mouth. How enthusiastically these pseudo-intellectuals bully and badger the people has to be seen to be believed. To the people the administrative offices become a symbol of tyranny before which they tremble in fear, filled with a sense of their own inferiority. There is no need for the white master to assert his authority; these black agents before whom the people cower do the job all too well.

But that is not all. A fuller picture of the function of the policeman-intellectual emerges when we depict the structure of South African society. On top sits the white ruling minority; at the base is the vast majority of the non-whites, and sandwiched inbetween is a thin layer of intellectuals, who are the purveyors and transmitters of herrenvolk ideas to the people. They are the connecting link between the ruler and the ruled. In fact, they are the most useful instruments of ruling.

Consider what a problem any Government would have to rule the people without their assistance. Language alone stands as a barrier between the Government and the people. Any law in any society is a law because of the consent of the people. Without their consent the law is not worth the scrap of paper it is written on. To get the consent of the people is the very crux of the matter. Here in South Africa the task of procuring this consent is the function of the literate and therefore of the vocal section of the non-whites. The various Governments in this country have been able to rule the non-whites largely by virtue of the co-operation of the intellectuals, who have to make the most obnoxious laws palatable to the people. In this way the intellectuals stand guard over the population as policemen in the interests of their masters.

THE BOYCOTT AND THE INTELLECTUALS

From the above analysis it becomes clear that the intellectuals have now a stake in the present setup of South African society. They have a definite function to perform. In this scheme of things they play the role of collaborating with the oppressor in working the machinery of oppression. It is their acceptance of this function that determines their attitude to the boycott weapon of the people. If they intend to continue collaborating with the oppressor they must view the people's boycott with alarm. For it hits at the root of their fundamental position, it threatens their very existence as collaborators.

The boycott is not in itself a policy. It is a specific application of the policy of noncollaboration.

It is this policy that the enemies of the boycott slogan are mortally afraid of. When they rail against the boycott, slander it and belittle it, they are in reality giving vent to their fear and hatred of this policy that spells death to their occupation – the policy of non-collaboration. Through daily hardship and bitter experience the people had at last discovered the true meaning of 'developing along our own lines'. It had led them, not to salvation, not to some mythical promised land or Black Utopia, but to the country of the doomed over whose gateway might well be inscribed, 'Abandon hope all ye who enter here'. It had led them to their present position, where they are without rights and without land; where they are ceaselessly harried by the pass laws, where they are being decimated by poverty and disease. They had learned that 'developing along our own lines' meant the acceptance of inferiority and segregation and that the segregated institutions created for a child-race were instruments for their own domination.

They resolved to reject the whole policy based on inferiority, with all that it implied; they threw off the shackles of the whole idea of the inferiority of the black man. They embarked on a new policy based on the equality of all men irrespective of colour and race. With this clear conception they gathered their forces together, ready once again to launch a determined struggle.

And once more the intellectuals were faced with a choice, either to throw in their lot with the people or with the rulers against the people.

A crisis developed in the ranks of the intellectuals and split them into two violently opposed camps. The best and most far-sighted amongst them threw in their lot with the people. They took their rightful place at the head of the people's organisations, helping them to clarify their ideas and formulate their policy, and putting the people's struggle firmly on the basis of principles. Such intellectuals brought their organisations within the fold of the people's federal bodies, the All-African Convention, the Anti-CAD and the Non-European Unity

Movement. Within these organisations they helped to educate the people as to the nature and origin of their disabilities and consequently the means and methods to be employed in the fight. They taught the oppressed to see the struggle in its entirety and to smash the artificial racial barriers created by the herrenvolk to separate them. This was to cross the Rubicon. This was to turn their backs on the rulers. It was to reject collaboration with the oppressor. It was to take their rightful place with their people.

But what of those short-sighted intellectuals whose vision was bounded by their own self-interest?

They were left in an unenviable position, and not even the resourceful liberals could find a way out for them. They were in a quandary. The people's eyes had been opened and the issues were crystal-clear. Those who operated the dummy councils were collaborating with the oppressor; they were the enemies of the people. When they were called upon to resign from these institutions, they could not, for to do so was to desert their master. Thus they resorted to blatant slanders and distortions of the people's boycott weapon.

IS THE BOYCOTT NEGATIVE?

We have said that the boycott is not in itself a policy but a practical application of the policy of non-collaboration at a specific time. It is particularly applicable at those moments when the quislings are engaged in the very act of luring the people into putting the noose round their neck.

The boycott has the effect of not only arresting the hand that carries the rope, but of holding it aloft for all to see. The quisling is, as it were, caught in the act, red-handed. In his fury he slanders the boycott, pours scorn upon it, reviles it. But all this vituperation has not worked. The people stubbornly continue to use the boycott, for they have discovered it to be an effective weapon.

The quislings have been forced to yield ground. Their latest distortion is that the boycott is negative. They argue that it calls upon the people to sit down and fold their arms, that it bids them refrain from action. Nothing could be further from the truth. Of course we are by this time familiar with the meaning that these valiant Knights of Action attach to the word. To them action means throwing themselves into dummy elections, it means labouring on toy councils, it means running up and down the country inciting others to ill-considered one-day strikes and then furiously organising Days of Mourning.

In short, to them action means any activity that distracts the attention of the people away from the main struggle, lures them out of their course and ends up by tying them the more securely to the herrenvolk parties. What a price the people have paid for those many calls to 'action'! It ill becomes the quislings to accuse the boycott of being negative.

The truth is that it is one of the most positive weapons that the non-whites can use at this stage. When an organisation advocates boycott, it cannot just pass a resolution to that effect and merely announce the fact to the masses. That would be meaningless. It takes upon itself the duty of going out to the people and carefully explaining to them why they must boycott a particular institution or elections to it. In this way it engages in political activity of the highest order. And this is not all. It calls upon the people to bestir themselves, throw off their lassitude and intervene in their own fate. With a consciousness arising out of a clear understanding of the issues involved, the masses take the positive step of boycotting. This is action. It is action of first-rate importance.

Deliberately and with a full sense of responsibility, they do two things; they cut the strings that bind them to the quislings, and secondly, they intervene in the plans of the rulers. By withholding their consent they frustrate these plans, which cannot work without their co-operation.

The ability to defeat the plans of the rulers in this way has in turn a further effect on the masses. It reinforces their rejection of inferiority; it restores their self-respect and gives them a sense of their own importance; it reveals to them their own strength born of unity in action .... Success begets success. There are other and more important fields in which the boycott could be applied. This is an important discovery. In the political struggle it could be employed with far-reaching consequences.

WHY THE BOYCOTT?

We have said that we do not choose at random our weapons of struggle. Each situation demands the use of a particular weapon according to the conditions prevailing at the time. We have unfolded how a chain of collaboration was started between the liberals and the intellectuals and led the people down the disastrous road of 'developing along their own lines'. At the end of that road they found themselves in a state of complete disorganisation and demoralisation. There was a mass of unorganised landless peasantry who fell easy prey to recruiting agents for the mines and white farms; there was a mass of agricultural labourers living under conditions of serfdom; in the towns were hundreds of thousands of unorganised workers who had no defence against exploitation. Those few – very few – who were organised into trade unions (unrecognised) could not even carry out their proper trade union function. They were stifled by the encrustation of a top layer of bureaucrats. In the political field rank opportunism had shattered and almost annihilated the organisations of the people. The few militants had become disillusioned by the irresponsible ventures of stunt-addicted opportunists. The people were left without hope. They had lost faith in leaders, and what is more, they had lost faith in themselves, in their ability to put up a struggle. This is the morass to which 'developing along our own lines' had brought them. To this desert, collaboration had brought them.

To get the people out of the morass it was necessary to sever the link that bound them through their leaders to their oppressors. It was necessary to cut the chain of collaboration. This is where the boycott proves itself a most effective weapon. It is the hammer and chisel that snaps the chain.

It is in this sense that we say the boycott is necessitated by the objective conditions in this country, that the need for the use of the boycott weapons arises out of the living realities of a whole system of racial oppression in the so-called Union of South Africa.

Once the stranglehold is loosened and the people are free to think for themselves, they can examine their position, review their past mistakes and on the basis of this choose the proper course to follow. The successful use of the boycott weapon gives them the necessary confidence and builds up their morale. If it is used simultaneously by all sections of the oppressed, it has a unifying force. It puts them on their feet, gives them a sense of their own power and this helps them to embark on more difficult forms of struggle. They develop self-reliance, independence and a tradition of acting in unity.

United action at this stage is directed simply at defeating the plans of the rulers. But the policy of non-collaboration – of which the boycott is one application in specific circumstances – implies much more than this. In its larger aspect it means not only rejecting and defeating the rulers' plans for their oppression, but directing the people towards organising their own forces for a concerted struggle for liberty. In place of the herrenvolkism of the rulers they counterpose the concept of the equality of all men. At that stage their united forces will be directed towards building a society in South Africa in which all men and women, irrespective of colour and creed, shall have equal rights and opportunities. Then only will the true Union of South Africa begin to take form. This will be the Nation of South Africa.

The boycott weapon, then, has a very positive part to play in building the nation. And all who oppose the boycott stand condemned before the people as defenders of herrenvolkism, with all the destruction that it brings in its train. The intellectuals have to make their choice: either to continue as collaborators or take their place alongside their people, and together with them go forward to the task of building the nation, a nation free from race hatred and oppression.

III LETTER TO NELSON MANDELA: PROBLEM OF ORGANISATIONAL UNITY

Editor's Note: At this time Tabata was particularly concerned with the problems of the youth who were clamouring for action but were completely lacking in political understanding of the forces involved. This concern prompted his longest book, The Awakening of a People, which is a history of the emergence of the ANC, the ICU, and the All-African Convention and the Unity Movement, each marking the progression of political consciousness. It prompted also the following letter to Nelson Mandela, a young kinsman who was an active member of the Congress Youth League and had visited Tabata, obviously concerned with the necessity for unity in the struggle. Tabata followed up the discussions with a lengthy postscript which he subsequently sent to other members of the Congress Youth League, including Robert Sobukwe, then a student at Fort Hare College. A political dialogue of this nature was all too rare. The two men were separated by considerably more than the physical distance of a thousand miles and the extremely different environments of Johannesburg, where Mandela had set up practice as a lawyer, and the Cape Province where Tabata carried out a great deal of his organisational work both in town and country. Mandela was on the threshold of his career in the African National Congress, which was under the control of leaders of the old generation. Tabata had already fought his first battles ten years earlier with this same leadership, which by tradition constituted the natural heirs of a policy of collaboration.

16th June 1948

My Dear Mandela,

.... Now to the discussion on the question of organisation, which is every day assuming greater importance. My experience has taught me – as you, too, must have perceived if you have pondered over it – that it is absolutely necessary for every individual to ask himself the question: What purpose does this or that organisation serve? It is not what the members say or think about an organisation that matters. It is not even a question of the good intentions of the leaders. What is of paramount importance is the programme and the principles of the organisation. To put it another way, it is not the subjective goodwill of the leaders that matters, but the objective function of the organisation, what effect it has on society. The question to ask is: Whose interests does the organisation serve objectively? This is the correct approach to the discussion on the present organisations.

I ask you to use this test. Apply it to yourself and the organisation to which you belong (The African National Congress). If you use it honestly and rigidly, without prejudice and without emotion, you are bound to arrive at the correct conclusion. You will remember that when you were here I asked you the following question: Can you give me any good reason, political reason, why you joined the African National Congress? – apart from the fact that your father or your father's father belonged to it – an argument that is purely sentimental and falling outside the realm of politics. I can have no quarrel with any organisation which is built for the purpose of fighting for liberty. Such an organisation, if it is true to its principles, will seek to unite the oppressed people and will at the same time follow a course of non-collaboration with the Government. But I am totally opposed to any organisation whose policy is to collaborate with the Government and disunite the people. And this is the crux of the question.

Let me state here that when I talk of the African National Congress I exclude the Congress Youth League. Politically it does not belong to the Congress. It is one of those peculiar anomalies which arise in a political situation where there is a lack of crystal clarity in political thinking. If the Youth League followed its political principles to their logical conclusion it would land itself outside the fold of Congress, so that, though you regard yourselves as Congress, I am more correct from a political standpoint in drawing the distinction. In fact the Congress is rooted in the past, whereas the Youth League is the product of modern conditions, with a modern outlook. It is not my purpose, however, to develop this point at this stage. I am more concerned with posing the problem of organisation in a proper way. My task is not a difficult one because recent political events which have taken place amongst the African people have served to open the eyes of many who have laboured under past illusions. All the same, I feel it necessary to give you a résumé of the past, for I am conscious of the fact that, because of your youth, you did not have the opportunity of living through the events leading up to the 1936-48 period. You have therefore been dependent on information from the older men who are all too prone to give you a distorted picture of the events and the issues involved. They do this, not because of any innate propensity for lying, but because of the necessity to justify their personal political position.

Let us therefore briefly recapitulate the past. The beginnings of this century closed a chapter in our history — the end of the resistance of the blacks by military means. It opened up a new chapter with new forms of struggle, the political form of struggle. The year 1912 saw the first creation of an African organisation (the ANC) on an individualist basis, with the breaking up of tribalism.

This was a progressive step, as compared with the past. But though in form the Congress had broken with the past, it had not shed completely the tribalist outlook. It could not be otherwise, for an organisation is the product of its time. However, it ushered in a new outlook more in keeping with the times and therefore deserved the support of all progressives. Many other organisations sprang up on an individualist basis of membership. There were the political and professional organisations, trade unions and civic bodies, all of which had one purpose, the fight for freedom. But the fight for freedom was undertaken by each organisation in isolation from the rest. The struggle was uncoordinated and this led to disaster so that by the 1930s all the African organisations had disintegrated and become completely atomised. The characteristic feature of this stage of development was a mutual suspicion, rivalry and hatred between the various organisations. Thus all political fights degenerated into personal squabbles and the leaders exhausted all their energies in fratricidal strife.

Then came 1935, which opened up a new chapter. It was the year of the notorious Hertzog (Slave) Bills, the fraud of 'Native Representation', the Native Trust and Land Bill and the Urban Areas Amendment Bill. By now it was evident that the organisations which had sprung up had come to stay. All of them were necessary in the various spheres. But what was needed was a body that would co-ordinate their struggles and create a unified leadership which could give direction to their multifarious activities.

Now the African people spontaneously created the ALL-AFRICAN CONVENTION. The political exigencies of the time and the crisis of the Slave Bills forced the people to organise on a nation-wide scale. So without any premeditated theory the people gave birth to a form of organisation which could knit together a whole people into a single compact unit, a fighting force.

The predominant idea at the time was unity. And this was a higher political level. Each leader was to bring his followers to this body and together with leaders of other organisations was to form a single leadership with a common aim and a common purpose. This was a turning-point in the organisational history of the African people. It was expected that this would constitute a point of departure for all our activities and that any further political development would have as its basis the form adopted in 1935.

The ruling-class, however, was fully alive to the danger to itself inherent in this development in this idea of unity. It could prove the basis for a new outlook. And they are aware of the interconnection between the form of organisation and a political outlook. This cleared the road for a national outlook, which was the logical outcome of this stage of development. A national outlook of an oppressed people constitutes the first stage of a threat to white domination. Such an outlook had to be stopped by the ruling-class at all costs. What I am trying to emphasise to you is this, that if the African people had progressed from 1935 as a unit, they would by now have reached a stage whereby their whole outlook, their propaganda and agitation, their energies and manual resources would have put them in a position to challenge the existence of the ruling-class (herrenvolk). It was to stop this that the ruling-class did their best to sow confusion amongst the African people. The idea of the All-African Convention had to be smashed at birth. It was comparatively easy for them to succeed, at least in part, for the idea had not yet become part and parcel of the people's thinking. They found a willing stooge in the person of the late Dr Dube. He was the first one to break away from the All-African Convention and with him went practically the whole Congress branch of Natal Province. The white press acclaimed him as a great statesman, a moderate, a practical politician, an epitome of all the virtues. Others of the same brand followed suit. This was a brilliant move on the part of the oppressors. But in order to break the new-found unity an organisation was necessary. Thus the Congress was resuscitated by these very individuals, and they wrenched it away from the Convention.

By this time the late Dr Xuma, an ex-Vice-President of the All-African Convention, was head of the Congress. The white press proceeded to build him up as a great leader, a great champion of the cause of the African people. This they did with an end in view. He shouted unity from the house-tops and the press helped him to unite people under the African National Congress. Why?

Because that was the surest way of disuniting the African people. The oppressors had to foster and support by every means at their disposal an organisation which sets itself up in opposition to the All-African Convention in order to kill the very spirit of real unity on a higher plane of development. What the rulers succeeded in doing – and this the younger intellectuals do not know – was to plunge the Africans back to the pre-1935 stage, that whole epoch in which the struggles of the people were reduced to a stalemate by fratricidal strife. It is this that bedevils us to this day.

I know you have often wondered why we are so intransigent, and yet we say we want unity. In fact I suspect that you think we are plainly bigoted and obstinate. The truth of the matter is we are defending a position which was conquered by the African people in 1935. We want unity on that basis, a unity which will serve as the basis for a further development leading to a truly national movement uniting all sections of the non-whites – so greatly feared by the rulers. This is the very antithesis of sectionalism or racialism. When you consider what might have been accomplished by this time, if this retrograde step had not been taken, then you become aware of the enormity of the crime committed by the Congress against a whole people.

Up to now I have not said anything about the divergence of political outlook between the Congress and the Convention, the yawning gap that separates the two organisations in the matter of principles. This is not because I think that political differences are of lesser importance; it is simply because I want to give you some idea of the past history of our political development. At the moment I can only add that those organisations which are affiliated to the Convention are facing in one direction while the Congress is facing in the very opposite direction. The first group have rejected the superiority of the white race over the black; they have rejected the trusteeship with all that it implies: segregation, sectionalism and tribalism. Many critics of the Congress often say, 'The trouble with Congress is that it has no policy'. There could be nothing further from the truth. The Congress has a definite policy, only it is not openly stated, for it cannot bear examination. One can divine this policy by watching the activities of the Congress over a long period. At every critical moment the Congress has played into the hands of the Government, either by directly siding with it against the people, (for example, in the boycott of elections of white representatives) or by sowing such confusion amongst the Africans that all efforts at gathering them together for a concerted fight against oppression are rendered ineffectual. And now they are bringing disruption into the ranks of the non-whites who are striving to come together. (Section omitted. Ed.)

Finally let me mention one aspect of your position which I feel sure you have not considered. You and your fellow members in the Congress Youth League are talking with two voices at one and the same time. As members of the Youth League you speak the language of the modern intellectual, progressive, independent and rejecting inferiority. But as members of the Congress your language is the very negation of all these things. You accept the theory of inferiority and trusteeship with all its political manifestations. For example operating segregated institutions like the Native Representative Council, Advisory Boards and the Bunga, etc. I can hear you protesting that never at any time did you and the rest of the Youth League accept these things. Yes, you may not have done so in words, but you have done so in fact and in deed. The Youth League is part and parcel of the organic body of Congress which does these things. It remains an entity within Congress, and voluntarily. This makes you political Januses with two heads facing in two different directions at one and the same time. This in politics is known as opportunism, and opportunism is the worst disease that can infect any political organisation. It is the canker that has claimed the greatest toll of all our organisations up to the present day.

It is possible that you are not aware of your contradictory position, or, if you are aware of it, you excuse yourselves by some such argument that you want to keep the people together. But this kind of argument is the essence of opportunism. Any attempt at unity without a principled basis and programme can only lead to confusion and political paralysis, and end in ultimate disunity.

Principles are the backbone of any Movement. To put it another way: any organisation which is not founded on the solid rock of principles is a prey to every wind that blows. It was the failure to recognise this fact that was primarily responsible for the fall of so many of our organisations in the past. We have had large organisations which were at first hailed with enthusiasm. But they have vanished away, leaving no trace behind.

Now, Mandela, if you curse me for having written you so long a letter, remember that you have yourself to blame! I have added this last page because I think it is of paramount importance for a man, and especially a young man entering politics, to establish the habit of basing his actions on principles. He must be ready if necessary to swim against the stream. Thus armed, he is protected against the temptations of seeking popularity and ephemeral success. (*See Appendix 2*)

Extract from letter to The Afro-Asian People's Solidarity Organisation

Editor's Note: The full extent of the counter-revolutionary role subsequently played by the African National Congress leadership both at home and abroad was summed up in a letter addressed to the Afro-Asian People's Solidarity Organisation (AAPSO), June 1966, accusing the ANC (within the AAPSO) of exercising the veto clause 'to exclude from membership of the AAPSO nationalist organisations which it knows to be anti-imperialist. In this respect it performs the work of imperialism'. It must be understood that the Unity Movement, in attacking the leadership of the ANC in its present role abroad, has never included the rank and file. Exigencies of space exclude the long letter to the AAPSO, but there is one passage that provides a tragic postscript concerning the fate of Nelson Mandela. At the same time it confirms Mandela's deep concern for unity. The letter cites the Congress Alliance of the CP of South Africa with the ANC, the Coloured People's Congress, the Indian Congress and the (white) Congress of Democrats as a Liberal-CP tactic to divert mainly the rank and file of the African National Congress away from the revolutionary road of struggle. We quote:

"It was after Nelson Mandela's return from a visit to several African States (1962) that he fought for the disbandment of the Congress Alliance. He had realised that the ANC was being used as a tool and that this Alliance, far from uniting the African people, was in effect splitting them and atomising the struggle. It was shortly after he succeeded in disbanding the Alliance that he was arrested in mysterious circumstances. We may add here that both Mandela and Robert Sobukwe (Leader of the Pan Africanist Congress which broke from the ANC) stood for unity. This is a fact despite protestations to the contrary by their followers abroad. But they differed in their approach to this complex problem of unity. Sobukwe was convinced that the prerequisite to the unity of the African people in South Africa was the total destruction of the African National Congress. He felt that the ANC had reached a point of no return. It would be impossible to unite the population as long as the ANC existed. Mandela, on the other hand, felt that if the destructive elements could be removed and the leadership restored to the Africans, it would still be possible to rebuild the African National Congress into a body capable of playing an important role of unifying the population. We are not here concerned with the correctness or otherwise of their views. We are concerned only with re-establishing the political integrity of these two men, whose followers abroad have done everything to turn them into caricatures. They have not scrupled to exploit for selfish reasons their names as martyrs, while hiding the truth about their real aims and the purpose of their actions."

IV   ADDRESS TO THE FIRST NATIONAL CONFERENCE OF THE AFRICAN PEOPLE'S DEMOCRATIC UNION OF SOUTHERN AFRICA (APDUSA), 1962, CAPE TOWN

Editor's Note: The birth of the African People's Democratic Union of Southern Africa in 1961 — where 'African' signifies all sections — confirmed the proletarian character of the Unity Movement, of which it is the political wing. The way for it had been paved by the several streams of resistance in the struggle against the Rehabilitation Scheme, the Bantu Authorities and Bantu Education, as well as the boycott of the bogus elections under the Native Representation Act. At the same time the minority groups of coloureds and Indians (though by no means united) were increasingly restive under the steady erosion of their few rights with such laws as the Group Areas (segregation by law as well as by custom) and the Coloured Disfranchisement Acts. The advancing juggernaut of fascism, however, scared many of the intellectuals; there was a retreat both outside and inside the Unity Movement and defectors carried a sector of coloured organisations with them. A number of these intellectuals, white and non-white, left the country in a characteristic mood of disillusionment. And today in Europe and elsewhere they are to be found airing their opinions as 'experts' — albeit ignorant and out-of-date, on the South African situation.

The Unity Movement, then, had purged itself of dead wood and moved forward to find its proletarian level. Through the widespread response to the APDUSA in the early sixties the development was both quantitative and qualitative. The organisation reached new layers of workers: Indian and African workers in Natal Province, African workers in the largest industrial area in the Transvaal, and, for the first time, African workers in the mines and even on the white farms. Utilising the fact of migrant labour, it linked a vanguard of African workers in the cities with the peasants in the Reserves.

This had far-reaching results. The now widespread resistance of the peasantry in every province began to be channelled and gathered together into 'the Nation'. This is the peasants' word for the APDUSA, and APDUSA means unity in the struggle. At last the peasants had accepted as their own the slogan: Land and Liberty. It was peasant leaders in the Transkei (Cape Province) who took the initiative. It is from this nucleus slowly built up over the years by the All-African Convention that new channels of unity radiated out into the districts of Zeerust and Sekhukhuniland in the Northern Transvaal as well as in Northern Natal. It is of course a process that is not and cannot be complete, spread as it is over so vast an area and under conditions of the most severe repression, where white police and the army vigorously support the local tyrants, the chiefs, who were invested with new powers both as agents of forced labour and as judges and jailers of their people. Thousands of peasants languish in jail without trial; others are in hiding in the mountains; there is torture and death of peasant organisers. So great is the lawlessness of 'law and order' in the so-called independent Bantustan, the Transkei, that the people have lost their respect for the law, and their fear of it. Since the Pondoland revolt in 1960, the Government has had to maintain martial law in the Transkei. The people defy Bantu Authorities; they mock the Baboons' Parliament; they continue to resist the Rehabilitation Scheme.

It was in 1964 — by which time Verwoerd was able to boast that he had routed the African National Congress, the liberals and the Communist Party with the Rivonia and other trials — that a delegation of peasant leaders from the Transkei, who were now firmly linked with the APDUSA, contrived to make their way, travelling over a thousand miles, to Johannesburg. There they met a delegation of peasants from a number of areas in the Northern Transvaal, comprising one of the largest organisations in the country and including mine-workers, factory workers and labourers from the white farms. These joint delegations held meetings with groups of mineworkers, including men from the neighbouring British Protectorates, Swaziland, Basutoland (now Lesotho) and Bechuanaland (now Botswana) and as far afield as Nyasaland (Malawi). 'The ideas of APDUSA,' said one of them, 'will unite not only Southern Africa but the whole of Africa.' At a further meeting of the delegations from the north and south with representatives of the Unity Movement, a significant point of disagreement was thrashed out. Peasants from the Northern Transvaal, with a deep distrust of the whites, were not happy about the non-racial policy of the Unity Movement. It was the peasants from the Transkei who put them right on this, confirming from their own experience that it wasn't the colour of a man's skin that you judged him by, but his actions. Some whites had assisted them in their struggle; and there were blacks who had betrayed them. Thereafter peasant representatives exchanged visits to their respective areas, north and south calmly indifferent to all the impediments of a police state. What emerges from the necessarily scanty reports is the indomitable spirit of freedom which sustains these peasants under one of the most oppressive regimes in the world. They made clear their determination to fight for their liberation. And they recognised the imperative necessity for unity in their struggle.

Said a peasant from the Northern Transvaal, 'The unity I saw there (in a part of the Transkei) I would like to see throughout the country. We must bring the people of Witzieshoek (Orange Free State) into the Nation (APDUSA). When all the people speak the same language, unity, we can be sure that liberation cannot be far off'.

It is significant of the growth of the Movement in the sixties that in a second wave of terrorism the Nationalist Government sent armed forces into Pondoland to crush the APDUSA which, it said, was a new name for the old 'Kongo' (peasant organisation). The 'Kongo' used to hold its meetings in the mountains and had led the first Pondoland revolt.

From: Presidential address to the AFRICAN PEOPLE'S DEMOCRATIC UNION OF SOUTHERN AFRICA, at first National Conference, April 1962, Cape Town (abridged).

APDUSA is a political body affiliated to the Unity Movement of South Africa. (Introduction omitted. Ed.)

VITAL ROLE OF WORKERS AND PEASANTS

The central theme of this Address is chosen to bring home to the membership the vital importance of those classes who are generally accorded a lowly status in society, the toiling masses who carry society on their backs. Clause (c) of our Constitution, under programme and policy, states:

'The democratic demands and aspirations of the oppressed workers and peasants shall be paramount in the orientation of the APDUSA in both its short-term and its long-term objectives.' This is the first time to my knowledge that such a clause has been included in the Constitution of any of the organisations of the Unity Movement. This alone marks a development in the outlook of the Movement, and in this way also reflects the times we are living in. If this Address should succeed in illuminating the full meaning of this clause, I shall be satisfied.

SOCIAL CRISIS MUST BE RESOLVED

When capitalism is faced with an acute crisis it tends to move towards a totalitarian dictatorship. But a totalitarian regime of the fascist type is a condition of an unstable regime. By its very essence it can only be temporary and transitional. Naked dictatorship is a symptom of a severe social crisis. And society cannot exist permanently under a state of crisis. A totalitarian state is capable of suppressing social contradictions during a certain period but is incapable of perpetuating itself. A ruling class, like a wounded lion, becomes more vicious as it feels itself drawing near to its extinction. The more vicious it becomes, the more monstrous become the laws against the oppressed, the greater grows its sense of insecurity. The very condition of an acute social crisis means that the forces operating in society can no longer be accommodated within it.

IT IS TIME TO CHANGE THE OLD SOCIAL RELATIONSHIP.

Only that class which is called upon to do so, by virtue of its historical role, can help to solve such a crisis. It is the toiling masses, and in this country in the main the non-white oppressed, those millions of workers and peasants toiling on the land, in the mines and factories, who are destined to lead the country out of the crisis and create a more rational social order. It is they who create the civilisation and lay the basis for a cultural development. They, by virtue of their contribution, should be accorded their rightful place of dignity and worth in society. They should participate in the governing of the country for which they have done so much. Without their labour, all this magnificence, all this spectacular development, this wealth and progress would have been impossible. We shall try to convey to you how all society is indebted to the labour of those it so often despises.

It is time that our people recognised that they are not step-children of the so-called civilised nations and that there is no such thing as 'Western Civilisation' created by the Westerners alone. There is only human civilisation to which man all over the world contributed. The people of Africa made as large a contribution to the sum total as any others. If, as we hold, human labour is the originator of all wealth, then we might justifiably claim that the people of Africa contributed a large share in laying the basis for the emergence of what is known today as 'Western Civilisation'. By the basis of Western Civilisation in this context we mean the series of events that led to the emergence of industrialism in Europe, with its accompanying Industrial Revolution.

SLAVE LABOUR AND THE INDUSTRIAL REVOLUTION

It is our contention that the Industrial Revolution would have been impossible at the time and in the manner in which it took place, if it had not been for limitless slave labour drawn from the continent of Africa. The discovery of the New World with its vast potential of sugar, cotton and tobacco had the effect of accelerating the slave trade. As countries like the West Indies, Cuba, Haiti – the whole of the Caribbean Islands – and Central and North America were developed by means of slave labour, the slavers intensified their rape of Africa with a ferocity hitherto undreamt of in history. It is estimated that in four centuries covering the 16th to the 19th century, fifty million slaves were transported across the Atlantic from the continent of Africa. So great was the concentration of slaves in some parts of the recently discovered New World, that in countries like Brazil and Venezuela more than half the population consisted of African slaves, ex-slaves and 'Mulattoes'.

Basil Davidson in his book *Black Mother* reports that by the end of the 18th century 'the value of British income derived from trade with the West Indies was said to be four times greater than the value of British income derived from the trade with the rest of the world.' It was not only the profits made on the sale of slaves as commodities that made the slave trade so lucrative. It was the profits made from the slave-grown sugar and cotton. By this time the economy of the European countries, which was a mercantile economy, was dynamically and inseparably linked with the slave trade. Speculation was the great fury of the age. Great profits were made, the average being 300% on investment. With this dramatic rise in the slave trade there was a tremendous impetus in shipbuilding. In 1719 the port of Liverpool had only 18,371 tons of registered shipping, but by 1792 'this rose to 260,832 tons, and it was the Great Circuit trade of consumer goods, slaves, sugar, tobacco and rum that commissioned most of the tonnage.'

We might explain here what is meant by the Great Circuit trade. Slaves in the main were bought from African potentates. The media of exchange were all sorts of trinkets and other European manufactured goods. Chief amongst these were cotton goods and textiles. Slavers' ships on their outward journey were laden with cotton goods and yarn to be sold mostly in exchange for slaves in Africa. On their return journey the ships crossed the Atlantic Ocean laden with the slave cargo which was sold in the Caribbean islands, where depots had been established for supplying the rest of America with its quota of slaves. From this point the same ships carried back to Europe the products of slave labour in the form of sugar and cotton to be sold at high prices on the home market. This completed the circuit. It is not difficult to imagine how, with this rapid exchange of commodities en route and the quick turn-over, tremendous profits were made, sometimes reaching the fantastic figure of 700% on the original capital investment.

This slave trade had a powerful effect on the European economy. It was not simply that it earned large sums of capital for reinvestment in the citadels of Europe. It also created new demands which in their turn set in motion tremendous activity directed towards the building of factories for manufacturing goods. New towns sprang up with their shops, banks and business houses; commerce thrived, providing a home market for the newly created cheap merchandise.

The same development took place in France and indeed the whole of Western Europe. To the merchants the great circuit trade was returning a regular high profit. Private fortunes were made, public opulence appeared, industries were founded, towns were built and a new class, the bourgeoisie, appeared on the scene with all its glory. This was the time of the great Industrial Revolution. It was the time of industrial inventions. All these inventions were the work of craftsmen struggling to meet an apparently inexhaustible demand for cheap consumer goods.

Export figures provide eloquent testimony to the extent that Britain benefited from this demand by way of accumulation of capital during this period. At the beginning of the 18th century British exports in textiles stood at about £23,000. At the end of the century the exports had grown to five and a half millions.

'Industrialism was born,' writes Basil Davidson, 'and it was the West African trade in all its ramifications that presided over the event.'

We have drawn this picture not merely to establish our claim to the sum total of the civilisation and culture of mankind today by virtue of the contribution made by our forbears, but also for a much more important reason, namely, that it was the labour of the millions of nameless slaves that made possible the transformation of a mercantile economy in Europe to an industrial manufacturing economy, that is to say, from a primitive economy of a backward society to an advanced industrialism. And this gave birth to new ideas that were to transform the nature of society itself. The new and powerful class, the bourgeoisie, could no longer tolerate the autocracy of the feudal aristocracy. It demanded such reorganisation of society as would give it state power commensurate with its economic power. With this in view philosophers from this class worked out a system of ideas that were to be the guiding principles in their fight for dominance in society.

Democracy was demanded as a condition of existence, without which no self-respecting man could live. The great revolutions in Europe were the logical sequence of the Industrial Revolution.

These, then, were some of the consequences of the great slave trade. Those nameless slaves who died in the sugar plantations, the cotton fields and the coal mines did not know that their labour was to lay the foundation for this magnificent structure, today known as 'Western Civilisation', with all its culture, science and technology. The ignorant backvelder may claim that his forbears alone built it, but the facts give the lie to his boasts.

If we have not mentioned the contribution made by the millions of equally nameless white wage-slaves who were consumed by the Moloch of industrialism, it is because time and space do not permit us. We have no reason to minimise their contribution. We claim them as brothers to our forbears in suffering, fellow slaves who lost their lives in the march of the progress of mankind. The point we are making is that labour, and labour alone, whether it be manual, intellectual, or technical, is the creator of wealth and civilisation. Only those who are actively engaged in the complex of production, administration and research are necessary to human progress. The rest are drones and parasites that feed on society.

NON-WHITE LABOUR IN SOUTH AFRICA

We are in a position to see by looking into the past what labour has done for mankind. Let us now turn our attention to our own country, South Africa. It was mainly the labour of the non-whites that transformed the economy of the country in a short space of time from a pastoral agricultural economy to a mining industrial economy. The curious thing in our country is that while industrialism has taken root, the social relations insofar as the non-whites are concerned are those of a feudal economy. While the non-whites have contributed the lion's share in creating wealth and civilisation in this country, the herrenvolk have excluded them from enjoying the fruits of their own labour. Flying in the face of history, they are at this moment desperately trying to legislate into being a dead and long-buried tribalism or barbarism. About this later ....

It is almost a platitude to say that wealth in this country has been and is being built up by the slave labour of the non-whites. This is easy to see. What, however, is not sufficiently appreciated, even by the non-whites themselves, is that the whole of the industrial life with all its ramifications rests almost entirely on the African, coloured and Indian sweated labour. If we accept this to be the truth, as we shall presently show, then it follows that all the super-structural activities, such as trade and commerce, communications, aviation, defence, social and cultural services, education (including 'white' education) and all those activities which flow from an industrial economy are made possible in this country, thanks to the existence of a vast depressed non-white labour force.

This means that the national income itself, which provides luxuries for a section of the whites and the protected high wages for the white worker, rests on the sweated black labour. In his book, The South African Predicament, F P Spooner devotes a whole chapter to what he calls the vulnerability of the economy. The world 'vulnerability' is well-chosen. We, too, shall devote a chapter to the vulnerability not of the economy but of herrenvolkism. Spooner states:

'The progress and strength of a country's economy are usually measured by the growth of the national income .... A special feature of this development (in South Africa) has been the growth of the manufacturing industry, which today contributes more to the income of the country than either mining or agriculture. Its contribution for the year 1956-7 was not far short of the contribution made by the other two taken together.' **(Detailed figures omitted. Ed.)**

There are three main things to note here:

1. That three industries, namely agriculture, mining and manufacturing constitute the foundation of the country's economy.

2. That only 51.4% of the national income comes from these three industries. The rest comes from the superstructure, that is to say, from those activities which are themselves dependent upon those three.

3. That the income from manufacturing industry alone is almost equal to the other two put together.

From this last most people draw the wrong conclusion, that it is the manufacturing industry that sustains the country's economy today. That this conclusion is wrong is revealed when we examine the balance sheet of exports and imports of the different industries. It must be remembered that all these groups in varying degree depend upon the importation of raw materials and equipment. Spooner gives us the balance sheet of 1955 as follows:

Credit Balance:

1. Agricultural Industry £23 million

2. Pastoral industry £76 million

3. Precious Mineral industry £215 million

4. Base Mineral industry £36 million

5. Others £8 million

But secondary industry shows a debit balance of £175 millions, leaving an overall credit balance of only £183 millions available for direct imports. These figures reveal that, far from sustaining the country's economy, manufacturing industry is in fact being carried by the other two, namely, agriculture and mining industries. The latter alone earns sufficient credit to pay for all the import requirements of the manufacturing industry.

In short, then, manufacturing industry in this country is running at a loss in so far as external balance of trade is concerned. That is to say, it is unable to stand on its own feet. Yet insofar as society internally is concerned, it is the manufacturing industry that provides the biggest national income, the bulk of which goes to the white section of the population, who constitute a minority in the country. In brief, it is out of this income that the whites are afforded an artificially high standard of living, while the great majority, the non-whites, are languishing in poverty and perishing from preventable diseases, because they earn less than a living wage.

We have already shown that manufacturing industry is carried by the agricultural and mining industries. The question then is, who are the producers in these industries? For it is they who, in the final analysis, carry the whole country on their backs. In the agricultural and pastoral industries, which according to Spooner, earned £99 million for imports in 1955, there were in 1957, 11,071 white employees, but 952,551 non-white workers. In the mining industry, including gold, diamonds and coal quarry mines, the biggest earner of foreign exchange which made available for direct imports a sum of £251 million in the same year, there were in 1959 a total of 62,025 whites and 187,982 non-whites. That means eight times as many non-white workers as white. These figures leave not a shadow of doubt that it is the non-whites of South Africa who carry the country on their backs.

Here we have a whole country, a prosperous white society, precariously perched on the backs of a discontented black labour force. The implications of this situation are frightening to them, particularly as the non-whites are now beginning to be aware of their worth and power. But this is their problem, not ours. What we are concerned with here is to show how this economic structure dictates a certain course of action on the part of the herrenvolk.

THE MINES AND CHEAP BLACK LABOUR

Long before Verwoerd came to South Africa, (he was born in the Netherlands) imperialism had mapped out a political and social order that would maintain and perpetuate the existing economic structure. Every herrenvolk government is charged with the duty of protecting the mining industry as the primary industry round which others revolve. All laws passed by every parliament of the herrenvolk had to bear this in mind. Gold mining consumes a terrific amount of unskilled labour. Therefore Parliament had to see to it that the whole of the non-white population, from which its labour is drawn, was kept mainly illiterate or semi-illiterate. This became the policy of every successive government since Union. The mines demanded cheap labour. They had to make huge profits for the investors as well as provide foreign currency for import requirements for secondary industry. Therefore the wages of the whole non-white population have to be depressed.

It became the task of whatever Government was in power to keep the non-white wages low, no matter in what category or industry they were employed.

The mining industry, by virtue of its primacy in the economic life of the country, dictates the wage policy for all its potential employees, no matter where they happen to be temporarily working. This is the source of the wage differentiation according to racial groups in South Africa.

Long before the term apartheid was known, the Government of the day created a special department, the Native Affairs Department (NAD) to work day and night at this problem of labour. It had created what are known as the Native Reserves in which they enclosed that section of the population which was expected to work in the mines. It was not for lack of land that these Reserves were made small. They were overcrowded by design, so that the population, unable to support itself, would be forced to seek work in the mines at low rates of pay. These in turn demanded more labour. The Government had to legislate for these new demands. Thus more laws against the non-whites came fast and furious on the statute book. For a time, when the South African economy was mainly agricultural and mining, it had been hoped that African labour alone would suffice. Consequently the Governments of the period concentrated their racial laws mainly on the Africans, leaving the attack on the other non-white sections in abeyance. But when the economy changed into an industrial manufacturing economy, it became obvious that the African population alone would not be sufficient and that the other two sections of the non-whites, the coloured and the Indian, would have to be roped in. The tremendous expansion that took place after the last world war did not alter the basic structure of the economy. It merely expanded it.

But all this expansion of activity drew its labour from the same limited source. Since the very existence of the secondary industries depended on the gold mines, they could not afford to deprive the golden goose of its life-blood. Parliament had to make available other sources of labour.

THE NATIONALIST GOVERNMENT

When the Nationalist Government took over, it created nothing new. It had no plans different from its predecessors. How could it? It was faced with the same problems that were dictated by the economic structure of the country. What was new in the situation was the greater urge for super-exploitation and a much more acute labour shortage. The Broederbond (Nationalist) Government, unimpeded by any necessity to pay lip-service to democracy, took the machinery created by its predecessors and used it with a ruthlessness beloved of fascists. They did not depart one whit from the policies of the previous governments. If anything, they pursued them with a brutal logic characteristic of men with a narrow vision, untrammelled by the wider implications of their policies.

The point we are making is that without a radical alteration of the socio-economic set-up in this country, it is not possible for any herrenvolk Government to depart from the so-called traditional policy, whether it is called apartheid, segregation, multi-racialism, or by any other name. For it is not the names that politicians give to their policies that matter, nor is it the smooth, oily tongues or vulgar formulations that decide the issue. It is the hard economic factors that dictate the policy and programme of the Government in power.

Those woolly-minded non-white politicians who fail to grasp this fact, will always remain abject sycophants of this or that section of the herrenvolk. Those simpletons who cry nostalgically for the return of the United Party days, **(under Smuts. Ed.)** on the ground that they are the 'lesser evil', reveal abysmal ignorance of the forces at work. If the 'lesser evil' of yesterday were in power today, under the pressure of the prevailing urgent problems it would long ago have transformed itself into the 'greater evil'. That is why it is so ludicrous to see some non-white intellectuals and politicians denouncing the Nationalist Party and in the same breath appealing to and even aligning themselves with the United Party and the ex-United Party now organised as Progressive and Liberal Parties. This is tantamount to appealing to the old Nationalist Party of more peaceful days as against the present-day Verwoerdian (Nationalist) Party, as though there were any intrinsic difference between the two.

It is not that the Nationalist Party is especially vindictive towards the non-whites, nor that it is actuated by a desire to settle scores with them for some past grievances, nor is it actuated by hatred against all people of colour. Such motives and feelings are irrelevant to the practical questions of government. The Nationalist Party happens to be in power at a time of crisis both internal and external. For the moment we shall pursue the internal problems which it is desperately trying to solve

We have shown above how the whole economy of the country is precariously perched on the mining industry. But events today, both internal and external, are threatening the main prop. The mines, unable to find sufficient labour within the Union of South Africa, had been in the habit of recruiting labour from the neighbouring countries beyond its borders. For years the Portuguese Government has been making a roaring trade with South Africa by hiring out its black colonial subjects – slaves – to work in the mines. The Tomlinson Commission reports that 60% of the labour force in the gold mines of South Africa comes from the countries outside its borders. Now, with the revolt of the oppressed Africans under the Portuguese iron heel, coupled with the agitation against the South African herrenvolk Government by all the emergent African States, the danger to the South African economy becomes apparent. If all the neighbouring States decide to broaden their boycott of South African goods so as to include the stoppage of their labour supplies, it is not difficult to imagine the reeling blow that would be dealt to South Africa by such a decision.

With things as they stand today, a sudden dislocation of the mines would send the whole economy of the country toppling down with a crash. It is the threat that this situation holds that hangs over the herrenvolk like the Sword of Damocles. It is the fear of the collapse of the country's economy that is haunting the herrenvolk and making them act like demented men. We are not at the moment dealing with the larger and more important cause of their apprehension, namely, the political upsurge threatening to abolish herrenvolkism itself. We are still pursuing the economic aspects of the matter, the threat of an economic collapse. The herrenvolk, acting through the ballot box, handed over the state power to that section which has distinguished itself by its ruthlessness in dealing with the oppressed.

SIGNIFICANCE OF GROUP AREAS AND BANTUSTANS

Their first duty was to ensure that they removed the threat to the economy of the country coming from the neighbouring territories. They have to do everything in their power to make the mining industry independent of foreign labour. For this they have to comb the population of every able-bodied male and female amongst the non-whites and make them available for work in the respective places of employment, the mines, the white farms and industry.

The Broederbond Government passed the Group Areas Act and promptly declared the whole of South Africa one huge White Group Area, throwing all the non-whites into little enclaves labelled respectively 'Bantustans', 'Coloured-stans' and 'Indian-stans'. These are labour reservoirs from which they will be able to draw all their labour requirements.

The Group Areas Act enables them to scour the country with a fine comb to drive every non-white out into his segregated group area. Those who own property and have an independent means of livelihood, like the Indian merchants for instance, will have to lose all that and move into the concentration camp.

Within these enclaves law as it is known in any civilised country, with the right of *habeas corpus*, will be abolished, and the policemen-chiefs in the Reserves will wreak their vengeance on the people, controlling and regimenting their lives. For only in this way will they be put in a position to supply the required quotas of labour at any given time. The same system of drafted labour that the Portuguese used before the revolt in West Africa will be introduced into these segregated 'stans'. This is the system that is being recreated in South Africa under the grand name of 'Self-Government'.

It is not accidental that in the 'Bantustans' (for Africans) the system of law itself is going to be changed. The introduction of that tribal law is one of the most sinister aspects of the whole plan. First it is intended to deprive the population of the protection of law, as known in any civilised community. Secondly it is designed to enable the chiefs to carry out any order against the people issued by the herrenvolk Government. Thirdly – and this is important – it is designed to abrogate the legal rights to property, together with all those property relations which are established by law in any capitalist system. It is designed to throw the whole population into a tribal milieu, to be governed by tribal law wherein individualism and individual effort are outlawed.

SOUTH AFRICA AND WORLD CRISIS

The herrenvolk of South Africa have far greater problems to worry about than the local ones. They are caught in the grip of a world crisis. While they are still struggling to maintain feudal relations in South Africa, the world in general has reached a stage in which capitalism, having attained the highest peak in its development, imperialism, is now engaged in a battle for survival. The East, with its socialist economy, headed by the Soviet Union and China, is locked in a life and death struggle against the capitalist West under the hegemony of America and Britain. The two systems cannot exist side by side indefinitely. Either socialism, or capitalism, must survive in the end. The battle of these two systems, as represented in these opposing Titans, is rocking the World. All countries are being drawn into it in one way or another. South Africa is now feeling the effects of this war. As this matter was fully dealt with at the recent conference of the Non-European Unity Movement (NEUM) we shall not cover all the ground again. We shall limit ourselves to those aspects which closely concern us here.

South Africa is divided into three main political camps. The two herrenvolk camps, having the same aims, differ only in their methods of achieving those aims. The third camp, that is, the oppressed, is fundamentally opposed to the other two. The divisions amongst the local herrenvolk are sharpened by external events which flow from the larger war between capitalism and socialism. Both sides are preparing for an all-out war which will settle the dispute between the two systems. In these preparations each side is trying to win over as allies the so-called uncommitted countries. This is of the very essence of the 'cold war'. The United Nations Organisation as a public forum, reflects the manoeuvrings of the two camps and affords the world an opportunity of gauging the varying fortunes in the battle for the so-called uncommitted countries. The West finds itself with certain definite disadvantages. All the emergent States still remember the centuries of oppression and humiliation to which they were subjected by Western imperialism. To them colonialism is not yet dead. Every act on the part of the Western powers is watched with grave suspicion. The colonial and ex-colonial peoples have not forgotten the feel of the whiplash administered by those same people who today offer the hand of friendship. The socialist East presses home its point of vantage. It accuses the West of hypocrisy. It argues that imperialism has not changed and cannot change its rapacious nature. If it can no longer afford to hold down its colonies by force, it will enslave its colonial people by economic means.

It was imperialism in its hunt for super-profits that originally introduced the colour bar and placed a stigma on all people of colour. It was imperialism that originated the theory of the inferiority of the non-whites. To this accusation the West has no reply. It is now trying its best to bury its past. It is in a hurry to establish new exploitive relations with its ex-colonies under the guise of a new so-called independence. In this way they seek to establish capitalist exploitive relations without the stigma of racism. In the battle to win over the non-whites throughout the world, imperialism is trying to forget its racist policies. It is in this respect that South Africa has become the polecat in the comity of western nations.

The South African Government under the leadership of the Nationalist Broederbond, untrammelled by the wider considerations of the 'cold war', has taken a granite stand on its racial policies. It upholds herrenvolkism as a noble ideal and defends it with the fanaticism of a people waging a holy war. But this 18th century mentality is an embarrassment to imperialism. It would like a more enlightened section of the herrenvolk to take over the reins of government and bring South Africa into line with the rest of Western policies.

It is this intervention of imperialism that has sharpened the division between the two herrenvolk camps. The Progressive and Liberal Parties, acting as agents of imperialism, are offering crumbs to a section of the oppressed non-white leadership in order to win them over to the camp of imperialism. That is why a number of intellectuals, together with non-white merchants, are veering over to these parties. In so doing, they are renouncing the battle for liberation of the oppressed and throwing in their lot with imperialism in its fight for survival. It is not necessary here to explain that a replacement of one herrenvolk Government by another would not make a tittle of difference to the sufferings of the workers and poor peasants. Neither the Progressive Party, nor the Liberal, nor any other herrenvolk party can bring about a radical change as long as the present economic and social structure remain unchanged.

Verwoerd with his Broederbond sees the salvation of herrenvolkism in the retribalisation of the non-whites, splitting them up into various ethnic groups and presenting each one with its own policeman-chief. These policeman-chiefs are going to be the frontline of defence of herrenvolkism in this country. In the same way the intellectuals constitute the front line in the defence of imperialism.

The rest of the oppressed must turn their backs on both sets of agents, on those defending herrenvolkism and those defending imperialism. APDUSANS recognise that neither imperialism nor South African herrenvolkism will ever assist them in the struggle for liberation. Only the oppressed people themselves, together with those who have irrevocably cast in their lot with them, can solve their problems. APDUSA believes that in any society the people who create wealth and civilisation and are therefore responsible for the progress of mankind, are those who provide labour in its many forms. Here in South Africa the bulk of the people who create the wealth of the country are precisely those despised and neglected workers in the gold and coal mines, those workers on the sugar plantations, the white farms and in the 'Native Reserves'. We are not saying that the white worker does not make his contribution, but we are saying that it is the majority of the oppressed non-whites who contribute the lion's share to a civilisation, the fruits of which they are not permitted to enjoy. It is those nameless millions who have been reduced to a position of 'Calibans' who carry the whole of South African society on their backs. Our belief is that those who create must decide what is to be done with what they have created. The producers of wealth in a society must be in the Government of the country. This is our attitude.

I shall sum up this address with a few remarks on the trade union question. But let me first emphasise the theme of my address by quoting once more Clause (c) of our Constitution:

'The democratic demands and aspirations of the oppressed workers and peasants shall be paramount in the orientation of APDUSA both in its short-term policy and long-term objectives.'

Our Constitution enjoins us to put in the forefront of our work the problems of the workers. In order to gain their confidence we must not only find out their special problems but actively participate in their daily struggles in the factories, the mines, the sugar plantations and the farms.

First of all we must examine those organs which are supposed to belong to the workers, namely, the trade unions. As things stand today, every officially recognised trade union has agreed to partition its members according to race. This alone renders them incapable of performing the function of true trade unions. In this sense it is justifiable to say that there are not, and never have been, true trade unions in South Africa.

What does exist are workers' organisations created by law and ringed round with legislation in such a manner that they serve only the interests of the bosses. The law of the country excludes the majority of the workers from trade union organisations. The minority who are allowed to organise themselves can only have their trade unions recognised if they split themselves up according to their racial groups. From this alone it is clear that such organs cannot possibly serve the interests of the workers. They are emasculated bodies kept for the convenience of the bosses and the ruling class as a whole.

The so-called trade union movement in South Africa is merely part of an intricate machinery for negotiation created by the bosses themselves for the control of the workers. The leadership cannot by any stretch of the imagination be regarded as leaders of the working class. Its function is not only to deceive the workers into thinking that they have organisations to fight for their rights, but to curb their militancy and direct it into harmless channels of negotiation. Such leaders are the policemen who stand guard over the interests of the employers.

The very fact that the leadership of the official trade unionism has agreed to the partitioning of the workers according to colour, as a condition for recognition, means that they have consciously sold themselves to the bosses. It means that they have agreed to the tying of the workers hand and foot and placing them at the mercy of the employers.

It is time that the whole concept of 'recognised' trade unions was examined. APDUSANS should pose the question before the workers. What does the term 'recognition' mean? It means that only those trade unions would be recognised by the Government and the employers which have committed themselves in advance to be the tool of the bosses. Only those unions would be recognised which agree to the terms and conditions laid down by the Government, including the renunciation of the strike weapon. It is obvious from this that, if the workers are to build effective organs for their protection, they can only do so outside the framework of 'recognised' trade unions. The only legitimate recognition which must be the concern of the workers is not the recognition by the Government but by the workers themselves. For a trade union is their own weapon.

APDUSANS, then must go to the factories to discuss these matters. When the workers understand what a trade union should look like, they will build their own organs of defence and attack in the fights for their rights. In these organs they will have no colour bar.

In conclusion I should like to say that if this address succeeds in directing the thoughts of Conference towards the necessity of finding a solution to the crisis that faces this country, and convinces the members that only through the efforts of the toiling masses is it possible to put an end to this crisis, I would be satisfied.

We believe that only that class which has a historical future can lead society out of the crisis. History has placed the destiny of our society in the hands of the toiling masses. If we are to succeed in our task of liberation, we must link ourselves dynamically and inseparably with the labouring classes. Without them we are nothing. With them we are everything, and nothing can stand in our way. No power on earth can hold us back in our march.

V. VERWOERD'S ASSASSINATION

From *APDUSA*, September 1966, Vol.2, No.5

The assassin's knife that plunged into Verwoerd's body did more than end the life of the Prime Minister of white South Africa. It has ripped wide open the facade of white unity and revealed the irreconcilable conflicts which beset the white ruling caste in South Africa and which have penetrated right through Afrikaner Nationalism, reaching its inner core, the Broederbond, that secret society which epitomised the desperate fanaticism of Afrikaner Baasskap (bossdom).

We are not at this moment concerned with what bloody hand used the assassin as an instrument. We are concerned with the political setting of this deed and the dynamic of the unfolding situation in South Africa. The fact is that, behind the facade of great prosperity, economic boom and the apparent stability of white domination, looms a dark cloud over white South Africa. The spectre of the black man rising to claim his rights haunts them. The whole of South African society is charged with tremendous tensions. Over a period there has been a state of ferment that is now reaching bursting point.

White South Africa is, in a political sense, living out of step with the world. In the midst of the atomic age it is inevitably attached to the industrial complex of the Western world, but nevertheless clings to political ideas that belong to a feudal age. Nearly four-fifths of the population comprising the oppressed Africans have been forcibly thrust back into tribalism in order to facilitate colonial exploitation, while the rest of the colonial world in the East, the Middle East and Africa is forging a path towards true independence.

The oppressed non-whites, regarding themselves as part of the forward movement throughout the colonial world, can no longer tolerate their condition of serfdom. They are gathering their forces to break through the shackles of oppression. In this process spontaneous outbursts inevitably take place. Verwoerd's only reply has been violence and more violence, so that today the whole country has been turned into one vast concentration camp for the non-whites. The Verwoerd regime governs by naked force which penetrates every aspect of life in South Africa.

Present-day legislation itself serves one purpose – to legalise this state of violence, regimentation of a people, torture and downright murder. It is the force and power of the growing movement of the oppressed population from below that has created the crisis within the white ruling caste. Their great problem is how to meet this crisis.

The key to the understanding of the complex South African problem is that there are two struggles on two different levels going on simultaneously. Their aims are diametrically opposed to each other. The first, and the most relentless and fierce, is that between the non-white oppressed and the white herrenvolk. The white-controlled press of all shades of political opinion does its best to conceal this struggle, though everything that takes place within the white group is directly influenced by it. Even the intensity of their own internal quarrels springs from the main battle, nay, the ceaseless war between oppressor and oppressed.

The second struggle is between the two main sections of the white ruling caste. It concerns two different methods of maintaining white domination. There is no doubt about their common aim – that is the perpetuation of exploitation and oppression of the non-whites. The differences in their approach to the problems are embedded in the history of South Africa ....

Politically, white South Africa is an independent State in which only the white minority have the franchise. This means that only one-fifth of the population decides which section of the white rulers shall sit in Parliament. Economically, South Africa is a colony of Britain. Its riches are owned in the main by British financiers, with American financiers fast infiltrating the economic scene, while at the same time gobbling up Britain and turning it into a semi-colony of this colossal octopus.

Nearly eighty percent of all economic activity in South Africa is in the hands of the English-speaking section of the whites, and is dynamically linked with the British economy. This factor determines their political approach and reinforces their traditional outlook, i.e. the so-called British democracy. But again, for reasons of the earlier betrayal of the black man and the Smuts sell-out in the passing of the Native Acts of 1936, this British section, though economically the most powerful group, cannot be returned to power through the ballot. This is the section – the Oppenheimer mining group together with the white liberals – that constitutes the spokesman of imperialism, i.e. of international finance.

As the crisis in South African society deepens, the clash between the two methods of white domination is sharpened. The English-speaking section believe that their methods will not only ward off the impending explosion but will also stave off the economic crisis that looms behind the apparent present-day boom. They believe, too, that the racial excesses of the Afrikaner apartheid policy seriously interfere with the natural economic expansion of the country and that theirs will provide a more efficient method for maintaining high profits.

The Afrikaners (Boers) on the other hand, when confronted with a crisis, fall back on their old traditions – tie the kaffir (nigger) to the wagon wheel and lash him with a whip. This means, in modern political language, employing fascistic methods, dispensing with parliamentary procedures and ruling the non-whites by proclamation and the use of naked force. This is the meaning of all their legislation today, beginning with the Population Registration and Group Areas Acts, which deprive the whole black population not only of citizenship but of the right to belong to South Africa. It is the meaning of their 90-Day Detention Act, now replaced by the 180-day Detention laws; Bantu Education Act, their Job Reservation, their Proclamation 400 applied to Africans, which authorises any policeman to arrest without warrant, any black man or woman at any time of the day or night and hold him in jail indefinitely, without trial. This is the meaning of their Native laws Amendment Act of 1964, Verwoerd's crowning apartheid law, which reintroduced a system of chattel slavery without the mitigating aspect of that vile system whereby the slave-owner in his own interest found it more profitable at least to keep his chattel alive.

The Verwoerd regime represents the Afrikaner petit-bourgeois, backed by the white-collar worker and the large semi-literate white civil service. It got into power through the appeal to fanatical Afrikaner racialism as against the English 'rooineks' (red necks) and a vicious race propaganda against the whole of the oppressed non-whites. In every sphere they set up purely Afrikaans organisations, churches, trade unions, teachers' organisations, schools and students' organisations; an Afrikaner Chamber of Commerce and banks. At the core of Afrikanerdom was the secret Broederbond which penetrated every sphere of activity, placing their own men in key positions, in state or other concerns. The intellectuals, including leading figures in the Afrikaans universities, provided the pseudo-theoretical justification for the barbarity of the Afrikaner outlook and policy. In this they were backed by their religious leaders who provided the biblical justification for the immorality of their vile racist creed. The Afrikaner industrialists supplied large funds to the Broederbond .... It is against this background that the present-day conflicts between the English-speaking representatives in South Africa and Afrikaner Nationalism must be seen.

All seemed to go well for Afrikanerdom until they captured political power in 1948. Even after this they continued to move upwards to their pinnacle of power. But then the class interests within Afrikanerdom began to assert themselves and cracks began to appear in the monolithic structure. While they kept the facade of unity, behind the scenes internal dissensions and rivalries emerged. International finance, fearing that the Verwoerdian granite policy was putting into jeopardy their vast investments in South Africa, took a hand in the affairs of the country. It is true that, in its usual manner of double-dealing, imperialism adopted a dual policy. It openly criticised Verwoerd's apartheid policy while continuing to underwrite his regime and indeed arm it to the hilt, since there was no alternate government in sight more politically suitable to them.

At the same time, however, they started a policy of undermining it. Oppenheimer, the mining tycoon of South Africa, whose multi-concerns are interlocked with British and American capital, threw the door wide open for the new Afrikaner financiers. He offered them participation in the mining industry and thus drove a wedge between the Afrikaner financier and the rest of Afrikanerdom. With their new status the dictates of self-interest clashed with their allegiance to the sacred Volk (the People). They withdrew their financial support of the Broederbond, the very core of Afrikanerdom and its driving force. Always the first to catch the straws in the wind, the Afrikaner intellectuals began to be beset by doubts and misgivings about their previous positions.

This in itself reflected the extent of the crack. Although in the Afrikaner general struggle for power, the intellectual occupied an unusually important position, now, when faced with a crisis, he reveals the natural traits of the petit-bourgeois, a propensity to vacillation, always looking ahead to see which group or class is likely to win and provide the security so dear to him.

All these internal dissensions have a momentum of their own. The sharper these become, the more the extremists are pushed to the limit. This is precisely what is taking place today within the governing party in South Africa. The fire-eater of yesterday is today regarded as a tame lamb. And so the process goes on .... Under the inexorable law of progression operating in a period of world crisis and the enormous pressures of the liberatory movement within South Africa, Verwoerd himself began to appear tame in the eyes of some of his fiery followers. Strange as it may seem, this fanatic proponent of apartheid, who was notorious for his granite policy, his utter disregard for the life of a black man in the pursuance of his genocidal schemes, was actually dubbed a 'kaffirboetie' (nigger lover), by the still more extreme members of his party. It was a foregone conclusion that after his assassination, Verwoerd would be succeeded by Jan Balthazar Vorster, that rabid racialist and Hitler-worshipper, for whom only one name is appropriate – The Butcher.

The unanimity with which Vorster was elected prime minister should not deceive anybody. It is a desperate attempt on the part of the inner circles to conceal the flashing knife-blades behind the scenes. It is significant that the only candidate put up in opposition to him was Ben Schoeman, a man who was once an admirer of the pro-British General Smuts. The very fact that his name was proposed indicates the pull of the new Afrikaner financiers, who have become a factor to be reckoned with. He would have been a compromise candidate, marking a half-way house on the road to a unification between the Afrikaner nouveaux riches and international finance capital. He would have been a useful stop-gap until a premier was found who could express the coming together of a Rupert, tobacco-king and symbol of the new Afrikaner finance group, and Oppenheimer, the South African representative of international finance, both of whom are vitally concerned with the full expansion of the South African economy, freed from the artificial barriers imposed on it by the Verwoerd-Vorster political dogmas.

The appointment of Vorster as premier solves nothing. But this does not by any means reflect the present relationship of forces within the wider circle of Afrikanerdom, and much less within the white section as a whole. Vorster's election will simply intensify the internecine strife.

Imperialism will not let the situation rest at that. It must take over real power, through whatever agency that is willing to do its bidding, whether Afrikaans or English-speaking. This does not, of course, imply that international financiers will automatically withdraw their capital, now that Vorster is in power. On the contrary, if we know the nature of the beast, with its habits both of double-dealing and ruthlessness, imperialism will continue to pump capital into the South African economy and supply more arms to the already bursting arsenal of that country. But the same imperialism will not scruple to throw to the wolves the same Vorster and his ilk, should another power arise which is more amenable to its policies and can guarantee its large investments in South Africa.

We have mentioned above that the conflicts within the white minority section arise from two different methods of maintaining white domination. The growing militancy of the oppressed masses of South Africa, their determination to break the chains that bind them, exacerbates these conflicts. We know, of course, that as against the oppressed, the herrenvolk always stand together. Any threat from that quarter immediately makes them close their ranks. The assassination of Verwoerd is not going to make any difference to the bondage that weighs upon the black man. It is not this group or that group of the herrenvolk parties that will relieve the pestilence of poverty, the relentless exploitation, the deprivation of human dignity and the sheer violence that is an integral part of the existing system of society.

In the final analysis, it is the oppressed people themselves who will rise up and liberate themselves. This is not to say that all white people are evil or are exploiters. But the burden of lifting the age-long yoke rests squarely on the oppressed masses. It is their will and power that will draw in those whites who will be prepared to throw in their lot in the struggle for the achievement of a new South African society, where men will not be judged by the colour of their skins, but by worth; a society freed from the sickness and corruption of racism, a society where the main purpose will be to satisfy the human needs of all its citizens, and men will unite in building a harmonious society.

Our slogan is: WE BUILD A NATION.

CHAPTER FOUR:

The political forces and their orientation

I   NEW METHODS OF STRUGGLE

From: *The Boycott as Weapon of Struggle*

OUR STRUGGLE IS NOT UNIQUE

The struggle of the non-whites of South Africa for liberation is not unique in its general form.

Every aspect of it has in some form or another been experienced by other peoples of the world during some stage of their development. The South African economy with its inherent contradictions, the unequal distribution of wealth, the existence of lavish wealth side by side with extreme poverty is centuries old in Europe. The herrenvolk disease that riddles the political, economic and social structure of the country has also been known in Europe and Asia. It has cost mankind millions upon millions in human lives. The struggle of the oppressed in this country is similar to the struggles of all the oppressed people throughout world history. It is part of the struggle of mankind in its long and arduous march towards progress.

Now man has forged weapons of struggle in this process, such as the strike weapon, the boycott, etc. But each of these has its proper time and place. We do not choose our weapons at random. The oppressed people in each country are faced with particular conditions that dictate which weapon should be used at a given time. In fact, it is an important part of the art of leadership to know which of these many weapons to use at any given moment. This implies a thorough examination of the existing situation and the historical past of the objective as well as the subjective conditions. The non-whites in South Africa at this stage of development are not called upon to traverse entirely new terrain. What may be unique in the situation is a different combination of forces which calls for an adaptation of the old methods.

To give just one example of the different rates of development in the various countries, we may mention the position in South Africa itself. Here we find the relics of barbarism co-existent with the last word in modern technological advancement; we find social institutions, such as the relics of pre-feudal times, tribalism, side by side with the most up-to-date machinery for the extraction of gold in the mines. There are relics of feudal and tribal relations in the midst of industrialism.

This fact gives rise to a strange phenomenon: in South Africa the foremost industry, gold mining, the very flywheel of the economic structure, is dependent upon migrant black labour; heavy industry is dependent on peasant labour, or more correctly speaking, on the labour of a landless African peasantry. It is not necessary for our purpose to elaborate on this particular situation arising out of what may be called a telescopic development. All we want to bring home is that these particular conditions have to be borne in mind when we consider the form and method of struggle. When, for instance, we think of the trade union problem, the peasant problem, the relation between the workers and the peasants, and the national problem, these objective conditions invest the situation with what may be called a unique quality. It is in this sense, and only in this sense, that there is a uniqueness in the problems of the non-whites in South Africa.

Nevertheless, the struggles of the oppressed in South Africa are basically the same as those of the oppressed throughout the history of mankind. It is a struggle at this very moment convulsing Asia, Europe and the Middle East; North, Central, East and West Africa — everywhere where people are striving to throw off the yoke of oppression.

The need for the use of the Boycott weapon at this stage of our development must be seen as arising out of the objective conditions of South Africa. It is dictated by the living realities of racial oppression facing the non-whites in the so-called Union of South Africa.

THE AGRARIAN PROBLEM

From: *An Address to the Society of Young Africa*, May 1954. (SOYA is affiliated to the Unity Movement and consists mainly of young urban workers and intellectuals.)

Some of you may have come here expecting an exposition of the day-to-day problems and difficulties of the peasantry on the land. But I do not intend to deal with them today. Let us deal with the fundamentals. We have first to understand the nature of the problem itself. Many people engage in politics without having a clear idea of where they are going. They have no fundamental theses to serve as a touchstone in all their activities, to use as a test of the correctness of their lines of action. Quite often they throw themselves enthusiastically into some activity, only to find that at the end of it all they are further off than ever from their goal. Lacking a clear understanding of the problem, and therefore a clear policy, they live a hand-to-mouth existence, veering now towards the policy of one group and now towards another. Such people are prone to indulge in one venture after another, leading to the inevitable result – frustration, despondency and disillusionment. Thus it is important for us at the outset to have an overall picture of the problem before us, the forces at our disposal, the method of struggle and our goal.

There are two main problems that lie before us and require immediate solution. They are the agrarian problem and the national problem. It is our task to examine them and show their interconnection. The one is intimately related to the other and their solutions are likewise closely linked together.

First of all, let us examine the distribution of the population and the type of work the people are engaged in. South Africa is still predominantly an agrarian country. The bulk of the population is to be found on the land engaged in agriculture. But the overwhelming majority of the people are African peasants, who own no land at all. Thus the problem for this country is the land or agrarian problem. To see our problem in all its acuteness, let us look into the distribution of the land. With the exception of 2,071,551 urbanised Africans living in locations **(segregated city slums. Ed.)**, the rest are peasant in character, notwithstanding the fact that they are forced to go and seek work in the towns for shorter or longer periods. On the white farms the number of Africans employed as labourers is 2,528,214. These live in virtual serfdom. The remaining 3,935,576 are over-crowded in the 'Reserves'. It must be borne in mind that out of the so-called urbanised Africans fully one third are miners living in (segregated) compounds. They are migrant labourers, that is, peasants recruited under contract for limited periods and living apart from their families.

According to the statistics in a government paper, every white man, woman or child in the rural areas owns on the average 177 morgen of land, while every African in the Reserves occupies (not owns) on the average 2½ morgen. And this is not the whole picture; for all the Africans in the towns and on the farms are by law regarded as living there temporarily only for as long as they are employed, since their home is presumed to be in the Reserves. **(For recent statistics, see Appendix B. Ed.)**

The agricultural census figures are illuminating. They show not only the poverty of the blacks as compared with the whites, but also the poverty of a large section of the whites in the rural areas as against the few rich farmers in whose hands the bulk of the land is concentrated. **(Details of census omitted. Ed.)** The figures make it clear that the fundamental problem in this country is the agrarian problem. Furthermore, they reveal an important fact that must not be lost sight of, namely, that a section of the white farming population suffers from land-hunger. It is in their real interest to have an equitable redistribution of the land. And in fact land-hunger cuts across the colour pattern. This brings us face to face with the real and fundamental divisions in society, namely, the rich and the poor. All colour divisions in this or any other sphere are a superimposition calculated to blur the real dividing line of classes and to reinforce it.

The agrarian problem is not the only one facing us. We have also National Oppression. The non-whites are without political rights; they are excluded from Parliament. All legislative, executive and judicial power is in the hands of the small minority of whites, who use this power for the domination of the blacks in order to facilitate their exploitation. Thus all the non-whites are nationally oppressed. The two problems are interconnected and their solutions are bound together.

Let us now examine the consequences of the appalling distribution of land. From the outset I shall state categorically that landlessness is an instrument for economic exploitation and national oppression. It is the cornerstone of the whole economic edifice of South Africa.

From landlessness flows a train of evils – the migratory labour system, which sends the African like a shuttlecock from the starving Reserves to the mines and back again; the forced labour system on the farms; and depressed wages in every sphere. We must not be deceived by those who shed crocodile tears over the evils of migratory labour and suggest all sorts of palliatives to alleviate the lot of the black man. Such people are either well-meaning fools or hypocrites who would pour ointment on a cancerous sore. They tinker with the superficial effects of the evil without ever getting down to the core. We must know that no amount of talk or goodwill can ever induce any herrenvolk (ruling class) government in South Africa to alter the distribution of land in order to relieve the position of the black man. Land shortage is necessary and fundamental to the whole economic structure of South Africa. The oppressed and exploited people alone can and will alter that situation.

*Editor's Note: **The speaker demonstrates how the system of racial legislation channels African landless peasants into the white farms and the mines. (See also Chapter 3, Section IV.)***

As a result of this dammed up African labour there have arisen certain characteristic features in the South African economy. The main feature is the great gap between the wages of the unskilled and the skilled workers. In this country this means the gap between the black workers and the white labour aristocracy, which has an exclusive monopoly of skilled jobs. The ratio of skilled to unskilled wages over the whole range of industries is four to one. In the mining industry, taking all types of mining, it is eight to one, but in the Witwatersrand gold mines the ratio is ten to one. In South Africa super-exploitation is made possible because all political power is in the hands of the employing section and all non-whites are without political rights. It is possible, also, because of the acute land-hunger of a whole people herded into the Reserves.

When we have understood the underlying motive for all the oppressive legislation and administrative measures against the non-whites, it becomes clear to us what our attitude must be.

It becomes obvious that no amount of pottering with them or improving them will alter the fundamental position. Those who want to improve these laws are our enemies; for they, in effect, want to perpetuate the status quo. Our demand is for the total abolition of all discriminatory laws, a full and equal franchise, an equitable redistribution of the land for all men and women irrespective of colour, religious creed or 'race'. Anybody who falls short of these demands must be seen as an enemy who wants to come close to us in order the better to divert the struggle from its purpose.

Let me repeat once more; the agrarian problem is the fundamental problem in this country. It is the pivot and axis of the national movement. The intellectuals and petty shopkeepers must be made to realise that the agrarian problem is their problem. Whoever flounders on the agrarian question is lost. Such a man will inevitably attempt to lead the movement into the swamps of opportunism. We must guard the movement against such individuals.

Our immediate objective is to create a machinery that will be capable of measuring up to the gigantic task of re-organising the whole of the political and economic structure of South Africa in such a way that the people are assured of getting Land and Freedom. This means that we have to set the whole of society into motion. This is a mighty task. The question is: how is it to be done?

What is the political programme necessary for this purpose? And what is the organisational structure most suited to the task? There is a direct connection between the programme and the form of organisation.

We already have our programme, the Ten-Point Programme. Its first point is a demand for full and equal franchise. Point seven demands the abolition of serfdom and the right of every citizen to acquire land anywhere in the country and to live wherever he chooses.

What we need is to work out a method of putting this programme into action. We have to link up the agrarian aspirations with the national aspirations. We have to arouse the peasantry throughout the country through their demand for land. In order to draw the landless peasantry into the movement we must unreservedly throw in our lot with them in their struggle for their right to the land. At the same time we must teach them that the national, i.e., the political question is the key to the solution of their problems. In the given conditions of South Africa these two questions are inseparably bound together. For the landless peasantry are by and large the same people who are nationally oppressed without any political rights. The two problems must be solved together.

On the question of the form of organisation, we have already evolved the structure which we consider the most suitable for the task. If we think of gearing the whole of society into motion, we must find channels that will penetrate all the layers of society. No single political party can carry out this tremendous task. As we know, there are in existence numerous little organisations representing many different interests at all levels. Each one works in isolation from the rest. Our task is to get to the people through these organisations and draw them into the main stream of struggle. We have to give these organisations a new political content, and that content is the Ten-Point Programme. By these means we can unite the population; the organisations in the country will unite with the organisations in the towns. We shall then be able to build a truly national organisation which will reflect the aspirations of the country as a whole. What I would like to bring home to you is the magnitude of the task confronting us. We must not think in terms of our own little local organisations. We must learn to think in terms of the movement as a whole. In all our activities we must continually keep before us the larger issues involved. Whatever we do must be calculated to bring nearer the solution of the agrarian problem and the national problem. This means Land and Liberty for the people.

NON-COLLABORATION IN ACTION

Editor's Note: At the 1946 National Conference of the Unity Movement, Tabata, after reviewing the national situation and moving a resolution for the adoption of the policy of non-collaboration, said:

"It is the duty of Conference to give directives that are in line with the Ten-Point Programme. The Conference should adopt the policy of non-collaboration with the oppressors. Let us make a clean break with the past, cut the umbilical cord that ties us to the oppressor and wrench off the intellectual and political influences of the herrenvolk which have so long dominated us. Let our policy be non-collaboration with the oppressors in our fight for full democratic rights."

Subsequently he stated, "This policy provides a sharp line of demarcation between the genuine fighters for liberation and the many compromisers and opportunists, the wolves in sheeps' skins."

PEASANTS USE BOYCOTT WEAPON

'With the challenge of the boycott we opened up a new era of struggle.'
From: *The Awakening of a People*, Chapter 9.

Having defined its tasks and formulated its programme, the Convention was in a position to carry its new policy to the masses. The reaction of the people was a measure of how well it had given expression to their needs. Years of bitter hardship and deep disillusionment had convinced them that their old leaders had led them into a political swamp. With a perception sharpened by experience they recognised that the new policy answered their needs and aspirations. This did not mean that they fully understood what the new road of struggle would involve. They had to learn the meaning of the new policy in the day-to-day struggles. Concretely it meant in practical politics the application of the policy of non-collaboration.

In 1945 the African people in the Reserves were presented with what was called the Rehabilitation Scheme, described by the Secretary for Native Affairs as 'Ensuring a better life for the inhabitants (peasants) in the future'. The Convention published a pamphlet, The Rehabilitation Scheme: a New Fraud, which places the Scheme against the background of the whole 'Native Policy' of the rulers, with its system of laws for the regimentation of African labour.

The people themselves did not find it difficult to realise that when the scheme had been put into full operation, many families would be landless and driven out of the places of their birth .... The root of all this destitution of man, of beast and of the soil itself was land hunger.

The majority of the people of the Transkei − where the scheme was first applied − opposed it.

The acceptance of the scheme by the Bunga (council of chiefs) more than anything else opened their eyes to the function of these institutions in collaborating with the government. By this time the leading organisations in the Transkei were members of the All-African Convention. They took the opportunity of explaining to the people that segregatory institutions like the Bunga should be rejected, not only because they had accepted this particular scheme but because they are foreign to a democratic system of government. They were part of the system of trusteeship and in this sense were instruments of oppression.

The resentment of the people mounted as the Rehabilitation Scheme was more and more applied. All over the Reserves the people resisted with a stubbornness which was new and all the more significant coming from the section of the population which was traditionally regarded as the most backward. In the Transkei the Amaxesibe, in the district of Mount Ayliff near Pondoland, threatened to take up arms in defence of their stock. The majority of the people, too, repudiated those chiefs who had accepted the Scheme. They held meetings in the hills under their newly-formed organisation, the Kongo. The following year a member of the Convention was arrested and charged with inciting the peasants against the Rehabilitation Scheme. In Pondoland the people were strong in their protest against their chief, while the surrounding villages totally rejected the Scheme.... in the Middledrift and Debenek districts in the Ciskei a number of villages repudiated the claim that they had accepted the Scheme and strenuously resisted its imposition. A number of arrests were made. In some villages the people formed their own People's Committees and collected money for the defence of the arrested men. All over the country resistance goes stubbornly on. It is a grim fight whose story has still to be told.

Editor's Note: *The arrested man here referred to was Tabata himself. He had been holding a series of meetings in the Reserves and was arrested at Mount Ayliff in Pondoland (Transkei) after addressing thousands of peasants gathered on the mountain side. His trial* was to have repercussions in the whole of the Transkei and beyond. The peasants came from far and wide to attend the trial and express their solidarity with the Convention. He rejected his lawyer's advice to have himself acquitted on a technicality and demanded that the trial, in full view of the peasants, should be used as a test of the legal validity of the imposition of the Rehabilitation Scheme, arguing that he could not be charged with inciting people against a government policy that had no force in law. In acquitting Tabata the magistrate was at pains to explain to the listening crowd of peasants that although there was nothing in law to enforce acceptance of the Scheme, nevertheless all those villages that had accepted it, through their chiefs, headmen or government-recognised village leaders, were guilty of an offence if they resisted its application. The peasants were jubilant at the verdict and of course chose not to hear the latter part of the magistrate's injunction. What concerned them was that this government scheme was not law. Practically every district in the Transkei and the Ciskei defied the Scheme, whether or not some quisling chief or headman had accepted it. The militant temper of the peasants in that area was shown by the fact that they had come to the trial armed with their spears and other traditional weapons, fully determined to rescue the prisoner. The law was amended, but resistance continued to spread, first to Zululand in Natal, and thence to the Reserves in the other provinces. The more the government applied savage repression, the stiffer became the resistance of the peasants. Such is the structure of South African society that the militancy penetrated all layers of the African population both in the towns and in the countryside.

Subsequently in an unpublished article entitled **The Conspiracy against the Real Liberatory Movement**, Tabata has this to say about the peasant resistance at that time.

'The peasantry applied the boycott weapon with such vigour that in some villages in the Reserves they nearly brought the administration to a standstill. In this way they discovered their own strength. It gradually dawned on them that they had been operating the instruments for their own oppression. They extended the boycott weapon to the so-called Rehabilitation Scheme, a new government device for robbing them of their stock, their grazing and agricultural land.

'The struggle gathered its own momentum and spread to far-flung areas that had not been touched as yet by the Convention. It spread to Witzieshoek in the Orange Free State, where the Smuts Government had mowed the people down with machine guns. Later it spread to Sekhukhuniland and Zeerust in the Northern Transvaal. As might be expected, the wave of the peasants' boycott struggles spilled over into the towns. The migrant labourers on the gold mines, who are drawn from the landless African peasantry, went on strike in 1946 and were once more brutally suppressed.

'The Convention linked the peasants' economic problems with their political problems. It flooded the rural areas with pamphlets and leaflets which pointed out that their landlessness and their low wages were all tied up with their lack of political rights. Their struggle for land, therefore, was indissolubly bound up with the whole struggle for political rights. In short, their struggle was a national struggle. It is this new approach that captured the imagination of the population and laid the basis for a series of outbursts leading up to 1960, the year of the Pondoland revolt and the Sharpeville massacre.'

LAND AND LIBERTY – UNITY MOVEMENT CONFERENCE, 1951

Editor's Note: After a report from the peasant representatives from Zululand (Natal) and from those of the Transkei (Cape Province), Tabata spoke as follows:

'The important slogan, Land and Liberty, emphasises the inseparability of the struggle for land from the struggle for the franchise. If Conference leaves with only this idea, it will have achieved a great deal. It is essential that we of the Non-European Unity Movement understand the place of the peasant in the struggle. The Land Problem is at the core. Coloureds and Africans depend on the land indirectly even in the towns. The town is dynamically related to the country. We have heard here of the struggles of the peasants, many of us for the first time. Recently we read about the peasant disturbances in Witzieshoek (Orange Free State), but the full import did not come home to us because the two struggles, of the workers in the towns and the peasants in the country, were not connected and seen as one struggle. The Witzieshoek martyrs are those who have gone into the battle first.

'In 1947 others in different parts of the country faced the same position. Consider the case of the Amaxesibe (Pondoland) who were summarily told to get rid of their stock. One village after another rose and took up arms. The country as a whole did not know of these incidents. The only Press which mentioned it was our own. Yet the battle of the Amaxesibe – and of those in Zululand and Witzieshoek – is the battle of the non-whites. They are fighting our battle. We must understand and demand to know what has happened in Witzieshoek. They belong to us. We do not yet understand that it is they who are fighting our battles." *(Tabata continued his speech in Xhosa. Ed.)*

'I want to say a few words to those of Zululand. We are glad you are here. For the first time you have come to your home. You have realised that we are your people. The first thing I want to say is that this Rehabilitation Scheme is able to operate because we have lost our human rights, our independence, our manhood. We are pinning our faith on what died long ago – the chieftainship.

'Is there a single chief amongst us who is a chief, determined by the will of the people? The very idea of a chief being paid by the Government is ridiculous. Let us strive to achieve our former state of manhood where the men themselves discussed their problems – and let us have our women too, for they also are workers. Whenever any problem arises it must be discussed by all the people together by themselves, and then only must their decisions be taken by elected delegates to the authorities – and not by the chief, who can be bought over. We advise you not to send chiefs to face the authorities. In all the villages tell the people that there must be People's Committees.

'The Rehabilitation Scheme does not operate unless the people accept it. If the people did not accept it, how did it begin to operate? Through those who receive their monthly pay from the authorities. No paid servant of the Government should be the mouthpiece of the people. Go all over Zululand and say this is the position and this is what you must do. And tell them also that the same things are happening in the Transkei. Keep in touch and work with the people .... We are glad to know that there are still men in Zululand who demand their human rights. Whoever is trusted by the Government is a mere white man's dog and should be treated as such.

'Go home and tell your people that there are men here with you, here in the Non-European Unity Movement. We shall watch and always keep an ear open for news. Get your people into this fold. It is a long road and it means hard work, work all over Zululand and further. Remember that in the Transkei you will find men like you and like us.

'To those from the Transkei I shall add these few words: We are watching you. We are hoping that when the people follow you – as they do – you will live up to their trust in you. We are aware that some are toying with the idea of collaborating with the government officials. If you are going to take advantage of the people, you would be betraying the Movement. The people have confidence in you. Go home and work as you have done hitherto, and even more. Carry the torch from this Conference to penetrate all the corners of the Transkei, from Gealekaland, through to Pondoland and right down to Zululand and Natal as a whole. Go home, not to sleep, but to work.'

GROWTH OF BOYCOTT MOVEMENT

'It is the masses who understand non-collaboration. It is the masses who are taking the lead.' From: The Awakening, Chapter 9.

The determined rejection of the Rehabilitation Scheme was only one manifestation of the new outlook of the people. It led also to the rejection of all those institutions which were part of the machinery of segregation. And for this they employed the weapon of the Boycott. The main point of attack was the Native Representative Council (NRC), the newest and most exposed of these institutions. The Transkei Organised Bodies (TOB) took this up and carried it to the people. The struggle went on in earnest. The Transkei Voters' Association (which is part of the Cape African Voters' Association) twice met and twice repudiated the sham representation under the Native Representation Act. In January 1947, the biggest and most representative gathering of Africans seen in the Transkei for many years was held in Umtata under the joint auspices of the TOB and the Transkei Chiefs' and People's Association. It decided by an overwhelming majority that the members of the Native Representative Council should resign forthwith. It was at this conference that a rift in the whole of the Transkei became clearly evident, between the people on the one side and the chiefs, headmen, Bunga members and members of the NRC on the other.

BOYCOTT CALL

Issued by the Transkei African Voters' Association, Executive Committee.

Editor's Note: Convention organisers had brought about a transformation in the Transkei African Voters' Association and in the TOB, both of which were now affiliated to the Convention.

The TOB, comprising chiefs as well as peasants, had been created simply as a means of tying the peasants to the Bunga, but the germ of the new ideas burst the TOB apart.

TO THE AFRICAN VOTERS OF THE TRANSKEI CONSTITUENCY!

Fellow African voters, we are addressing you on the subject of the coming Parliamentary Elections. As you probably know already, a mass meeting held at

Umtata 23rd May 1947, representing twenty-two out of the twenty-seven districts in the Transkei, decided by ninety-four votes to twenty-nine, to boycott the coming elections. In communicating this decision to you, we feel we ought to let you know why the African voters have made this momentous decision.

The Native Representation Act was passed in spite of the opposition of the African people. This Act deprives us of our vote, the last vestige of political rights which we had in the Cape Province.

It took from us the right to buy land where we please, go where we please, live where we please without having to carry paper badges of slavery. Instead we were given a dummy council, called the Native Representative Council. African 'representation' in both Houses is a farce and a mockery. Three whites to represent eight million Africans, while two million whites are represented by one hundred and fifty.

SHAM REPRESENTATION – WHY?

To ensure, first of all, that the interests of the white 'aristocracy' are served without any serious opposition from African representatives. Secondly, it is calculated to make the Africans believe that they are represented, and to live in hope of justice. But these so-called representatives have been sent to Parliament not to see justice, but to make laws to suit the mine owners and the big farmers, to force the Africans to go to the mines and the farms as cheap labour.

The Government makes this pretence at representation because, if it doesn't, the African will turn away from the white parliament and seek to build his own organisations into a powerful weapon which alone can free us from the chains that bind us.

Why should we feed our own people the illusion that we have representation? Let the people know that we are voiceless. Let the world know that we are voiceless. We are voiceless! Let us use the only weapon we possess at the moment, the boycott weapon. Let us refuse to collaborate with the Government in our own oppression.

The African people have decided to boycott the elections, not merely as a demonstration but as a positive act in our fight for freedom.

Let us be vigilant. Those who are not with us are against us. Every vote cast in this election will be an act of treachery to the African people.

Boycott the elections! Nothing less than full democratic rights!

From *The Awakening of a People*, continued:

The mounting tide of opposition was so great that the African National Congress, which had stubbornly set its face against the boycott movement, was threatened with either being drawn willy-nilly into the stream or swept aside .... The Communist Party of South Africa, too, (at first) fell into line.

It was the eve of the dummy elections, and all the organisations took up their positions on the burning issue of the boycott, ranging themselves unmistakably according to their acceptance or rejection of inferiority and trusteeship. The African National Congress reversed its previous resolution, decided to break the boycott and thus declared for collaboration with the oppressor.

Needless to say, they found a formula which attempted to disguise their true intent. That is when they invented the notorious meaningless slogan, 'Return the Boycott Candidates' – as if one could both boycott the elections and take part in them. The Communist Party followed suit in reversing the boycott decision.

Now the battle breaks out into the open between the protagonists of the two policies. The campaign for the boycott is intensified and hundreds of meetings are held all over the country.

The organisations in the Convention go to the people and around the question of the boycott pose the larger issue, the position of the black man, whether he shall accept inferiority and helotry or claim equality and full democratic rights. The people rally to the Convention policy. The AAC demands the expulsion of all quislings from the affiliated bodies, and announces that no member of the Native Representative Council can be a member of the Convention. At a joint meeting the Transkei Organised Bodies and the Transkei Voters' Association expel from their organisation all members of the NRC, and call on all candidates to withdraw 'in deference to the people's will'. With this decisive action the Transkei set an example to the country as a whole.

II. THE ROLE OF THE COMMUNIST PARTY OF SOUTH AFRICA

Editor's Note: The militancy of the masses in the boycott struggle posed the issue so sharply that it placed all the collaborators, the opponents of the Unity Movement, on the horns of a dilemma, with the result that they showed all the zigzags of opportunism in their behaviour. The role of the Communist Party of South Africa in this period calls for particular comment.

It was in 1921 that the Communist Party of South Africa had been established, merging with the International Socialist League, which had resolutely turned its face towards the blacks. The CPSA came into existence before the degeneration of the Stalinist bureaucracy in the Soviet Union had supplanted Lenin's programme of workers' democracy and international socialism. But so great was the weight of white herrenvolkism — which means racialism — in South Africa that the CPSA fell down on its very first test. This was the 1922 Rand strike of white miners in the Transvaal province. The strike developed into an anti-black struggle with the slogan, 'For a White South Africa!' The CPSA enthusiastically supported the white workers. Then, when the Rand strike brought down the Smuts (pro-British) Government, the CPSA supported a pact between the Hertzog Nationalist (Boer) Party and the Labour Party, which was itself completely committed to a racial policy. The irresistible current of white herrenvolkism resulted in the making of strange bedfellows. This Nationalist Party was the forerunner of the Verwoerd-Vorster Party against which the Communist Party and the Liberals in the late fifties were to organise the African National Congress in the name of Anti-Apartheid. The pact Government of the twenties, then, was responsible for the passing of a series of racial colour-bar Acts reinforcing the position of the white aristocracy of labour. For example, the Industrial Conciliation Act excluded 'Natives' (Africans) from the category of employees. In all this the Communist Party occupied the position of the left wing of a completely reactionary Labour Party. The position was neatly summed up by a Labour leader, Bill Andrews: "I'm a white man first and a socialist afterwards".

The subsequent concentration of the CPSA on the trade union movement was consistent with its reformist position. It was a struggle emasculated from the outset because racially separated trade unions could not defend the workers even in the economic sphere, and still less since they were prevented from taking part in the political struggles of the oppressed. It was characteristic of CPSA policy that when the Unity Movement sent out to all organisations, including the trade unions, its call for a national conference, the central committee of the CPSA circularised the following instruction: 'All our districts and branches are instructed to refrain from sending delegates to the Non-European Unity Movement Conference (December 1945). If possible, all organisations under the influence of the Party should be persuaded also not to send delegates.' (Signed, Moses Kotane, General Secretary, 13 November 1945). The African National Congress and the trade unions under the CPSA control obeyed these instructions.

The CPSA vied with the liberals for position as white 'Native Representatives' under the segregatory Native Representation Act and was as ardent as they in trying to control the oldest African organisation, the African National Congress, through its leaders. The influence of the Congress had waned since the early twenties when the militancy of the African masses after the first imperialist world war had resulted in the rise of a new organisation, the meteoric Industrial and Commercial Workers' Union (ICU). The crisis of the Slave Bills had given the Congress the opportunity to revive on the crest of a new wave of militancy, but its leaders, ignoring the unanimous decision of the rank and file of the federal body, the All-African Convention — of which they were executive members — to reject the Bills, had sold out for a compromise of 'giving the Acts a trial'. What was here involved was not simply rejecting the Slave Bills in toto, but the repudiation by the African people of the whole concept of the inferiority of the black man, of segregation and, in a word, white domination. The sell-out on the part of the Congress leaders had put the liberatory struggle back at least a decade. And now, utilising the general militancy of the masses who had responded to the boycott call by the Unity Movement, the CPSA made the African National Congress the focus of a variety of ad hoc bodies in an attempt to set up a counter-activity to the Unity Movement, calling for anti-pass campaigns and one-day token strikes, while knowing the complete atomisation of racial trade unions. They also supported the unity pact between the President of the African National Congress, Dr Xuma, and the leaders of the merchant-dominated South African Indian Congress.

It was in this situation that the leadership of the Unity Movement considered it important, especially for the young intellectuals clamouring for action, to understand the role of the Communist Party of South Africa, as well as that of the liberals. Thus, in The Awakening of a People, a book published by the All-African Convention at the height of the boycott struggle and providing the historical background of the emergence in turn of the African National Congress, the ICU, the All-African Convention and the Unity Movement, Tabata cited several examples of CPSA tactics in utilising the very leaders who had rejected unity on the principled basis of full equality laid down by the Unity Movement. He cited the fiasco of an anti-pass campaign at the head of which the CPSA placed Dr Xuma, President of the African National Congress. When he backed down and the campaign collapsed, it brought bitter disillusionment to the Africans who had responded to it by burning their passes. We quote from **The Awakening of a People** (Chapter 12):

'The fact of the matter is that in this instance Dr Xuma had become a tool in the hands of the Communist Party. In all the foregoing one can trace the pattern of their tactics. It has long been the CPSA line either to control or kill an organisation. It cannot tolerate a movement or organisation which is not dominated by itself. Every time there is political excitement over some oppressive measure, the CPSA is the first to set up a hue and cry against it. They do not call upon the existing organisations of the non-whites to fight the issue.

'They either organise the people round the CPSA itself or set up an ad hoc body or committee in which their own men play a leading part. When the campaign comes to an end they dissolve the ad hoc body – but with a few new recruits to the credit of the CPSA. The people's organisations themselves are not allowed to develop because they are not allowed to fight the issue under their own banner and thence grow into a permanent, independent force. In other words, the people are kept defenceless so that when the next onslaught takes place the CPSA can always appear as their champion. At all times the CPSA gets hold of one or other of the leaders of the non-whites and uses him as a decoy.

'The question to ask is: Why does the Communist Party of South Africa behave in this manner? – a party that is supposed to stand for the workers.

'The few non-whites in the CPSA have by and large joined it by filling in the membership form which is publicly distributed, without having the slightest idea of what Communism really means.

'The preponderating conscious element in the Communist Party is drawn from the white petitbourgeois intellectual section. It is this element which is responsible for formulating its policies.

'And it is just this section which is particularly susceptible to ruling-class ideas. Their daily existence connects them with this class in manifold ways, through social and economic bonds. In fact it is the very milieu of their existence. Even those few trade union functionaries operating in the working class are themselves limited in their social contacts to the trade union bureaucrat and the white worker, who constitutes an aristocracy of labour in South Africa, and is himself riddled with the herrenvolk prejudices and ideas. This is why in every political crisis the Communist Party of South Africa finds itself standing four-square on the side of the herrenvolk parties.

'Consider the war question, for example. During that whole period, beginning at the time when the Soviet Union entered the war, the CP was indistinguishable from General Smuts' Party. In the 'Friends of the Soviet Union' and allied bodies the members of the CP and the Bishop Lavises, etc., were all of one fraternity.

'With equal zeal they mobilised man-power, labour, industry, in one grand war effort. From pulpit to social club, from factory to rural village they were busily engaged recruiting the oppressed to join the army – even as baggage-warriors – in order to defend 'their country'. At this time a favourite argument on their lips was that nothing must be done to embarrass the

Government in its prosecution of the war, and General Smuts was proclaimed as the greatest leader in the 'fight against Fascism'.

'In the political crisis that arose during the late forties the Communist Party once again took up its position on the side of the herrenvolk.' **(The writer refers to the boycott struggle under pressure of the increased economic exploitation of the blacks after the war. Ed.)** 'The CP strained every effort to break the boycott. They advanced spurious arguments to defend their line. But no amount of eloquence could disguise the fact that.... to keep the segregatory institutions alive is in the interests of the ruling-class.'

From *The Awakening of a People*, Chapter 13

Editor's Note: The writer lays particular stress on the remarkable volte-face made by the CPSA together with the Congress leaders, as elections drew near. From declaring support of the Boycott they swung into a virulent campaign against it, again taking up the same positions as the liberals.

Both put forward candidates for election. The course of events strikingly demonstrated the totally divergent interests of the white as against the African section of the Communist Party.

At this period all and sundry were forced to advocate the boycott. The CP, too, fell into line. True to their tactic, they shouted the loudest of all to demonstrate their zeal for the people's cause. In fact they so out-did themselves in their zeal that it was subsequently to prove embarrassing when the time arrived for one of their all-too-frequent about-turns. It was at this time that the CPSA, under the signature of its General Secretary, Moses M Kotane, who was also an important leader of the African National Congress, issued a statement, 'The Boycott of Elections under the Representation of Natives Act', and expressed 'the readiness of the Communist Party to participate in any active campaign to make this decision effective'. In a fury of castigation against those who opposed the boycott, Kotane continued, 'If we are dominated by fear of stooges and reactionaries, and if we are to allow our actions to be conditioned by the attitudes of such persons, then it means that we can never agree to Africans embarking on a boycott. The best way to deal with 'Representatives' who get into Parliament against the views and interests of the people they claim to represent is to repudiate them publicly.

Again:

Those European "friends of the Africans" who, while they themselves enjoy full democracy and citizenship rights, are opposed to the boycott and are consequently against the Africans ridding themselves of something deceptive and achieving for themselves the full franchise which these Europeans enjoy, cannot escape from being looked upon by the Africans as representatives of white supremacy.

It was not long before the Communist Party was to make a desperate attempt to swallow these heroic words, which stubbornly stuck in their throats. Even at the moment when they were taking a decision to boycott the elections, a white leading member of the CPSA was preparing to launch his candidature as 'Native Representative'. He was associating himself on the political platform with those whom the CP was castigating as having 'flouted the decision of the Transkei African Voters' and therefore must be 'looked upon by the Africans as a representative of white supremacy'. The pattern of contradiction here, too, is clear. (**The reference is to the Congress and its Youth League. Ed.**)

Within the CPSA itself are two currents running in opposite directions. The one wing – what may be called the Kotane wing – living closer to the people and carried along by the force of their demands, is pushed in the direction of non-collaboration, while the other, the dominant wing in the CPSA, represented by the white intellectuals whose roots are in the herrenvolk class, was being impelled towards the policy of collaboration and was already making openings for a retreat.

The curious phenomenon calling for comment at this period is the brazenness with which the Communist Party and the African National Congress made a political turn-about in the space of a few months and still had the effrontery to expect the people to put their trust in them. The CPSA now turned their vituperation against the boycott. Now that the logic of their own opportunistic policy placed them in the position of having to defend precisely those institutions which, in their own words, 'veil the enslavement, strangulation and degradation of the black man', they turn a somersault and say, 'The essence of the (boycott) campaign is that the Non-Europeans should turn their backs on political struggle, isolate themselves from the Europeans and, in short, accept segregation.'

What monstrous falsification is this? They who, by breaking the boycott, are in the very process of stabbing the political struggle in the back; they who are working the institutions of segregation and tying the people to them, shamelessly accuse the protagonists of the boycott of accepting segregation.

The flood of vituperation against the boycott was not limited to the

CPSA. The various Congress scribes vied with one another in their attacks against it. The herrenvolk opened the columns of their press to them. From the columns of the big dailies to the magazines, from church publications to the smallest local newssheets, attacks on the boycott were churned out for consumption by the intellectuals.

(*Some years later, in summing up this period, Tabata made the following comment. Ed.*):

The liberals likewise intensified their efforts to break the unity of the African people under the All-African Convention, smash the boycott and draw the population within the ambit of the Government plans. Let it be said that the liberals by themselves would never have succeeded in pulling the Congress out of the All-African Convention – for they were working from the outside – if it had not been for the able assistance of the Communist Party of South Africa.

ANTI-APARTHEID

Editor's Note: The common purpose of the liberals and the Communist Party acting in the interests of the liberal bourgeoisie took clear form under the banner of Anti-Apartheid in the ensuing period after the coming into power of the Nationalist Party, the fascist wing of the ruling class. The Unity Movement leadership exposed the fallacy of choosing 'the lesser evil' implied in the Anti-Apartheid slogan, or alternately the slogan of 'defending democracy against fascism'.

Writing in Ikhwezi Lomso (Morning Star), an independent paper of the Movement, Tabata stated, 'The aims of the oppressed and those of the liberals are totally irreconcilable. To be lured on to the liberal bandwagon is to relinquish their own struggle and to be hitched on to the fight (of the liberal bourgeoisie) for the removal of the Nationalist Party from power. For as long as the leadership of the non-white organisations remains in the hands of those who, though in opposition to the Nationalists, seek to maintain white domination in South Africa, so long will the struggles of the people be brought to naught.'

This warning was particularly pertinent when the CPSA launched what it called a Congress Alliance consisting of the CPSA and the African National Congress with the addition of the small CPSA-dominated Coloured People's Congress, the Indian Congress and the Congress of Democrats containing white CPSA and Left liberal elements. It announced a 'Freedom Charter', but its real intent was to use the non-whites as a pressure group and at the same time split their ranks. Verwoerd hit back at the Alliance leaders with the five-year Treason Trial. The CPSA succeeded in leading the African National Congress into a political cul-de-sac.

Since the period to which the foregoing extracts refer, *evidence of the wider ramifications of CPSA policy, in the African continent is explored in:* The Conspiracy Against Southern Africa's Liberation (Chapter 4.5). *The present heirs of Stalin in the Soviet Union, the usurpers of Leninism, are seen to prostitute the function of the Communist International. The theory of 'socialism in one country' has dictated for forty years a devious foreign policy.*

III. THE PAN-AFRICANIST CONGRESS ADVENTURE IN PERSPECTIVE

A Unity Movement Pamphlet, September 1960 (Abridged)

Editor's Note: 1960 was a year of high political tension in South Africa. It witnessed the Sharpeville massacre of a peaceful crowd of African men, women and children when the police shot dead sixty-nine people and wounded a hundred and eighty; the declaration of a State of Emergency by the Verwoerd Government and the revolt of the Pondoland peasants which marked the mounting resistance of the African peasantry, not only throughout the Transkei and the Ciskei (Cape) but spreading into the Reserves in every province. Sharpeville hit the world headlines, while there was almost complete censorship on the peasant revolt. As a corrective to this unbalanced picture of the situation in South Africa, a very different assessment was placed before the Liberation Committee of the Organisation of African Unity in a memorandum presented by I B Tabata (leader of the delegation), N Honono and Miss J Gool as representatives of the All- African Convention and Unity Movement (December 1963):

At this stage it is important to correct a misconception that has been created in the outside world. The dramatic event of the Sharpeville and Langa (Cape Town) massacres in 1960, resulting from the passive resistance campaign of the young Pan Africanist Congress, has been presented as the starting-point of the struggle of the African people for liberation. Far from this being so, these events were an overflow, a spilling-over of the tidal wave of resistance that had engulfed practically all the Reserves in the country. The interesting fact is that the men who marched in the Cape Town demonstration from Langa Location were not the townspeople. They were practically all living in the segregated barracks in the location, that is, they were the migrant labourers who had been forced to leave their families in the Reserves. It was the grim struggle that was going on in the Reserves that influenced them to join the march. It was at this point that the imperialist press, with a blaze of publicity, stepped in, falsifying the true perspective of events in their sum total. They gave the impression that this was the beginning of the struggle; they isolated it from the main stream and succeeded in capturing and harnessing it to the battle of imperialism (finance capital) against Verwoerd (petit-bourgeois Nationalists). While the imperialist press focused attention on the so-called new struggle in the towns – of which they had full control – it has kept a blanket of silence on the struggle in the Reserves .... Both imperialism and Verwoerdian fascism were united in an attempt to crush this peasant struggle. The army would surround a village, mow the people down, rape their women and destroy their crops in the fields.

But the imperialist press maintained its calculated silence on such outrages. Why? Such a struggle was undermining the very basis of the economic structure. Whoever organised the peasantry was interfering with the vital source of labour for the mines, farms and industry. This Movement had to be crushed at all costs. And even more than this was at stake. This was the real national struggle that is fighting against both Verwoerd fascism and imperialism. In short, it is the struggle that is fighting for the overthrow of the whole political, social and economic system of the herrenvolk.'

The memorandum adds:

Today most of these village committees that participated in the Pondoland revolt belong to the All-African Convention, and the leaders have come in as individuals into the African Peoples' Democratic Union of Southern Africa (APDUSA), a national political organisation which is itself affiliated to the All African Convention, and the Unity Movement.

THE PAN AFRICANIST CONGRESS ADVENTURE IN PERSPECTIVE

With Sharpeville and Langa, 21st March 1960, the PAC (Pan Africanist Congress) adventure exploded on the South African scene. Sharpeville, a hitherto unknown location in the Transvaal, hit the world headlines with the news of the police shootings and the ground strewn with African dead. For a brief moment the world gaze was turned on South African affairs. South Africans themselves, the whites, suddenly became aware of the teeming black millions in their midst.

People asked in amazement what had happened. Some said that Sharpeville marked a turningpoint and it would never be the same in South Africa again. Others even spoke of a South African revolution. People everywhere were shocked and puzzled at the turn in events. Prices on the share markets came down sharply and the national reserves dwindled by the day. Industrialists, kings of commerce and big farmers alike for once raised their voices in urgent chorus and sounded the tocsin of alarm. Not the least shocked by the results of their actions were the PAC leaders themselves.

In a spirit of reckless bravado and adventurism they had launched their anti-pass campaign, which was somehow to bring freedom to more than ten million people by 1963. It was to be a 'non-violence' campaign, they proclaimed. With enormous political naïveté they saw themselves as discovering a new political method of disarming the herrenvolk with the minimum of expenditure, a method of liberating a whole people without the loss of a single drop of blood. They were the first to be stunned with shock when their 'non-violence' march provoked a burst of gunfire, followed by an orgy of brutality from a police force armed to the teeth and supported by the army. They were no less taken by surprise at the eager solicitations of a section of the herrenvolk itself, the Parliamentary opposition, the Progressive Party and the Liberals. Nor could they explain why the world press, including that of British and American imperialism, expressed such strong criticism of the policy of the Nationalist government and concern for the state of the Union. Yet it is a fact that the events, which a few years ago would have been allowed to pass unnoticed, today produced such sharp and widespread attention.

What, then, really happened in those March days? And what lay behind the events that prompted the Nationalist government to take the drastic step of declaring a State of Emergency?

To understand and assess these events, it is necessary to have some idea of certain historical developments in South Africa. For the past lays the basis for the political conflict and the emotional content of events in the present.

Editor's Note: *Tabata briefly traces the historical background to the interlocking of British and Boer capital in the coalition between Smuts (United Party, representing the Chamber of Mines) and Hertzog (representing the rich farmers).*

Now Dr Malan, who had refused to be drawn into the Hertzog-Smuts deal, broke away and sought support from the small farmers, railway workers, government employees, small business men and intellectuals: in a word, the Afrikaner petit-bourgeois.

This section belongs to that class which, wedged in between the two fundamental classes in society, the bourgeoisie and the working class, is unstable and susceptible to spurious propaganda. They are all the more prone to fall for catch-phrases because of their precarious position in society. Malan then, appealed to the racial passions of a fanatical group dedicated to the salvation of the Boers.

It was a narrow, rabid racialism that was given the grandiloquent name of Afrikaner Nationalism. It was the Nationalist Party, controlled by the Broederbond (the secret junta) that won the parliamentary elections in 1948. The Malan victory was the victory of a party controlled by the petit-bourgeois. For the first time in the history of South Africa the big financial interests found themselves ousted from the Government.

Here, then, we have the phenomenon where the big bourgeoisie is represented by a minority in its own parliament. And it is the ruling Afrikaner section of the petit-bourgeoisie that considers itself at war with the big financier; it is still fighting the Boer War. This Broederbond government can think and behave only as a petit-bourgeois. There is altogether a devastating preoccupation with pettifogging legislation. Job reservation (for whites only), Bantustans, etc., are a sop to party supporters. But all these are an irritant to big business. They have the cumulative effect of seriously interfering with the natural flow of capital and clogging the economic development of the country. This pettifogging legislation, then, which is made in the interests of a petit-bourgeois utopia and a racial myth, produces tensions which in turn make it necessary to employ strong-arm methods. The State of Emergency, where the rule of law is replaced with rule by edict, is a step towards a permanent state of fascism, not only for the blacks as hitherto, but applied to all.

(*For the later stages of the conflict between finance capital and the Afrikaner petit-bourgeoisie, see* **Verwoerd's assassination, Chapter Three. Ed.**)

The situation as it is now, under the Nationalist petit-bourgeois government, is intolerable to finance capital. It must get rid of the stranglehold of the Broederbond. This was the state of affairs — a state of conflict between the bourgeoisie and the petit-bourgeoisie — when the PAC adventure burst upon the South African scene.

IMPERIALISM STILL SEES A FUTURE

Imperialism, for its part, firmly believes that it still has a future in Africa and that there are vast fields for the investment of capital and possibilities of development that will give a new lease of life to world capitalism. Any attempt to move into fascism at this juncture has the effect of jeopardising the whole process. Imperialism visualises the end of one era and the beginning of a new one. Macmillan's 'wind of change' speech (**when the British Premier toured Africa. Ed.**) came as a shock to the Nationalists. It was an expression of the new trend in imperialist tactics. It marks the end of the old colonialism and the beginning of a new relationship with the emerging African States. All this, of course, is directed to the continued existence of capitalism, i.e. to its expansion and the increase of heavy investment.

In other words, imperialism is deeply concerned with the economic domination of Africa. This means that, while granting the African States constitutional independence, it ensures the economic stranglehold over them. It is in this context that we must view the conflict in South Africa between the big bourgeoisie, i.e. the financiers and the industrialists on the one hand, and on the other the petit-bourgeoisie, i.e. the functionaries now running the government of the country.

The local industrialists, backed by international finance, are calling for a revision of the old crude baasskap (master-race) attitude. The non-whites are to be granted some concessions and treated in a manner more commensurate with the current demands of the emergent States. This does not mean, however, that the industrialist is actuated by any philanthropical feelings towards the non-whites. First and last he is concerned with self-preservation and the maintenance of his investments. It is because he considers that the petit-bourgeoisie at the head of the State are endangering these interests and heading the country for disaster, that he can no longer tolerate them and must have them removed.

If that section of the Nationalist Party which speaks for the new Afrikaner finance houses does not succeed in ousting the Broederbond, then finance capital will have to get rid of the Nationalist Party itself from power. Many behind-the-scenes attempts were made to bring pressure to bear on the Broederbond, but they would seem to have failed. With this it became evident that the defeat of the petit-bourgeois Broederbond would involve a more protracted battle, and stronger methods would have to be used.

It was in this situation, with the big bourgeoisie and the petit-bourgeoisie poised for a fight, that the PAC incident happened. As soon as the PAC launched its Anti-Pass campaign, the two opposing sides moved into position. The Government acted with a promptness and violence quite out of proportion to the PAC 'provocation'. Sharpeville was its reply, not simply to the PAC but to its opponents. Those shots that reverberated throughout the world were fired in the battle between the last-ditch elements, the Broederbond, and finance capital. The liberals, always very vocal, placed themselves at the head as champions and spokesmen for the interest of industry.

They grasped the situation with both hands. Here was an opportunity of forcing the issue. They planned on the one hand to sweep the Broederbond out of power, clear the field for big capital and place it firmly in the saddle, in a government representative of its own interests. At the same time the liberals seized the opportunity of reinstating themselves and once more establishing a footing among the non-whites. They were eager to recapture the leadership of non-whites organisations.

The PAC adventure, then, came in most opportunely as an instrument in the fight between the Broederbond and industry. The same PAC that had broken away from the African National Congress on the ground that the latter was dominated by the liberals, now became a pawn in the hands of these very liberals.

PAC NON-VIOLENCE CAMPAIGN

The story of the PAC is simply told. Less than two years ago the PAC broke away from the parent body, the African National Congress. It set itself the task of organising on a racial basis. Its criticism of Congress was that it allowed the other racial groups not only to become members but also to be in the leadership. Since they had no real political difference with Congress, they had no distinctive rallying cry with which to draw membership to themselves as against Congress. In fact they had to fall back on the adventuristic tactics typical of the ANC. They had to out-Congress Congress.

While there was an overwhelming sense of urgency and a readiness to engage in battle against oppression, the people had not yet learned to recognise the genuine as against the spurious form of struggle, they had not yet grasped the crucial importance of the when and the how; and above all, they had not learned to weigh and discriminate in choosing their leadership.

On the 21st March 1960, the PAC launched their Non-Violence Anti-Pass campaign. The people were asked to leave their pass books at home, march peacefully to the nearest police station and hand themselves over for arrest. **(Robert Sobukwe with several of his followers was thus incarcerated from that morning.**

He knew nothing of Sharpeville, the massacre later that day, nor of its repercussions. Ed.)
The emphasis was on non-violence. This was in some mysterious way to bring
about freedom by 1963. Let it be stated that the PAC put forward two demands:

a) the abolition of passes;

b) the payment of a specific wage to every African, to wit, £8 3s 4d. per
week.

How these demands, and how the fulfilment of them could transform
the State and bring about freedom in three years, or even thirty, the PAC alone
knew. The leadership of the PAC showed complete ignorance of the nature of
the tasks before them. They did not pose the question of the kind of society
they visualised, or the nature of the State in which these freedoms they
proposed could be enjoyed. For the method of struggle is dynamically related
both to the nature of the society the people are up against and the society they
are striving for. The starting-point as well as the objectives must always be
clearly defined. The degree of responsibility of the leadership in an organisation
is measured by the way in which it poses these tasks and faces up to them.

It is little wonder that the PAC did not even examine the nature of the
'weapon' of nonviolence they so cavalierly brandished. Nor did they stop
to consider its effect, first on the authorities who promptly unleashed their
police terror on the people, and then on the people whom they had
disarmed, both psychologically and literally, tied hand and foot and
delivered over to the authorities. The whole conduct of this PAC adventure
showed not only reckless irresponsibility but an ignorance that made them
prey to the more wily and experienced politicians of the liberal party. They
became, as we said, pawns in their hands. Their state of mind when they
launched their campaign is revealed in a statement made by one of their
leaders under cross-examination during the Commission of Enquiry. When
asked how the PAC proposed to effect a change and achieve their aims, he
replied that 'All Africans could do was what the PAC had planned: get
arrested for not carrying passes and stay away from work until industry was
forced to approach the Government.' (Cape Argus, 11/6/60). He went on,
'The only thing, we felt, was to exert pressure on the industrialists who
have the vote and who, with the pressure on them, can appeal to the
Government.'

The imagination almost boggles at this display of infantile naïveté. The
above statements imply that, from the outset, they would hand over the
responsibility to the enemy, to the very industrialists who are their employers

and exploiters. What is more, the people must stand aside and wait patiently while their bosses 'appeal' to the Government on their behalf. This is tantamount to handing over the leadership to the liberals, who in this case speak for the industrialists. In short, what the PAC leaders advocated from the start was no less than a betrayal of the people. Night and day without ceasing, men and women are tasting the bitterness of that betrayal.

LIBERALS TAKE OVER

Let us return to the March days. As soon as the liberals had assessed the PAC adventure, had determined its scope and limit and made sure that it was controllable, they took over the leadership. From then on they directed the course of events. The Liberal Press swung into action.

It will be remembered that very few centres responded to the PAC call on Monday, 21st March. It was only afterwards that a number of other places reacted as a result of the reports of Sharpeville and Langa. The Press, which is notorious for spreading a blanket of silence over the activities of independent non-white organisations, suddenly came out full blast. Events rapidly followed one another with a snowball effect. The Government, for its part, promptly replied with nation-wide police raids, seizing documents and arresting members of the Liberal Party, the Congress of Democrats (controlled by the CP) and the African National Congress. The following week the tempo of events sharply increased. Luthuli, the president of the ANC, was brought into the picture. Monday, 28th March, was his nation-wide 'Day of Mourning'. Then on 30th March, 30,000 Africans from the Langa and Nyanga locations marched into Caledon Square, Cape Town.

The Government introduced a Bill to outlaw the ANC and the PAC and on the Thursday a State of Emergency was declared. But this did not halt the increase of incidents throughout the country.

Feeling ran high. In Durban (Natal), thousands of people marched to the jail, demanding the release of their leaders, and were mowed down by machine guns. Similar incidents took place in Johannesburg and other cities. The police, backed by the armed forces, let loose a reign of terror on the people, arresting more than 18,000 Africans by 6th May. (**These wholesale arrests included members of all non-white organisations. Ed.**)

The Government had reacted to the situation with the utmost ruthlessness. Now let us look more closely at the moves and counter-moves. We have said that Luthuli was placed in the limelight. What was his function? Up to the Day of Mourning the PAC leaders had occupied the centre of the stage.

The liberals, however, realising that the young PAC leaders were a bit of a dark horse, decided to fall back on the old and tried ANC leader. Luthuli, whose popularity had been waning, had no machinery for making his 'decisions' known to the people. As a banned man he lived in isolation. He had neither the organisation nor a press of his own by means of which to address himself to the country. The liberals and the liberals alone, could enable him to gain access to the powerful English Press.

This they did, and with great effect. The Day of Mourning was a resounding success. Industry and commerce suffered heavy losses; there was a dramatic drop in shares on the stock exchange and a spectacular flight of capital. Both the British and the American Governments voiced the anxiety of finance capital in the strong protests they made against Government policy. And the Nationalist Government had no answer to this. With the Day of Mourning the liberals had made their point: if the Afrikaner industrialists were to save their business concerns, they would have to get rid of Verwoerd and his Broederbond. At this stage they could have called off the PAC venture.

Now, however, the liberals proceeded to play their typical role. They had to lay the very 'monster' they called forth to use against the Government. We shall concentrate on what happened in Cape Town to demonstrate their machinations. To continue after the Day of Mourning was to upset a precarious balance. The spectacle of 30,000 Africans marching down on the city produced widespread alarm among the Europeans. But after a parley with the police the liberals persuaded them to go quietly back to the locations. They were inveigled into marching back into what proved to be natural concentration camps. Yes, they were to learn a bitter lesson as to what a location is – nothing less than a concentration camp. And now was the signal for the second round of violence.

The army took over, threw a cordon round the locations of Langa and Nyanga, sealed them off from the rest of the community and subjected the Africans to untold terror. The third round of violence took place when the police went on the rampage through the streets of Cape Town, ostensibly looking for 'loiterers and intimidators'. With baton and sjambok they hit out right and left at every non-white in sight. The spirit of the people had to be broken; they had to be whipped to their knees; they had to be starved into submission.

But violence breeds violence. The situation throughout the country became tense and many whites were ready to reach for their guns. In the continued State of Emergency the Government was filling the jails to overflowing; police and armed forces co-operated in creating a state of terror and confusion.

And now the same Press that had blazoned forth the Sharpeville and Langa shootings began to underplay the widespread police-terror. So scanty was the reporting that the overseas Press accused the local Press of timidity. But it was not a question of timidity. What was involved was a change in direction; their aim and purpose had shifted. It was one thing to have called forth the power of the people to threaten Verwoerd and his Broederbond, but it was quite another to allow them to become fully conscious of their own power. The strike weapon was a Sword of Damocles hanging over capitalism itself. It was now the task of the liberal bourgeoisie to break the very spirit and idea of the effectiveness of a strike. The heroes of yesterday had to be stripped, humiliated and returned to their ignominious anonymity.

Let there be no mistake about it. The liberals were concerned with more than the defeat of the Broederbond. They were conscious of the larger issues; they were aware of the movements taking place throughout the continent of Africa and beyond. And, like the good servants of imperialism that they are, they had to anticipate the dangers. Their actions were calculated to call out the movement prematurely so as to bleed it to death. This is the sum total of the havoc wreaked on the people, and it is they who have to pay the heavy price for the venture originally triggered off by the PAC and exploited by the liberals.

The next move further reveals the complex function of the liberals and the subtle role they play in the deception of the people. Although the liberal bourgeoisie and the Broederbond had started out as opponents, with the Africans as a pawn in the game, the developing situation had made them aware of the common danger. It must be understood that, beyond a certain point, the basic identity of their interests transcends their internal and temporary conflicts. The awakened sense of power in the people constituted a threat to the herrenvolk as a whole; over against the common enemy, the oppressed, they are united. The liberals had made a gesture. The Press had piped down on the ruthless suppression of the people. And the Government appreciated this. That is why it allowed them to play the 'Good Samaritans" in the blockaded locations. The liberals were the only ones permitted to pass the army cordons and take in food to the starving people.

VOICE OF INDUSTRY

There has been a whole spate of fine speeches from many anxious representatives of industry and commerce in South Africa. But the people would be very much mistaken if they thought these were uttered in their interest. The tussle between the Broederbond and the representatives of finance capital flared up strongly and this time it was unmistakable that the whole of the business world, i.e. all of industry, commerce and mining concerns, were on the one side against what they called the extremism of the Broederbond junta in the Government. For the first time the Nationalist Afrikaner business institutions raised their voice openly in criticism of Government policy. This struggle now raging within the Nationalist Party itself was brought into the open. It revealed a rift in the Cabinet and indicated the sharpness of the feud within the Nationalist Party.

(*The author cites several speeches by representatives of industry and mining, both English and Afrikaner, demanding some easing of the pressure against the Africans. We quote only one of these warnings. Ed.*)

Mr H F Oppenheimer, uncrowned king of the mining industry, a skilled and suave politician to boot, expounds his views at some length in his Chairman's address to the Anglo-American Corporation of South Africa. 'New methods and new policies are urgently needed if we are to build a truly united South Africa,' he said. (*Cape Times*, 2/6/60). Firstly, a modified form of the Pass Laws, not their abolition, since 'they are necessary for good government and are very much in the interests of the Africans themselves.' Secondly – and he regards this as most important – the creation of a special class of 'exempted Natives'. Here it is clear that the creation of the 'exempted Native' has become the pivotal point of their policy. In other words, the buying over of the non-white intellectuals is seen as a sine qua non for the maintenance of the status quo.

In their struggles against the Broederbond and their attempts to worst it, the spokesmen for the various financial interests will appear bold, courageous and even revolutionary in their criticism of the Government. But jackals cannot, by their very nature, work out salvation for the sheep. If the people learn that the liberal bourgeoisie, together with the rest of the herrenvolk, depend for their existence on the exploitation of the oppressed, they will realise that it is a form of political suicide to follow them, hang on them for advice and expect assistance from them. Once they understand that their interests and those of the herrenvolk are diametrically opposed, they will be effectively insulated against the pernicious influences of the liberals.

LESSONS TO BE LEARNED

The year 1943 marked a turning-point. When the All-African Convention took the New Road together with the newly-formed Anti-CAD, and the Non-European Unity Movement was born, a new leadership crystallised certain ideas which were profoundly to affect the struggle. First of all, they saw themselves as part of a larger struggle of the oppressed throughout Asia and the rest of the continent of Africa. The people learned to identify their struggle for liberation with that of all those who were throwing off the yoke of imperialism, and in this way the happenings outside the Union affected their thinking and influenced their attitudes and actions in a very real sense. For many years the NEUM carried on campaigns in the towns and all over the countryside to boycott all institutions for 'inferior races'. As the political consciousness of the people heightens, as they build up their forces in preparation for a concerted effort against oppression, the Government for its part stiffens and tightens its grip, with the result that the atmosphere becomes more and more highly charged. A situation is then ready-made for opportunists to jump in. Opportunist stunts by their very nature must fail. And it is the people who must bear the brunt of that failure. Up to now every such failure has been followed by disillusionment and a temporary setback.

But the political climate has changed in South Africa as well as the rest of Africa. A close examination of events during the PAC venture reveals a pattern. It is significant that all those centres throughout the Union, which had participated in the Defiance Campaign and the Passburning organised by the Congresses, now did not respond to the PAC venture. The people in these places had obviously learned a lesson. It was centres like Cape Town, which had been conspicuous by their absence from the earlier stunts, that were now involved.

The response of various centres one after another, after the Sharpeville and Langa shootings, was not due to the PAC call. The people were reacting to the Government's brutal measures; they were expressing solidarity with their fellows. Throughout the country the tension had become enormously heightened. If the

Government thought to cow the people with its ruthlessness, it had miscalculated. Not even the subsequent failure of the PAC venture, which was crushed with such ferocity, could break their spirit. The temper of the people has hardened. It can be said that there is a qualitative change in the mood and outlook of the people in town and country. The slaves of yesterday had suddenly dropped their humility and presented themselves before the disconcerted magistrates (*at the many trials – Ed.*) like men who have sloughed off their chains.

Further proof of this change, and underlining the fact that it is widespread, comes from events in Pondoland, where peasants were shot dead as a result of their opposition to the Government schemes. Giving evidence before a Commission of Enquiry, one spokesman, who bluntly refused to give his name, said, 'We want to know from the Government: Is blood being spilt freely here? (*An accurate translation of the Xhosa would be: Are you asking for war? Ed.*) Because then we are prepared to die. We might as well be dead as alive.' He said again, 'If you wish to see peace and rest in this country, take this message with you: We do not want Bantu Authorities; take the Paramount Chief and his supporters away. Take him where he can administer affairs away from us.' (*Cape Times*, 26/7/60). These are the peasants talking in this forthright manner. They are the peasants in what the rulers regard as the most backward part of the country. But let us hear these same peasants speak for themselves, 'When the vote was taken away from us, the African people were not allowed to sit side by side with the white man in Parliament. This unrest has come to stay as long as the African people have not got representatives in Parliament to voice their grievances.'

PROBLEMS OF ORGANISATION

One thing that comes out clearly in the present crisis is that the people are ready to make sacrifices for liberty. But this in itself is not enough. They must learn to define more precisely what freedom means. Freedom from what? And for what? In other words, they have to learn to know where they are going. This is still not all. They have to learn how they are to achieve their goal, i.e. the nature and the method of the struggle in which they are engaged.

It is the task of the leadership to bring this knowledge to the masses. And this is bound up, among other things, with the problems of organisation. If the people learn to regard their organisations as instruments of struggle, then their whole attitude towards them will alter. Just as no man hastens to war without his weapons, so will the people cease to rush into action without pooling the resources of the nationwide organisation under the guidance of the united leadership of the National Movement. The leadership has to stress unceasingly the sustained national aspect of the struggle as against the sporadic, localised, isolated and sectional ventures. It is only when the people have recognised the indivisibility of oppression, when they have fully learned to see themselves not as Africans, coloured and Indians, but as a people seeking to abolish national oppression, that they will turn their backs on localised stunts. People must learn that colour, white or black, is irrelevant to membership of a nation. This is the responsibility of the leadership.

When the people have learned to think in terms of a nation and act as a nation, they will themselves shun precipitous action at the bidding of an irresponsible, local or sectional group. For such actions rushed into recklessly without forethought, without preparations, and virtually gambling with the lives of the people, have the effect of atomising the struggle and handing the people piecemeal to the Government. The tempo of events is such that they can no longer afford to lay themselves open to the costly pranks of the opportunists.

The task of the leadership, then, is clear. The people must be taught the meaning of organisation and all that is involved in belonging to it. They must be bound by organisational discipline. They must learn to act in the name of their organisation and under its leadership. The problem of organisation has assumed paramount importance. It can no longer be treated as an academic question. It is a problem that requires immediate solution. We cannot separate the political problems from the organisational. Hitherto the Movement has tended to lay stress on the ideas and the programme of struggle at the expense of the organisational question. It must be brought home to the people that political and organisational problems are aspects of one and the same problem. An organisation is not only a necessary instrument in the struggle but also a vehicle for the ideas of the Movement. The concept of a nation will remain an empty word without those vital channels of communication which an organisation supplies. A body without its arteries which carry the life-blood to every tissue, and without that network of the nervous system that alerts the body and carries impulses to its outermost parts, is a dead thing. An organisation must be seen both as an instrument of struggle and as a weapon of defence against the ceaseless attacks from all sides. Such an organisation gives the individual a sense of belonging, which strengthens him against insidious influences.

The people have to learn that it is idle to talk about liberation unless they are prepared to knuckle down to the arduous task of building and maintaining their organisation. They have to learn that each little organisation is a component part of the larger body, and if each is not pulling its own weight, the whole will suffer. The workers in the towns, with their problems, are part of the nation, as the peasants in the countryside are also a part. The workers will have to understand that the pass system cannot be sought in isolation, because it is one aspect of the segregated low wage system and an integral part of the whole machinery of oppression. The peasantry too will have to understand that the Bantu Authorities and the Rehabilitation Schemes are indissolubly bound up with the low wages in the towns, the pass system and all the Urban Areas legislation. In short, the land problems facing the peasantry, and all the impediments and lack of freedoms put in the way of the workers in the urban locations, are aspects of the sum total of national oppression. The organisations of the people have to reflect this dynamic interconnection.

The peasantry, then, will have to learn that it is not enough to organise the people in their respective villages or even districts. They have to see to it that their fellow fighters in the towns are similarly organised, and that both groups belong together in the National Organisation. The townsman, too, cannot afford to isolate himself from his fellow oppressed in the country. They must be aware of their common goal. In the prevailing conditions in South Africa this task is made easier by the fact that it is the same people who today hold the plough and tomorrow are wielding the pick-axe and the next day are employed as labourers in heavy industry. The system of migratory labour ensures continual contact between town and country. The National Organisation, then, must co-ordinate all these aspects of the struggle. It reflects at once the indivisibility of oppression and the unity of purpose on the part of the oppressed non-whites.

The people must bend all their energies to building an organisation that will be an effective weapon in the struggle for liberty. The Non-European Unity Movement is such an organisation. It was created precisely to break the artificial barriers that had separated the various sections of the non-whites and bring town and country together. The people are clamouring for unity: the coloured people, the Indians and the Africans in the towns stretch out their hands to their fellow oppressed in the country. The African peasantry, too, are turning their eyes to the towns in the knowledge that their co-fighters are eager to join them in the struggle for liberation. The leadership must provide the channels to give effect to this burning desire on the part of the people.

Editor's Note: Postscript on Organisation

From the outset controversy turned on the kind of organisation the Unity Movement leadership considered essential to a protracted struggle requiring the involvement of every layer of the oppressed population. One further passage completes the picture. We quote from The Conspiracy Against the OAU (Organisation of African Unity) and Nationalist Movements:

'The efficacy of this type of (federal) organisation for the task in hand has been tested in the crucible of history. The people of Algeria discovered it during the heat of the struggle. The example of Vietnam has more than demonstrated the point. The people of Vietnam would never have been able to sustain for so long the massive attack by the United States, the biggest military power in the world, if the political parties had not drawn the peoples' organisations together and conducted the struggle under a unified leadership.' (APDUSA, Vol 2, No 10, March 1967.)

IV. THOUGHTS ON WORKERS' DEMOCRACY

Editor's Note: Tabata attended the independence celebrations of Algeria at the invitation of the Algerian trade unions. He had discussions with the political section of the National Liberation Front (FLN) and brought greetings from the Unity Movement of South Africa. There is a tragic irony in these eloquent brief notes addressed, as early as 1962, to the victorious leaders of the FLN in Algeria as to fellow fighters in a revolutionary struggle for a common socialist goal. Tabata saw the armed struggle in South Africa as imperative as it had been for the people of Algeria in their seven-year war against the imperialist colonial oppressors. Like Frantz Fanon, whose writings were as yet unknown, he gave warning of the continued vigilant commitment required of a whole people after victory in the building of a true workers' democracy.

From: Some Notes on Political Problems, addressed to the head of the political section of the FLN, Algeria, 13th November, 1962.

In our discussions I told you how the socio-economic and political set-up in South Africa is unlike that of any other country in all Central or East or West Africa. It is highly developed and poses problems of a different kind. Following upon this, the only conclusion that can be drawn is that the pattern of liberation in South Africa cannot follow that of the now emerging countries of Africa. It must on the contrary develop along a different path. From its inception it must unfold itself as a national revolutionary movement with revolutionary social and economic objectives.

These very objectives, that is the aim and the end, determine the means and methods of struggle. The nearest parallel to this situation, the country that is most comparable to ours in the whole continent of Africa, is Algeria. And for this reason the Algerian revolution took a course quite different from that of the emergent African States. Instead of moving in the direction of neocolonialism, which signifies the continuance of the economic stranglehold by Imperialism under the guise of 'independence', it sets its compass on a course leading to complete independence outside the orbit of Western Imperialism.

That is why the struggle was such a hard one. Imperialism clearly recognised the direction of the Algerian struggle from the start and set itself the task of drowning it in blood. And when it failed it did not scruple to apply a scorched earth policy, divesting the country of all its civil service, dislocating its industry, ransacking its larder and its treasury in order to bring it to heel by starvation.

The idea is to confront revolutionary Algeria with the choice of one of two courses: either to disintegrate as a State through lack of means and the resultant confusion and mass dissatisfaction, or to become dependent on French and Western Imperialism.

All these things you know even better than I do; for you are faced with them concretely as a grim reality. We in South Africa have watched with bated breath the whole course of the Algerian revolution. To us the Algerian revolution is of special interest. In it we see the forerunner of our own. We in South Africa are vitally concerned about the manner in which you solve your problems or are proposing to solve them, in the period of reconstruction. This is not a mere theoretical interest on our part. It has a very real bearing on our own struggles in South Africa.

The difficulties that face you today will confront us tomorrow. We must, even at this early stage, be prepared for these hurdles and so adjust our struggles that we meet them with the greatest preparedness and the least possible cost to the movement.

In the absence of written literature and polemical discussions on the Algerian Revolution, we have to fall back on the spoken word. This is the reason why I was so keen to meet the leading people here in the political section of the FLN Party.

On my way to this country I was hoping that I would meet a group of politicos whom I would be able to address on the conditions in South Africa. The purpose was to familiarise our brothers and fellow revolutionaries here with the problems and struggles of South Africa. From this I had hoped would arise a general discussion which would broaden out to the examination of the similarities between our two countries. In such a situation I am sure I would have benefited immensely from the contributions of the local people who have actually gone through the experiences that still lie ahead of us.

There are other questions, too, that I would have liked to have discussions on, for my own clarification.

There is the problem of wrenching Algeria from the orbit of capitalism-imperialism — an Algeria which is an ex-colony and whose whole economy is tied to the French economy. This is an extremely difficult and delicate operation. For Imperialism is not just going to sit still with folded arms, watching itself being gradually smoked out and strangulated in the soil of Algeria. It is going to fight back with all the resources left in its command.

Among these are those nascent and sullen allies within the body politic of Algeria. That class in Algerian society whose economic interests are bound up with French Imperialism is mortally afraid of the Revolution and by this token it becomes the natural ally of French Imperialism. If, owing to recent history, the bloody history in Algeria, it cannot openly espouse the cause of French Imperialism, it will tend to flirt with Western Imperialism in general. This is a potential danger that faces the Algerian Revolution.

There is the problem of demobilisation. For seven long years the Revolution has built up an army that lived in the hills and whose job it was to fight a shooting war. Now that same army has to be integrated into the civil population and absorbed in the administrative work of government. I would have liked to know what problems were posed by this situation and what difficulties could have been avoided.

There is the problem of carrying the whole population from one stage of the revolution to another.

For seven years the people of Algeria were faced with a war with all the atrocities that a 'civilised' nation could invent. The mind is outraged at the thought of what the Algerians must have endured. And yet the war itself, with all its tortures and all the physical and mental sufferings, was a more straight-forward, a less complicated affair than the war of reconstruction now facing the people in the second stage of the revolution.

This period is more difficult in that the blows delivered by the enemy are not immediately visible to the people. The shaft of the enemy leaves no visible gaping wound as it enters the social organism to damage its vital parts, the heart of the socio-economic organism. For this reason the people do not rush to the defence of their institutions. They discover the ill-effects only long after the damage is done. At this stage the normal tendency, after the flush of elation in the first victory, is that the people, exhausted from the war, tend to relax their vigilance and leave things to the government in which they have implicit trust. They do not stop to consider the tremendous difficulties that confront the government, faced as it is with the task of constructing a new society on the wrecks of the old and at the same time contending with surreptitious sabotage from within and outright hostility and disruption from without. The sanguine attitude of mind on the part of the people if unchecked, may expose the revolution to grave dangers. For each difficulty encountered on the way may catch them unprepared and give them a sense of shock and disillusionment. Such a situation has its own logic. It provides a fertile soil for the propaganda of the enemy.

It is then that the hydra-headed monster of reaction may raise itself and stalk the land. The Government would then be compelled to employ repressive measures against the internal enemy. The enemy in turn, donning the self-righteous cloak of defenders of the people, defenders of democracy, freedom of speech, etc., will seize the opportunity to shout, 'Autocracy! Dictatorship! Totalitarianism!' – all shibboleths beloved of the treacherous imperialisms when denouncing and denigrating the struggles of the people for liberation. All this, then, is calculated to create confusion in the minds of the people and undermine the Revolution.

I am aware that the leaders are fully conscious of all these contingencies. I state them only to ask certain questions. And the answers will be of great value to us in our turn.

Here are some of the questions that exercise my mind: What methods is the leadership employing to anticipate such an eventuality as I have indicated? What techniques is it adopting to close the gap between itself and the population? How does it set about the task of creating that dynamic unity between the ideas (of a new society) and action, between the directives and their practical application? In short, how does it set about creating a sense of commitment on the part of the population, that is, involving them not merely in the carrying out of the tasks that must be performed, but something more? To put the matter another way – what methods does the leadership use to inculcate in the masses that sense of belonging, of being the masters in their own house – for which they have fought with their blood? It is only when the masses have developed this feeling that the Revolution will be insured against counter-revolution.

To give a homely example of the kind of problem I mean, the other day I had occasion to go to the post office. There were long queues. The young people behind the counter were struggling very hard at a job that was obviously new to them. There for the first time I came face to face with realisation that the French had committed a great crime against the people of Algeria by robbing the State of its civil service. My heart was at the same time filled with joy to see with what diligence the young people applied themselves to the job. But I thought to myself: how long will the youth maintain that diligence born of the revolutionary spirit that is now manifest everywhere? In time, will their work not become routine and boring, as it was to the previous civil servants? Is it not necessary to invest the kind of work they are doing with a new meaning? Is it not essential to make them feel that their tasks and their positions are vastly different from and superior to those of their predecessors? By this I mean, is it not necessary to devise some means of consciously and consistently reminding them and making them feel that they are not civil servants in the old sense, but that they are making a special contribution to their own collective State?

What methods can be found whereby the people in their various activities in the social services and the different sectors of industry and agriculture can be encouraged to realise that they are not just cogs in a machine, as is the case with all the workers in a capitalist society?

How can they learn to see themselves as indispensable parts in the great task of building a new society? They must be made to understand that the very content of their labour power is itself transformed and ennobled. For it now serves different aims and purposes on behalf of the whole community.

In this way the attitude to themselves and their work, their whole concept of their place and function in the new society will be transformed. When the people apply themselves to their work with this new outlook, then the latent genius and their potential energies will be released in all their spheres of activity. Thus a new man and a new society will be in the process of being made at one and the same time.

It is this dynamic unity between the people and their society, this identification of the people with their State, that will ensure their steadfast alertness against attack from any quarter. It will provide a bulwark against all the evil machinations of counter-revolutionary forces and bring about the consolidation of the revolution in the truest sense of the word.

There is much more that I would have liked to discuss with you in connection with this great task of a dedicated leadership in the process of creating a new society, where for the first time men and women of Africa, nay, of the whole world, will enter the threshold of a new age in history. It is a society in which they will be free of the exploitation of man by man and where each one will develop to the fullest those latent qualities that belong to him as a human being.

V. CONSPIRACY AGAINST SOUTHERN AFRICA'S LIBERATION

(*APDUSA* – March 1969)

Editor's Note: Tabata has often made the point that a sine qua non for the development of the national movement in all its breadth and depth is the complete elimination of the liberal bourgeois influence over the oppressed non-whites. This is why he has concentrated his fire, both inside and outside South Africa, on the South African liberals together with the Communist Party.

When he directs some of his attacks on the leadership of the African National Congress it is only because it allows the ANC to be used as an agent of disruption. The Unity Movement leadership has frequently said at conference, 'The people in the African National Congress are part of us'.

And now in the wider arena of the African continent, in the battle against imperialism, Tabata necessarily returns to the theme of betrayal again and again.

THE CONSPIRACY AGAINST SOUTHERN AFRICA'S LIBERATION

Reviewing the international situation leads one to conclude that the struggle of capitalism-imperialism versus socialism is dividing the world roughly into three main groupings: the highly industrialised Western capitalist states headed by the USA, the socialist states of which the Soviet Union is the most advanced, and what are termed the underdeveloped countries, which fall in between and cannot escape being pulled to either side despite protestations of non-alignment.

The nature of the involvement of these underdeveloped states is revealed by Walter W Rostow in the *New York Times* (5 January, 1969). He lists the outstanding achievements of the Kennedy and Johnson administration. The first on the list of successes is Cuba. He says, 'First we worked to isolate Castro. We have worked bilaterally and otherwise with some of the countries under pressure from infiltration from Cuba and managed to prevent the achievement of a guerrilla war base on the mainland of Latin America, which was – and remained – Castro's main objective. Some quiet preventative medicine was done here. There are many problems ahead. Castro is a nuisance, dangerous still – but manageable ....'

On Vietnam, Rostow makes a startling revelation, 'We had a side understanding with the Soviet Union that they would take responsibility for keeping Hanoi out of Laos but Khrushchev could not or would not implement that agreement.' He is even more startling when he says, 'Despite Vietnam and other crises, we have managed to move our relations with the Soviet Union from one of across-the-board hostility to a relationship in which we isolate areas of common interest to both sides and work systematically in those areas to produce agreement.' This is what the Soviet Union calls 'the policy of co-existence', which applies only as between the big nuclear powers. It is designed to prevent a direct military confrontation with each other while each is engaged in the serious business of extending its sphere of influence. This agreement extends to the Far East including Vietnam, Latin America, the Middle East and the continent of Africa.

MIDDLE EAST WAR

The Arab-Israeli war is to be seen in this context. It is of vital importance to imperialism to ensure that the Middle East oil, the life-blood of Western industry, is kept flowing to the heart of Europe and England on its own terms. Israel is part of this scheme of things. After the UAR had taken over complete control of the Suez Canal, and a bid was made to unite all Arab countries, i.e. the oil producing countries, it was inevitable that imperialism would redouble its subversion of that whole area. US imperialism armed Israel to the teeth, encouraged her to go to war and helped her to win. The events of the war are well known: the convenient presence of an American flotilla at the critical moment, the jamming of Egypt's radio system by the Americans, the decoding of Egypt's secret messages and passing of information to Israeli High Command, all of which resulted in the pinpointing of the vital Arab military installations and weaponry with an unprecedented accuracy. It is also known that both the United States and the Soviet Union were well informed of the impending Israeli attack, but this did not deter them from persuading the Arabs not to forestall the attack. The results of this conspiracy are common knowledge. Within six days Egypt lost nearly all her planes and military might.

The actions of American imperialism and its interests in all this are obvious. What is not so clear, however, is the behaviour of the Soviet Union.

Ever since the OAU was formed, an important part of the Arab world became politically bound up with the rest of Africa. By putting the Arab countries under her obligation and turning them into virtual client states, as she has done with her neighbouring socialist states, Russia entered the African arena and joined the legations of foreign imperialist countries whose main purpose is to subvert unity and progress of the continent towards real independence. The Biafra-Nigeria war provides a glaring example of this process. Russia is providing a tremendous amount of weapons and aeroplanes for the slaughter of Africans by Africans. The United Arab Republic has nothing to gain by assisting in the slaughter. But the Russian bomber planes are piloted by Egyptians. This is part of the price demanded by the Soviet Union for the support she gives her. In this regard the UAR is not acting as a free agent but rather in the nature of a victim deserving more sympathy than angry condemnation.

Already the unavoidable dependence of African states upon rich foreign countries has enabled imperialism to play havoc with the Organisation of African Unity (OAU). The appearance of the Soviet Union on the scene has served to create a worse confusion and greater rifts within that organisation. It is no longer a three-cornered contest between American, English and French imperialists scrambling over the body of Africa, with the obstreperous little South Africa nibbling away from the southern tip. The OAU has now become part of the battleground between Capitalism and Socialism together with its accompanying side quarrels between the various forms of socialism as typified by the rift between the Soviet Union and the Republic of China.

A corollary to the subversion of the OAU and sowing disunity among African states is the capture of nationalist organisations belonging to the unliberated countries. Here the aim is threefold:

(a) to use them to sow confusion and enmity amongst African states;

(b) to turn them into instruments of foreign policy of the major powers;

(c) to use them as a means of staving off the revolutionary process, in
other words, to sabotage the revolution in Southern Africa.

Nationalist movements from time to time present memoranda to the Committee of the OAU or issue public statements in which they inexplicably criticise some African benefactor countries.

The explanation for this lies in their desire to please whatever state provides them with the most funds. The net result is to sow suspicion among member states, often followed by accusatory innuendoes.

On the question of turning nationalist movements into instruments of foreign policy, it is our opinion that the Soviet Union has taken over complete control of some of the nationalist organisations. The most obvious of them all is the African National Congress of South Africa, and this is because she has been connected with it, through the South African Communist Party, since long before Congress leaders left home. In fact the complete take-over is not unconnected with the trouble that has now reached the dimensions of a deep crisis within the leadership of Congress.

The first time that the Soviet Union stepped on to the political stage in Africa was when she joined the Afro-Asian People's Solidarity Organisation (AAPSO). At that time China fought very hard to have Russia excluded on the ground that she was not an Asian country. The real reason of course was an ideological one. That struggle alone embroiled the whole of the third world in the Sino-Soviet dispute, which was never officially put on the conference agenda but nevertheless kept cropping up in many disguises and vitiating all discussions. It is common knowledge that Russia poured a lot of money into transporting large delegations favourably disposed to her and packed the conference. Upon her entry she immediately sought to weed out China.

The culmination of this process was reached in the unconstitutional Cyprus conference. Russia had managed to win over the leading officials of the organisation who gave the conference a semblance of constitutionality. A big split took place and the original AAPSO died for lack of support. Russia, however, had sufficient funds to maintain a skeletal body, under the same name, with the same leading officials, keeping the same headquarters in the same place – Cairo. But the body now consists almost exclusively of Russia's ardent supporters. The veto clause that had been abolished by the previous conference in Ghana was restored with the express purpose of excluding all opposition to Russian domination. Thenceforth only those organisations that are recognised by Russia could have full membership status. This body now became the mouthpiece of the Soviet Union's policy relating to the nationalist movements.

So great is the importance attached to the newly constituted organisation by its benefactor that the latter has seconded Dr Spatak, a leading Soviet diplomat, to the AAPSO headquarters in Cairo.

He is reputed to be the effective boss there. It was this AAPSO that convened a conference of selected nationalist organisations in Khartoum in January 1969 with all expenses paid by Russia.

African states were also invited. In spite of the refusal of the vast majority to attend, the Russianconvened conference received virtual recognition by at least one of the agencies of the OAU. The influence of the Soviet Union is evidently so great amongst some members or officials of the African Liberation

Committee that this Committee had to postpone its scheduled January meeting in deference to the Khartoum conference. Among the papers delivered there was one by a Russian delegate. This particular conference was evidently a sounding board, and apparently the omens were propitious, for it was followed by another conference in Morogoro (Tanzania), also consisting exclusively of the Russian-backed nationalist movements. This time the participants were bolder in their megalomaniac claims.

In one of their resolutions they request 'all governments of the world' (not progressive governments, mark you) 'to recognise as the sole official and legitimate authorities of their respective countries the following fighting movements.' They go on to name the chosen six.

Elsewhere the conference calls on all governments to recognise the named liberation movements as the alternative and future governments of the territories concerned. They have hardly begun the armed struggle – some like the ANC of South Africa have not yet fired a single shot in their country – but they are already deciding who the Government shall be and distributing portfolios among themselves. National Committees are going to be set up in all countries of the world and offices established for the favoured six. An executive committee consisting of the representatives of the six plus AAPSO and the World Council for Peace has been appointed to function as an *ad hoc* mobilisation committee operating from Cairo for the implementation of conference decisions.

Significantly the Secretary-General of this committee is the Secretary-General of the Russian-controlled AAPSO. It is clear where the directives come from and who will supply the funds for this global venture.

ARMED STRUGGLE WORTHLESS

The adroit handling of this whole scheme reveals a hand skilled in the art of manipulation and deception. The attention of the Russian-controlled nationalist organisations is being turned away from the scene of battle in their own respective countries and their gaze fixed upon distant pastures; their energies will be dissipated in fruitless activities in all the capitals of the world, protesting against a sports team going to play in South Africa, furiously organising demonstrations on this or that apartheid law and generally maintaining a facade of high militancy; anything and everything but going back to South Africa to fight for their liberation. Our information is that one of the main occupations of this Dr Spatak who controls AAPSO is quietly to convince individual leaders of the worthlessness of the armed struggle in Southern Africa. No country in black Africa was ever liberated through armed struggle which only results in unnecessary bloodshed, he says. The only effective method is to bring pressure upon the South African and Portuguese Governments by arousing world opinion against them.

In these words, Dr Spatak merely confirms what we knew to be the political position of Russia vis-à-vis the liberation struggle. We had known all along that the Soviet Union has 'a side agreement' with the United States whereby they will help each other to maintain 'peace' in their respective spheres of influence. They will not tolerate any interference with their main strategic positions. In Southern Africa, South Africa constitutes a vital base for imperialism, both from a military and an economic point of view. Russia is bound by the rules not to interfere in that domain.

At best, the two sides may countenance a controlled armed struggle in the Portuguese territories, as indeed the United States did in Angola for a while. But under no circumstances will imperialism tolerate an outright assault on its citadel – South Africa – and for that very reason the Soviet Union will not permit, let alone support, a revolutionary struggle in that country. If this basic fact is grasped, then all the seemingly contradictory actions of the major powers and the movements under their control become clear. The pieces of the jigsaw puzzle fall into place.

AN IMPERIALIST PLOT

A while ago American imperialism was reputed to be assisting the freedom struggle in Angola. She has given large sums of money to South African freedom fighters and has shown a marked interest in providing financial assistance to the OAU itself. The Soviet Union is known to have trained freedom fighters including South Africans. Most of Africa rejoiced at the announcement that the members of the African National Congress of South Africa were fighting in Rhodesia. To them this was the beginning of an assault on South Africa itself. Few people asked the question: how does it come about that an organisation completely under the joint control of the Soviet Union and Great Britain should now launch an attack on a British territory which constitutes the front line of imperialism's fortress? Still fewer people concluded that the announcement was part of a huge plot and a trap. We do not believe

that the ANC of South Africa ever intended to fight a conventional war against
the combined forces of Rhodesia and South Africa. The pitifully small numbers
it sent in supports this view. Such a venture would amount to criminal suicide.
The idea of making the announcement could only have come from their
political mentors to achieve a double purpose:

a) to reveal to the Congress its own impotence so as to stop the clamour
of the trained men to go home.

b) And this is important. The grossly exaggerated publicity giving the
impression that large numbers of armed South African freedom fighters were
fighting their way through Rhodesia to South Africa. The trigger-happy South
Africa racists seized the opportunity to brazenly take occupation of Rhodesia
with the tacit approval of British imperialism.

A VAST CONSPIRACY

For all military purposes South Africa's boundaries now extend to the Zambezi
in the North and by agreement with Portugal to the Northern boundary of
Mozambique in the East and the borders of the Congo on the West. This is
what the African National Congress announcement was intended to achieve or
provide a justification for. It is, of course, true that the leadership of Congress
benefited from the publicity in so far as it greatly facilitated its fund raising
efforts. But the struggle for liberation in South Africa suffered a tremendous
setback.

The most distressing thing in all this is that most of the African States do
not recognise the snare. Even as the imperialist hangman puts the noose round
the neck of Africa, they cheer and clap hands believing this to be a rope
thrown to a drowning man to save his life.

The logic of the situation now is, that those few African countries which
seek to escape from this stranglehold and come out in opposition to these
machinations will be accused by their gullible fellowmen of betraying the
struggle. Imperialism with the able assistance of the Soviet Union has entrapped
Africa in the coils of a vast conspiracy. The client States will beat the drums in
support of the plan in the fond belief that their benefactors are making a
contribution to the struggle for freedom. They will pour scorn on the true
defenders of the Revolution. They will be used to isolate them, little knowing
that by so doing they are playing a perfidious role and that they are the ones
who are being used as instruments for betraying the revolution in Southern

Africa. The contiguity of Zambia and Tanzania to the unliberated countries places them in a position not only to give shelter to all the freedom fighters but to serve as a corridor to the battlefields. The wrath of the enemy will be concentrated on them. All methods will be used to isolate them and so create conditions favourable to crushing them piecemeal.

The picture we have painted above is a bleak one. The situation seems hopeless. But this is so only to those who pinned all their faith on the ability of the OAU, as presently constituted, to save Africa, that is to say, only those who underestimated the power of imperialism. A shift of vision will reveal a totally different picture. The prospects of success are by no means slim, provided we discover the source of our own strength. It is futile at this stage to attempt to reform the OAU by force of argument. Deeds speak louder than words. It is not possible at present to initiate correct action within the framework of the OAU. But it can be done without in any way violating its tenets and decisions. Once a workable plan has been set into motion and can be seen to be producing results, many member states will give it their support. The longer they wait the worse the position will become. Sooner or later racist South Africa, using Rhodesia as a spearhead, must seek to destroy the bastions of non-racialism which constituted a source of inspiration to the oppressed majority within her borders. In that event the OAU will be helpless to come to their aid. Their only effective defence lies with the oppressed masses in South Africa itself.

FORCES OF LIBERATION IN SOUTH AFRICA

Here again we are constrained to spend time showing how the same conspiracy against the people of South Africa so succeeded that imperialism aided by the Soviet Union managed to persuade Africa – that same Africa so dedicated to the struggle for freedom of their brothers in the South – that she acted and still continues to act in such a way as to strengthen imperialism in South Africa. This may seem paradoxical but is nonetheless true.

Amongst the documents captured by the South African Police and used in the Rivonia Trial, were the Minutes of a secret meeting of what is known as The Centre, the most authoritative organ of the Communist Party of South Africa. The meeting was concerned with formulating a policy to be presented to the Congress Alliance consisting of the Communist Party, the African National Congress, the Congress of Democrats, an organisation of the white

Liberals (COD), the South African Indian Congress, an Indian merchant class-dominated organisation (SAIC), and the Coloured People's Congress, a body created by the coloured members of the Communist Party to represent the coloured people in the Alliance (CPC). The minutes contain, inter alia, the following: A picture .... has been taken advantage of .... to depict the ANC as a collaborationist organisation dominated by non-Africans. It is essential that this picture be corrected. All sections of the democratic movement should fully understand and appreciate this need, and co-operate in seeing that particularly in Free Africa, the African National Congress of South Africa, both in theory and in practice, comes forward and is accepted as the recognised spokesman of the entire democratic movement in this country. 'We ask all our members concerned in various organisations to give unqualified support to this ruling.' (their own emphasis). Having made quite certain that the ANC is under its complete control, the CP now calls upon all its members and its friends, the white bourgeoisie, to present the Congress as the only liberatory organisation in the country.

ORDERS FROM MOSCOW

Those who know that the CP of South Africa has always taken orders from Moscow realise all too well where this instruction came from. History has shown how well this injunction has been carried out. The white liberal functionaries have since bent all their energies to execute this task with the greatest zeal. Russia produced the funds to enable them to launch a propaganda assault on all Africa, Europe and Asia. As was the case at home, the Executive of the ANC in Dar es Salaam continued to maintain two political wings; the one, the major one, attached to Moscow and the minority to London, a convenient arrangement for bringing in funds. Moscow, following the dictum that money speaks, took no chances and saw to it that she contributed the largest share and that all such funds were channelled through her own trusted men, the old members of the Communist Party.

All members of the Executive were paid a fixed salary according to their status in the hierarchy. The positions became sinecures with salaries fantastically high as compared to what they could ever hope to earn at home. Some of those members who had been anti-communist found it convenient to change their faith in order to come to the honey pot. This was part and parcel of the means used to maintain control. It was also a method of undermining the morale of the leadership and corrupting it, so that the status quo became a way of life. Many African States belonging to the OAU were pressurised to fall in line with the plan. Even the individuals in the Liberation Committee and on the Secretariat could not escape the effect of the pressures. It is indisputable that amongst the South African organisations, the ANC has received by far the greatest financial aid from the OAU despite the fact that in seven long years it has produced no results and no accounting for funds received.

The irony of it all is that the ANC does not need what must be to them pin money. Many states now know that the ANC is a puppet of the Soviet Union but haven't the courage to reject it. The few who have turned away from it in disgust, have pinned all their faith in the PAC, without realising that this vociferous, unprincipled group has more members outside than inside South Africa. It is a head without a body. The point we are making is that so long as Africa spends all its monies in support of these organisations, so long will imperialism feel assured that the revolution will be aborted and its investments in South Africa safe. The matter does not end there. A state of tension cannot continue indefinitely. Any procrastination on the part of the revolutionary forces is tantamount to strengthening the position of racist South Africa and imperialism as a whole.

THE REAL STRUGGLE IN SOUTH AFRICA

Let us make it plain that it is not our intention to place all the blame on the African States. Many, perhaps most of the mistakes they have made, are due to lack of knowledge of the facts about the situation in South Africa, such as the relationship of forces as between the organisations of the oppressed; their respective programmes and principles; the relationship of forces as between the whole of the oppressed and the oppressor. They have no means of acquiring this knowledge for they depend for their information on the imperialist press and committed publicists whose job is to distort facts to bolster up their iniquitous system.

How are the African states to know for instance, that the widely publicised Sharpeville was but an insignificant incident as compared to the numerous slaughters that have been taking place long before and after it? How are they to know about the Masabalala massacre, the Bulhoek, the Pondoland, the Sekhukhuniland genocides, to mention but a few? What of the heroic struggles of the people in which they were forced to face machine guns and Saracens (mobile armoured vehicles) with sticks, spears and bare hands, struggles which have increased in frequency in the last decade? How is the outside world to know of the numerous organisations, big and small, that have sprung up in the last few years all formed for the purpose of self defence and to launch a struggle for freedom? Who, outside South Africa knows that the biggest organisations in the country are peasant organisations, the same peasants who have borne the brunt of oppression, exploitation, starvation and torture, torture because they have at last raised their voice in protest against the unbearable conditions of their existence? NO! No one knows outside South Africa. It does not suit the book of imperialism to mention all these facts. Does anyone know outside our country that out of need for self-defence most of those peasant organisations and all the biggest ones have now joined forces with the other organisations of the oppressed, federated in the Unity Movement of South Africa? The leaders of the various organisations are now drawn into a unified leadership which directs all their struggles in accordance with the principles, policy and programme hammered out in conferences during the days when they could still meet legally.

In the opinion of many African states and individuals racist South Africa is impregnable. So it seems from a distance. In truth it is, if one is thinking of a military confrontation on a state level.

From a purely military consideration white South Africa can take on all the African states south of the Sahara. She may not be able to conquer them but she can certainly defeat them. Indeed it would be suicidal to attempt to invade her. But there is a power in South Africa that is capable of challenging the white racist regime. This is not a facile assertion but a considered statement born of long experience and a knowledge of the situation.

No government is stronger than its own population. It can hold them at bay for a time, but if the majority of the people are committed to its overthrow it must sooner or later fall. In South Africa we have a situation in which the bulk of the population is committed and the majority of the organised population has reached the stage of total commitment to the overthrow of the regime. It is now a question of logistics. They not only know what they are fighting against, but more important, what they are fighting for. They have even created the political organisational structure most suitable for the prosecution of an armed insurrection. But they lack the military know-how. This is the only thing that is holding our people back. As it happens, this is precisely the one thing that the independent African states can give without much difficulty. But for reasons explained above, i.e. the conspiracy, Africa refuses to give military training to the only organisations that can topple the fascistic regime in South Africa. They spend tremendous sums of money supporting a Congress that is under the complete domination of powers that will not permit it to fight. They expend funds, time and energy trying to prop up a disintegrating organisation, the PAC, which is not by any stretch of imagination a factor to contend with at home. What is happening to the PAC outside is only a reflection of what happened to it at home some years ago. Nobody amongst the oppressed in South Africa even discusses the PAC. It was like a meteor that suddenly appeared in the firmament and as suddenly disappeared into oblivion.

What then can be done to help the struggle in South Africa?

Without going into this question in all its ramifications I shall simply make a bald statement.

South Africa cannot be defeated outside her own boundaries. This is possible only on her own soil. Besides, it is necessary to pin down the trigger-happy white soldiery within their boundaries before they come out to destroy the very base of all freedom movements. I am convinced it can be done.

Whether Africa or the OAU like it or not, the plain fact of the matter is that at the present moment the main political stream in South Africa is constituted by those organisations which are banded together in the Unity Movement of South Africa.

BIBLIOGRAPHY

Declaration of Unity – Preliminary Conference of Unity Movement of South Africa. December 1943. Cape Town, South Africa

Declaration to the Nations of the World – Statement by Unity Movement of South Africa. July 1945

Speech delivered at the first all-in National Unity Movement Conference. January 1945 (Summary)

Manifesto of the All-African Convention. November 1945

Resolution on the International Question, Unity Movement Conference. December 1945. Kimberley, South Africa.

Tabata, IB: **The Rehabilitation Scheme: A New Fraud**. 1945. All African Convention, Cape Town, South Africa

Tabata, IB: **The Problem of Organisational Unity**, Letter to Nelson Mandela.16th June 1948

Tabata, IB: **Memorandum on Native Education**. Cape African Teacher's Association. Teacher's Vision. June 1949.

Tabata, IB: **The Awakening of a People**. Peoples Press, Johannesburg, South Africa 1950. Reprinted: Spokesman Books, Nottingham, England 1974

Tabata, IB: **Land and Liberty**, Speech Unity Movement Conference 1951

Tabata, IB: **The Boycott as a Weapon of Struggle**. All-African Convention Committee. Cape Town, South Africa 1952

Tabata, IB: Address to Society of Young Africa, May 1954

A Call to the Conference of the All-African Convention, November 1958

Tabata, IB: **Education for Barbarism**. Prometheus Publications, Durban, South Africa 1959, Reprinted: Unity Movement of South Africa,Lusaka, Zambia 1980

Tabata, IB: **The Pan Africanist Congress Adventure in Perspective**, Unity Movement Pamphlet, September 1960

Tabata, IB: **A Baboon's Parliament**, Ilizwi Lesizwe, Vol. 1, No. 4 1962

Tabata, IB: **Presidential Address to First National Conference of African People's Democratic Union of Southern Africa**. Cape Town 1962. Reprinted in Tabata, IB: **Apartheid: Cosmetics Exposed**. Prometheus Publishing Company. London, England 1985

Tabata, IB: **Some Notes On Political Problems addressed to the Head of the Political Section of the FLN Algeria** 13th November 1962

Tabata, IB: Extract from letter to the Afro-Asian People's Solidarity Organisation, June 1966

Tabata, IB: **Verwoerd's Assassination**, APDUSA, Vol. 2, No. 5 September 1966

Tabata, IB: **The Conspiracy Against the OAU (Organisation of African Unity) and Nationalist Movements**, APDUSA, Vol. 2, No. 10 March 1967

Tabata, IB: **The Revolutionary Road for South Africa**. A Unity Movement of South Africa pamphlet. Partisan Press, England 1969

Tabata, IB: **The Conspiracy Against Southern Africa's Liberation**. APDUSA. March 1969

The writings of I.B.Tabata are lodged in the University of Cape Town, Manuscripts and Archives Department Unity Movement of South Africa/I.B.Tabata Collection, BC925

APPENDIX 1

From: **Declaration of Unity** at Preliminary Conference of the Unity Movement,
December 1943, Cape Town.

It is the duty of every organisation attached to this Unity Movement to unfold
to the people the meaning of the following programme, a programme not for
bargaining but for representing the minimum demands and fundamental needs
of the people.

THE TEN-POINT PROGRAMME

1   The FRANCHISE, i.e. the right of every man and woman over the age of
    21 to elect and be elected to Parliament, Provincial Council and all other
    divisional and Municipal Councils.
    This means the end of all political tutelage, of all communal or indirect
    representation, and the granting to all Non-Europeans of the same
    universal, equal, direct and secret ballot as at present enjoyed by Europeans
    exclusively.

2   Compulsory, free and uniform education for all children up to the age of
    16, with free meals, free books and school equipment for the needy.
    This means the extension of all the educational rights at present enjoyed
    by European children to all Non-European children, with the same access
    to higher education on equal terms.

3   Inviolability of person, of one's house and privacy.
    This is the elementary Habeas Corpus right. The present state of helplessness
    of the Non- European before the police is an outrage of the principles of
    democracy. No man should be molested by the police, nor should his
    house be entered without a writ from the magistrate. The same right to
    inviolability and privacy at present enjoyed by the European should apply
    to all Non-Europeans. All rule by regulations should be abolished.

4   Freedom of speech, press, meetings and association.
    This means the abolition of the Riotous Assemblies Act, directed
    specifically against the Non- European. It embodies the right to combine,
    to form, and enter Trade Unions on the same basis as Europeans.

5   Freedom of movement and occupation.
    This means the abolition of all Pass Laws and restriction of movement

and travel within the Union; the right to live, to look for work wherever one pleases. It means the same right to take up a profession or a trade as enjoyed by Europeans.

6 Full equality of rights for all citizens without distinction of race, colour or sex.

This means the abolition of all discriminatory Colour Bar laws.

7 Revision of the land question in accordance with the above.

The relations of serfdom at present existing on the land must go, together with the Land Acts, together with the restrictions upon acquiring land. A new division of the land in conformity with the existing rural population, living on the land and working the land, is the first task of a democratic State and Parliament.

8 Revision of the civil and criminal code in accordance with the above.

This means the abolition of feudal relations in the whole system of justice – police, magistrates, law-courts and prisons – whereby the punishment for the same crime is not the same, but is based upon the skin colour of the offender. There must be complete equality of all citizens before the law and the abolition of all punishment incompatible with human dignity.

9 Revision of the system of taxation in accordance with the above.

This means the abolition of the Poll-tax or any other tax applicable specifically to the Non- European, or discrimination between Europeans and Non-Europeans. There should be one, single, progressive tax and all indirect taxation that falls so heavily upon the poorer classes should be abolished.

10 Revision of the labour legislation and its application to the mines and agriculture.

This means specifically the revision of the Industrial Conciliation and Wage Acts, the elimination of all restrictions and distinctions between the European worker and a Non-European worker, equal pay for equal work, equal access to Apprenticeship and skilled labour. This means the liquidation of indentured labour and forcible recruitment, the full application of Factory legislation to the mines and on the land. It means the abolition of the Masters and Servants Act and the establishment of complete equality between the seller and buyer of labour. It also means the abolition of payment in kind, and the fixing of a minimum wage for all labourers without distinction of race or colour.

APPENDIX 2

Letter from Nelson Mandela to I.B.Tabata, 22nd May 1948

No 8115, Orlando West,
Johannesburg
22nd May 1948

Dear I.B.,

Please pardon me for delaying to write to you although this was caused partly by your absence in the Orange Free State and partly by the consideration of the fact that on your return, you would be busy preparing for the Conference of the Unity movement, a fact which would make it slightly impossible for you to give attention to some of the issues I would like to pose for your consideration and reply. I hope you will excuse me for this irregularity - - - I do not often commit such careless mistakes.

First, I should like to thank you most heartily for the hospitality you showed me during my visit to the Peninsula. I have not the slightest hesitation in saying that had it not been for you, my visit would not have been as enjoyable as it was. *Ungadinwa nangomso*.

Immediately after I had returned from the Cape, I heard that you were about and that you had invited some of our men to a discussion on the general political situation with special reference to the situation as it affects Africans. Unfortunately, I was not informed of this meeting until a few days after it had been convened. It is reported that the substance of your remarks was to the effect that in order to save the position the African National Congress must be destroyed and that a New Organisation must be build on its ashes. I was surprised to hear that you expressed this view since in all our conversations in Cape Town you have never put forward this contention. On the contrary, the basis of our discussions, it seems to me, was the finding of a common basis for cooperation between the African National Congress and the All African Convention. In this connection, I then intimated that I could use my influence with our fellows and suggest to them the acceptance of this view. I might mention that on my return I had conversations with various individuals with reference to the discussions I had with you, and it was the common feeling among these men that there was a necessity for some measure of cooperation between the two organisations. In the circumstances, I must confess, I was completely at a loss to understand your new approach to the subject. I know that you are a very busy man, but I shall appreciate it if you will be kind enough to enlighten me on this question.

The most striking feature of the political situation this end is the so-called 'FIRST TRANSVAAL-ORANGE FREE STATE PEOPLE'S ASSEMBLY FOR VOTES FOR ALL', a movement alleged to have been formed 24 hrs. after a Press Conference held by Dr. Xuma on the 5th of April, 1948. Councillor Mosaka and other important personalities are listed as sponsors of the new movement. In actual fact the Working Committee of the Assembly existed weeks before Dr Xuma's Press Conference. He subsequently made a statement in the Bantu World denying the allegation that he was sponsor of the movement. Councillor Mosaka followed suit. There is no doubt that the Communist Party is behind the movement but true to form and tradition they have decided to disguise its true nature and composition in order to deceive the public. I have not been able to ascertain precisely what the object of this campaign is. I know that by now you have made up your attitude towards this movement and I would be pleased if you could indicate to me what the attitude of your Organisation is towards it. If you have already made a Press statement in connection with it, I shall be pleased if you will kindly send me a cutting.

I have very little time at my disposal and I must now stop, but I feel that I will have failed in my duty if I did not repeat once again how deeply indebted I am to you for what you did for me.

I shall always remember it. Please convey my greetings to Miss Gool and the Jordans.

Yours Truly,

N.R.D.Mandela

* "Don't get tired tomorrow"

ABOUT RESISTANCE BOOKS AND THE IIRE

Resistance Books

Resistance Books is the publishing arm of Socialist Resistance, a revolutionary Marxist organisation which is the British section of the Fourth International. Resistance Books publishes books jointly with the International Institute for Research and Education in Amsterdam and independently.

Further information about Resistance Books, including a full list of titles currently available and how to purchase them, can be obtained at http://www. resistancebooks.org, or by writing to Resistance Books, PO Box 62732, London, SW2 9GQ.

Socialist Resistance is an organisation active in the trade union movement and in many campaigns against the war, in solidarity with Palestine and with anti-capitalist movements across the globe. We are eco-socialist – we argue that much of what is produced under capitalism is socially useless and either redundant or directly harmful. Capitalism's drive for profit is creating environmental disaster – and it is the poor, the working class and the global south that are paying the highest price for this.

We have been long standing supporters of women's liberation and the struggles of lesbians, gay people, bisexuals and transgender people. We believe those struggles must be led by those directly affected – none so fit to break the chains as those who wear them. We work in antiracist and anti-fascist networks, including campaigns for the rights of immigrants and asylum seekers.

Socialist Resistance believes that democracy is an essential component of any successful movement of resistance and struggle. With Britain and the western imperialist countries moving into a long period of capitalist austerity and crisis, deeper than any since the Second World War, Socialist Resistance stands together with all those who are organising to make another world is possible.

Socialist Resistance is the bi-monthly magazine of the organisation, which can be read on-line at www.socialistresistance.org. Socialist Resistance can be contacted by email at contact@socialistresistance.org or by post at PO Box 62732, London, SW2 9GQ.

International Viewpoint is the English language online magazine of the Fourth International, which can be read online at www.internationalviewpoint.org.

The International Institute for Research and Education

The International Institute for Research and Education (IIRE) is an international foundation, recognised in Belgium as an international scientific association by Royal decree of 11th June 1981. The IIRE provides activists and scholars worldwide with opportunities for research and education in three locations: Amsterdam, Islamabad and Manila.

Since 1982, when the Institute opened in Amsterdam, its main activity has been the organisation of courses in the service of progressive forces around the world. Our seminars and study groups deal with all subjects related to the emancipation of the world's oppressed and exploited. It has welcomed hundreds of participants from every inhabited continent. Most participants have come from the Third World.

The IIRE has become a prominent centre for the development of critical thought and interaction, and the exchange of experiences, between people who are engaged in daily struggles on the ground. The Institute's sessions give participants a unique opportunity to step aside from the pressure of daily activism. The IIRE gives them time to study, reflect upon their involvement in a changing world and exchange ideas with people from other countries.

Our website is constantly being expanded and updated with freely downloadable publications, in several languages, and audio files. Recordings of several recent lectures given at the institute can be downloaded from www.iire.org – as can talks given by founding Fellows such as Ernest Mandel and Livio Maitan, dating back to the early 1980s.

The IIRE publishes **Notebooks for Study and Research** to focus on themes of contemporary debate or historical or theoretical importance. Lectures and study materials given in sessions in our Institute, located in Amsterdam, Manila and Islamabad, are made available to the public in large part through the Notebooks. Different issues of the **Notebooks** have also appeared in languages besides English and French, including German, Dutch, Arabic, Spanish, Japanese, Korean, Portuguese, Turkish, Swedish, Danish and Russian.

For a full list of the **Notebooks for Study and Research**, visit http://bit.ly/IIRENSR or subscribe online at: http://bit.ly/NSRsub. To order the Notebooks, email iire@iire. org or write to International Institute for Research and Education, Lombokstraat 40, Amsterdam, NL-1094.

www.ingramcontent.com/pod-product-compliance
Lightning Source LLC
Chambersburg PA
CBHW060037030426

42334CB00019B/2365